The Twenty-First Century Left

The Twenty-First Century Left

Cognitions In The Constitution And Why Buckley *Is Wrong*

Second Edition

William P. Kreml

Carolina Academic Press
Durham, North Carolina

Library of Congress Cataloging-in-Publication Data

Kreml, William P.

The twenty-first century left : cognitions in the Constitution and why Buckley is wrong / By William P. Kreml.

p. cm.

Includes bibliographical references and index.

ISBN 1-59460-251-4 (alk. paper)

1. Political science--Philosophy. 2. Right and left (Political science)--United States. 3. Buckley, James Lane, 1923- 4. Campaign funds--Law and legislation--United States. I. Title.

JA71.K74 2006

320.51'30973--dc22

2006010123

Carolina Academic Press
700 Kent Street
Durham, North Carolina 27701
Telephone (919) 489-7486
Fax (919) 493-5668
www.cap-press.com

Printed in the United States of America

For

My Late Brother

and the

Early Syndicalists

Table of Contents

Table of Cases ix

Acknowledgments xi

Introduction xiii

Chapter 1. The Subatomic Tier 3

Chapter 2. Forms of Understanding 25

Chapter 3. Limits to Knowledge and How to Get There 35

Chapter 4. The Cognitive Triumph—Fission and Fusion 65

Chapter 5. Aristotle and America 85

Chapter 6. The Supreme Court and Cognition 125

Chapter 7. *Buckley v. Valeo* 147

Chapter 8. A Strategy 167

Notes 195

Bibliography 203

Index 207

Table of Cases

Baker v. Carr, 369 U S 549 (1962).
Brown v. Board of Education of Topeka, Kansas, 347 U S 483 (1954).
Buckley v. Valeo, 424 U S 1 (1976).
Carter v. Carter Coal Co., 298 US 238 (1936).
Charles River Bridge Co. v. Warren Bridge Co., 36 U S (11 Peters) 420 (1837).
Colegrove v. Green, 328 U S 549 (1946).
Dartmouth College v. Woodward, 17 U S (4 Wheaton) 518 (1819).
Dred Scott v. Sandford, 60 U S (39 Howard) 393 (1857).
Griswold v. Connecticut, 381 U S 479 (1965).
Marbury v. Madison, 5 U S (1 Cranch) 137 (1803).
McCulloch v. Maryland, 17 U S (Wheat) 316 (1819).
Miranda v. Arizona, 384 U S 384 (1966).
Moose Lodge No. 107 v. Irvis, 407 U S 163 (1972).
National Labor Relations Board v. Jones and Laughlin Steel Corp, 301 U S 1 (1937).
Nebbia v. New York, 291 US 502 (1934).
Reynolds v. Sims, 377 U S 533 (1964).
Richmond v. Croson, 109 S. Ct. 706 (1989).
Roe v. Wade, 410 U S 113 (1973).
Schechter Poultry Corp. v. The United States, 295 U S 495 (1936).
Shelley v. Kraemer, 334 U S 1 (1948).
Smith v. Allwright, 321 U S 649 (1944).

Acknowledgments

My thanks to the Department of Political Science at The University of South Carolina for assistance with this work, as well as to Daniel Sabia, Robert Thompson and Peter Sederberg of that department for their helpful comments. My thanks as well to Meili Steele and Bill Matalene of South Carolina's Department of English for their stylistic as well as substantive suggestions. My research assistant, Deniz Sevgili, helped with footnotes and bibliography while Pat Coate and Nancy Kreml assisted enormously with copy editing. Becci Robbins of Harbinger Publications assisted with the layout and substantive editing of the first edition. Karen Clayton did a wonderful editing job at Carolina Academic Press. My thanks also to Chicago's Bob Rudner for his assistance with the Red/Green coalition literature in Chapter One. Finally, I wish to thank the late Mike Avey, Chair of South Carolina's courageous United Citizens Party, for an early reading of this manuscript. Any errors are my responsibility alone.

Introduction

This work does two things. It describes an original political theory, and it applies that theory both to the structurally induced problems of the American government and the continuing problems caused by the way political campaigns are financed in this country. Rather naturally for a political scientist, I have always been concerned with what citizens think about politics and why they believe what they do. I have also been concerned with the degree to which citizens, at various levels of political interest, have been able to encase their beliefs in something of a theoretical framework. Influenced in my early academic years by the Yale political scientist Robert Lane's insistence that average citizens did have political ideologies, I have also tried to find to what degree such citizens understand why they believe what they do.[1]

Generally, most citizens' conscious political identifications are centered around their objective groupings. That is, citizens typically place themselves within the political arena as members of economic, ethnic, racial, gender, religious, sexual orientations, and the like. Frequently, they find more than one such objective identity to be politically important for them. Such identifications are significant and will continue to be significant.

But I am a theorist. For years I have worked on the development of a subjectively— that is psychologically based—political philosophy. We have known for some time that citizens' psychological orientations impact their political attitudes. What I try to do here is build a full-blown political philosophy on the bedrock of human psychology.

This work does four things. First, the work briefly assimilates what has until now been available only in separate, earlier writings that began my work toward a psychologically based political philosophy. Second, it adds substantial new material to the theory, essentially completing the broad philosophical outline. Third, it applies the theory to a specific area of public concern, that of campaign finance reform. Fourth, it intersperses the theoretical writings with brief descriptions of my own political experiences. I hope that these experiences, and the lessons I drew from them, further illuminate the theory by demonstrating how the kinds of things I have been involved in within the real political world reflect a new framework for political understanding.

Though not a member of the Green Party, then or now, I sat in on the final meeting of the Illinois Greens convention during the summer of 2000 in Chicago. The thirty to thirty-five people there were of different ages and occupations, and very different personal histories. The session seemed to be a wrap-up, reviewing what had been talked about and decided on in earlier conference meetings. The participants' ease of speech with each other and the group as a whole bespoke a harmony that I found inviting. These were people at peace with themselves.

What was only a little troubling, but disturbing nonetheless, was what so many of the participants said concerning their own theoretical orientations. In a session wherein individuals spoke frankly about specific concerns and unique political histories, all of them were stretching, I thought, to find a theoretical grounding for their current, in many cases still evolving, political beliefs. In the main, they seemed to be wrestling with how their new political identifications may or may not square with earlier theoretical orientations. Cognitive maps die hard. It is so much easier, particularly when one is well into adulthood, to make an adjustment or two to what one has built up over many years than it is to tear down the old model entirely and begin anew.

Many of the convention participants spoke of their former party affiliations, and I particularly remember one youngish man who described his experiences with the syndicalist Socialist Labor Party. The early syndicalists, influenced by the teachings of Daniel DeLeon in this country, believed in a kind of cooperative orientation toward production, rather than a state socialism. They advocated worker ownership and worker management. Sitting there, I recalled that my late brother had gone to Socialist Labor Party meetings in Chicago and liked the people he met there. If you think of early syndicalism as being terribly radical, think again. United Airlines, America's second-largest air carrier in spite of its recent troubles, and the Chicago and Northwestern Railway, now part of the Union Pacific aggregation but once America's seventh largest railroad, were both founded on syndicalist principles. You can still see the faint "Employee Owned" medallion on the old, yellow CNW boxcars that haven't been repainted. And you can see the shame on the faces of a selfish management, and even on those of the selfish pilots and machinists unions, who after September 11, 2001, brought United to much of its current difficulty.

At the Greens' meeting, virtually all who spoke included mention of their prior affiliations with the "Old Left" of the 1930s and 1940s or, as frequently, the "New Left" of the 1960s and 1970s. They all seemed to be bending those orientations now, at least partially, because of concerns over contemporary issues, such as the environment, international human rights, and industrial and postindustrial worker justice. At the same time, they maintained strong ties to past orientations, particularly those orientations that surrounded the always-knotty issue of the very justness of the political system itself.

So many of those who spoke that night incanted almost religiously about such things as the air and the water, the excesses of logging and mining companies, developers, and other ecological problems. But they also talked about larger inequities, the worker who does not receive her just due, civil rights protections not being enforced, and of course the problems of an American government that they saw as increasingly distant from them and ever closer to the large private corporations. Both as reminiscences and as statements of contemporary concern, their statements were powerful, almost in the sense of that wonderful Norman Rockwell painting of the young man speaking at a public meeting, which was on display at that time in the Chicago Historical Society, two miles away on Clark Street.

But, again, I found a troubling side to their heartfelt message. It was troubling because in spite of their struggle there was a disconnection, a failure of linkage really, between the grand, if now dated political theories that each of them may have held for a long time and the pattern of concerns that currently bedeviled them. Each speaker felt strongly about worthwhile things, but all seemed to fail at the task of fitting those concerns into their old political theories or creating a new theoretical understanding. Some realized it, speaking almost sadly of "what I used to believe" or "when I was a ______." What was going on was not so much a matter of old wine in new bottles, but more a matter of grapes and bottles, with no wine in between. I felt their need for a new theoretical map.

Indeed, in political meetings of all stripes that I have attended, and in individual discussions with citizens who are troubled by America's campaign finance scandals, the prostitution of our government by large private interests, and the increasing apathy of citizens as reflected by the decline in voting percentages, the absence of a theoretical framework always strikes me. Thus, what I offer here is a new theory, one that is based on who we are, not what we are. We have come to that time in history, I think, when we are entitled not only to know a great deal more about our own psychologies, but also to have our psychologies be much part of our political orientations. Ultimately, those psychologies should serve as the underpinning of an entirely new political philosophy. This is what I offer.

Please do not misunderstand. I know the risk of giving the political left one more theory to argue over. Anyone with the slightest knowledge of the left's history understands that ideologically based disputes have far too often crippled the efforts of those who meant to do much good. At most, I write what I do because I believe an increasingly complex twenty-first- century world needs a new left-of-center political philosophy. At a minimum, I believe the left needs at least a skeletal statement of novel theoretical principles that helps to reestablish basic equities within the United States, and within the increasingly interdependent human family.

What I have created, then, is an original political philosophy, a philosophy that I have struggled with over the years and that I fervently hope will be useful to what I have come to call the "Psychological Left" or, preferably, the "Natural Left". Partly to demonstrate how the theoretical insights I share grew within me, and partly to demonstrate how the necessary dialectic between the real world and the world of the mind works, at least for me, I will be interspersing my description of this political philosophy with brief remembrances of my own political activities. I have been involved in the real world of politics for a long time. My running for office and my being a part of other political activities, have been instructive for me. I hope the inclusion of such events will help illuminate my theoretical perspective.

I am concerned about the deep imbalances that have grown up recently in the American constitutional order. I am concerned, for example, that so much of the Bill of Rights is now misunderstood, perhaps deliberately, by those who see it as containing solely individual rights. The Bill of Rights contains far more than that, it being the foundation for the aggregated, small "d" democratic political activity of a free people. It is my hope that the sectoral and cognitive analysis I lend to constitutional interpretation, couched in the original political philosophy that I describe herein, will make clear what the Bill of Rights is really all about, and why the campaign finance reform denying case of *Buckley v. Valeo* (1976) is tragically wrong.

The Twenty-First Century Left

CHAPTER ONE

The Subatomic Tier

History

Throughout political history, various groups of citizens have brought grievances to their governments, seeking redress. As a part of that seeking, these groups have either repaired to already accepted standards of equity or have created new standards of equity that they felt placed their own cases for just treatment into the most supportive theoretical context. From the writings of Susan B. Anthony and Elizabeth Cady Stanton in the women's movement, to the writings of Frederick Douglass and Dr. Martin Luther King Jr. in the African-American struggle, to the more recent writings of those who argue for equal treatment for citizens of a different sexual orientation, for example, a general standard of equity must invariably underpin specific pleas for fair treatment.[1] I believe a better, general standard of political equity, one that transcends the specific struggles of those who have been treated unjustly, is now available. That standard is based on psychology. More specifically, it is based on the balancing of different psychologies and the very different cognitions that different psychologies generate which in turn produce very different visions of the world.

A new standard of equity for those whose psychologically generated perspectives on politics have not always received fair consideration is long overdue. Those of a particular psychological predisposition may well have been selected out of the political processes of this country or any country just as women, ethnic minorities, and others were at one time and to some extent still are selected out. It is overdue as well, I believe, because the development of a psychologically generated theoretical position is even necessary for maintaining the gains of those groups whose political advances are always in jeopardy. In short, I believe that a psychologically based theory of politics is a better guarantee of political equity for all who are or who have been excluded than any prior theory.

The last four centuries, roughly, have witnessed the creation of two grand schools of political philosophy. Let it be clear that the theory I present here does not reject the best from either of them. In significant ways, it stands on the shoulders of what came before it. Without the foundation of what these theories brought to our intellectual understandings, and to what real world political successes have existed for aggrieved groups, there could be no advancement of political philosophy. Without these first two tiers of theoretical development, in other words, there could be no third theoretical tier. Having said that, however, let it be clear that my political philosophy is distinct. It has its own roots, and its own superstructure. I believe it marks a discreet third tier of political philosophy. Conceptually, it is perpendicular to the objectively based political theories that have come before it, thus creating what I have called a warp and woof for the political left.

The first tier of political theory within modern Western thought is most commonly called "classical liberalism." Classical liberalism is the theory of a legally and politically free people. Over the period of its development and influence, the writings of Thomas Hobbes, John Locke, the Baron de Montesquieu, the early John Stuart Mill, and so many others delineated a set of personal liberties that protected citizens from unjust governments or the whims of monarchs, aristocracies, or even an established church. Over time, liberalism also ensured that citizens were entitled to participate in governmental decisions. Writers such as Thomas Paine and Samuel Adams, and political actors including Thomas Jefferson and Andrew Jackson were important figures during this development in the new United States. Let us not forget that much of the political progress of the Western world, and more recently even parts of the Eastern world, is owed to the core prescriptions of the liberal creed. I certainly embrace those prescriptions.

The West's second grand theory is generally not well labeled, in my view. It is frequently referred to as Marxism, but I find that label troublesome because Karl Marx focused overwhelmingly on the notion of capital ownership in his core writings, finding the concentrated and exploitive use of such capital to be the cause of all inequity. Though Marx referred to the impact that an exploitive economic system had on, say, women, he neither included all of the groupings of aggrieved citizens that we might embrace today in his political perspective, nor did he focus on other causes for inequity beyond the economic, such as racism, religious bigotry, and so forth.

As telling as the Marxist arguments were in the early times of economic exploitation, and even still today in the highly oppressive corners of the world, a political philosophy based on psychology, I believe, must not only go beyond the protection of economically exploited members of an objective class;

it must also further protect those who may have already won, or who are at least starting to win, some degree of economic justice, as well as those who have not.

What would I label the second-tier theories? I suggest that Marxism, along with all philosophies that argue against the injustices directed at any singular group, are best labeled as Whole Group Equity theories. This second tier, made up of the Whole Group Equity theories, argues for a redressing of the injustices that have been visited upon any collection of similarly situated peoples in a political society, those injustices resulting from mere membership in the group. The theories that underlie political movements like feminism, gay rights, civil rights, and the like all deal with a well defined, objective grouping of citizens and the discriminations that they have endured and, in too many instances, continue to endure.

To be sure, whereas Marx spoke largely of economic injustice in the context of nineteenth-century industrialism, latter-day Marxist and other objective group-oriented writers have now included concerns about the position of African Americans, women, and other targets of discrimination within an objective framework. A goodly part of these groupings, in one way or another, has now been incorporated into a kind of neo-Marxist liturgy. Though I agree that there is an economic component to the condition of whatever "outgroup" we refer to, there are many causes of injustice beyond the economic, particularly in the case of women, African Americans, gays, and so forth. And, there is more to it all than just these whole groups.

I argue that, just as Marxism does not deal adequately with all the causes of group-centered inequity, all Whole Group Equity theories stand on independent theoretical grounds, or sport some hybrid of indigenous and borrowed roots, and do not deal with all of the sources of discrimination. Thus, whereas the second tier, Whole Group Equity theories, properly illuminated the problems of classical liberalism in failing to ensure economic equity for groupings of citizens, they surely did not, and still do not, provide for an understanding of the psychological biases that often accompanied whole group discriminatory patterns. This is why I believe a third tier of left-of-center political philosophy is necessary.

In another context, I also have trouble with the Marxist position regarding the perversion of government. Marx, correctly in greater or lesser degree depending on the time and the country, held that liberal government was a sham, the real decisions on significant public matters being made privately by those outside government who owned the means of production. There is no question but that overweening economic influences still impinge on democratic government. Interests with the most economic clout, such as banks, insurance companies, the securities industry, and now far less frequently the unions, surely have great influence with legislatures as well as with chief executives, courts, and administrative agencies. But, again, I believe that the objectivist explanation alone is incomplete. As with whole group discrimination, I believe that the recent perversion of our government has a good deal more to do with an imbalance of psychology, or the imbalance in preferences for cognitive forms, than we have so far understood.

In short, I ground my original, psychologically based political philosophy on the twin suggestions that a) the worthy principles of classical liberalism alone do not ensure true equity, and b) the vision of Marxism and all other Whole Group Equity theories, whether Marxist, neo-Marxist or whatever, do not ensure true equity either. Put simply, if a political society were to possess all the qualities of liberalism and all the remedies for liberalism that Marx and subsequent writers have concerned themselves with, and if that society then dealt with all of the inequities that whole groups have endured, I believe there would still be inequity in that society. That is why I believe in a new philosophical tier that is wholly separate from liberal or Whole Group Equity theories. That tier, again, is based on psychology or, more specifically, on the most significant differentiations in human cognitions that exist among all citizens.

Curiously, I have always found it unfortunate that Marx so crisply dismissed psychology as an independent and relevant political force. Marx argued that the human personality is nothing more than the sum of that individual's social relations. In the context of a modern theoretical understanding, Marx would be known as an anti-essentialist, that is, someone who did not believe in an innate human core. Just as John Locke viewed the human mind as a tabula rasa, so too Marx believed that the human psychology is an empty vessel, to be filled and defined only from the outside.

I differ with Marx on this. In spite of the politics of the long-running argument over nature and nurture, and in spite of what for a long time was an almost automatic identification of the nature-based perspective with the irretrievable conservatism of social Darwinism, or even the excesses of so many sociobiology-based writings, I have always believed in a human essence. I think that in addition to the environmental importance of prenatal care, parental nurturance, nutrition, mental and physical stimulation, and safety and feelings of belonging, to name some circumstances, each of us possesses an innate personality.

We all possess different psychological characteristics. Some of these characteristics, contrary to a great deal of late twentieth-century nature/nurture hogwash, are inherited. They will survive as part of our personalities throughout our lives, barring torture, a serious brain injury or the like. I held this view even in graduate school thirty-five years ago, when one freshly minted Ivy League psychology professor told me not to use the word "personality" in his class. After class, I repaired to the office of an Asian-American professor from whom I had taken an earlier course, and we shared a good laugh. In my judgment, it has been counterproductive for the left to deny the role of inheritance. The better position, both empirically and strategically, is to accept the permanence and inheritability of personality and then argue for a just balancing of all personalities' cognitive, and ultimately political, preferences. The forms of how we think have a great deal to do with our politics.

I think that recent research concerning the human personality, as well as the everyday life experiences of people who deal with a variety of other people in their daily lives (or who are the parents of two or more children), confirms my position. Flawed as some of this research may be, the evidence on the capacity for cognitive complexity, for example, pretty well confirms that there are differences in personality among all of us.[2] The brilliant work of Steven Pinker, I think, further dispels any doubt that there is something within each of us that makes us unique and permanent.[3]

The simple fact is that the role of differentiated personality characteristics plays virtually no part in the core writings of classical liberalism or in the core writings of Marxism or other Whole Group Equity theories. Therefore, though I accept the contributions of classical liberalism and accept the descriptive claims if not the prescriptive remedies of Marx regarding the exploitation of employees who are not equally balanced in the bargaining for wages and benefits, we must now go further. Though the left should always hear the claims of those who have pleaded for one group or another's equitable treatment, it is now time for that third tier of psychologically based considerations to ensure a level of equity that will otherwise never be attainable. This set of considerations will ensure a greater level of equity, even for the whole groups that have typically argued solely for their own objective advancement.

The Core of the Theory

I will now briefly outline this psychologically based political philosophy, filling in the details as we proceed through subsequent chapters. Let it be understood at the outset that this psychologically based political philosophy is subatomic. The theory looks inside the atom of whole group identifications (class, race, gender, sexual orientation, etc.) just as Ernest Rutherford and Nils

Bohr looked inside the physical atom to find what they did. In its looking within the atom of any group identity, this theory relies, again, on an understanding of a clear division between the objective, or external, conditions of a citizen, on the one hand, and the subjective, or core, psychological predispositions of that citizen, regardless of his or her objective grouping, on the other.

As already noted, we are all influenced in our politics by our ethnic identities, our economic circumstances, our wealth, and by other non-psychological attributes that make us what we are. Without question, these attributes, which are best labeled "objective," have played and will continue to play a significant role in the kinds of politics each of us embraces. But equally without question, our personalities, our subjectivities, have been shown over and over again to play a role in our political orientations. I believe that the subjective orientation has now overtaken the objective orientation in American ideological identification.

In the year 2000, a truly historic milestone in the political identifications of Americans was reached. Whereas the most significant variable in the prediction of an American citizen's political identification had consistently been that individual's educational and economic standing, 2000 marked the first year in which the variable of whether or not an individual was a regular attendee of religious services, of whatever denomination, approached the social and economic standing variable as the best predictor of an American's ideological identification, at least in the white community.[4]

Although this indicator is only one of that family of subjectively driven political issues such as school prayer, aid to private schools, abortion, gay and lesbian rights, etc. that have grown to be politically significant over the last years, it is still a momentous watershed. Ever since the 1960s, there has been a fair amount of political science research on what was frequently called "post-materialism." Post-materialism described a circumstance in which certain members of the American population no longer voted, or engaged in other political behaviors, solely on the basis of their economic standings. These individuals' political activities appeared, rather, to be motivated by a variety of cultural, social, and what in a nonsystematic way were argued to be psychologically based attitudes.[5]

Many post-materialists, regardless of what objective group or groups they may have been part of, spoke out in favor of a society that, for example, no longer tolerated racial discrimination, wished to improve the status of women, or sought to protect the environment, regardless (up to a point) of whether those political views helped or hindered their own economic well-being. Most post-materialists were reasonably far up the economic, and social, ladder as a matter of fact.

It can be argued that because of their objective, or material status, these post-material citizens could afford to "be in touch" with their subjective selves and even to be magnanimous about such things as the payment of taxes and the support of safety-net provisions for the poor. And yet, when all was said and done, there still had to be a predisposition toward a more charitable view of their fellow citizens, their environment, citizens of other countries, and the like, even if the economic opportunity was there. A new kind of political identification seemed to be at hand. Something other than objective group membership was beginning to be important, for at least some portion of the population. My own view is that the subjective variable at the center of this theoretical perspective is not confined to those of means. The psychology of what I call the Psychological or Natural Left, as well as what should probably be called the Psychological or Natural Right on the other end of the spectrum, cuts through classes, races, genders, and the like, in a perpendicular way.

Another example of the rise of the subjective variable is the continued falling away of objective barriers to political participation, even at the highest levels. Whereas ending discrimination against women and African Americans as voters was among the principal accomplishments of the American democracy in the twentieth century, the opening of the twenty-first century found Senator Joseph Lieberman (CT-D), a Jew, on the presidential ticket of one of America's two major parties. It was well rumored, if never confirmed, that the just-retired army general Colin Powell, an African American, was the first choice of the Republican presidential candidate George W. Bush as his running mate. Powell was subsequently appointed the first African-American Secretary of State. Such events demonstrate the continued importance of objectively based political factors such as race, religion, etc. and at the same time demonstrate that the objectively based agenda has made considerable progress.

Further, it has been argued that the last decade's explosion of participation within the equities markets by so many American citizens—nearly half of us now owning stocks either directly or through 401(k) plans and the like—blurs to at least some degree the class distinctions that still existed in spite of a relatively classless American political rhetoric.[6] The distributions of income and wealth that now exist in America are increasingly troublesome, and will be discussed in a subsequent chapter. But for half of U.S. citizens an intimate political, and economic, identification with what used to be called the capitalist class is now a reality. I think that this objective fact, too, makes the addressing of the remaining inequities in need of a new, subjectively based theoretical perspective. The business TV station CNBC's principal propagandist, Larry Kudlow, speaks frequently of the "investor class," and he is correct that some citizens were, for a while in the 1990s, fooled enough by a booming stock market to join in on the anti-worker, anti-consumer, anti-tax, sentiment that already marked America's corporate boardrooms.

But, again, the fact is that though the United States has a ways to go in many political arenas, starting with the guarantee of fair elections, there has been at least a goodly amount of progress made along the lines of racially-based, gender-based, and other objective discriminations against citizens in this country. From the women's vote of 1920, to the 1960s civil rights and voting rights acts, to the more recent approval of such innovations as civil unions between gay and lesbian couples in, for example, Vermont, or same sex marriages in Massachusetts, objectively based barriers to full citizenship, even beyond the accessibility to high office of such figures as the almost Vice President Lieberman and later Secretary Powell, have continued to fall. I suggest that the progress the United States has made regarding many of these whole groups makes it more imperative that we dig deeper in order to discover and rectify the heretofore unrecognized causes of the remaining injustices. They clearly go beyond the biases of one objective group toward another. In my judgment, only the building of a subatomic, intra-objective, and ultimately trans-objective standard of subjective equity will do that.

In the overall, therefore, I suggest again that if the subjective variables' importance has increased to the point that they are now the primary variables of political identification within a politically advanced country such as the United States, then the building of a subatomic, psychologically rooted theory is the necessary next step toward understanding political equity. Recall that a subatomic theory looks inside every objective identification that a citizen may have, whether it be social and economic standing, ethnicity, sexual orientation, gender, or the like. I argue that within each of those objective identifications a range of subjective, that is, psychological, orientations exist.

To reduce it to a phrase, the best way to think of a subatomic, psychologically based political theory may be to suggest that *for every objectivity, there is a subjectivity*. Within every objective grouping of which you are a member, in other words, an internal range, or ranges, of psychological orientations exists that has an impact on the ideological orientation of that group, that ideology depending on the ascendance of certain psychologies over others within the group.

Put even another way, I suggest that within every objective group membership you or I might possess, there are citizens with perspectives that are very different subjectively, or psychologically, within that membership. I suggest that within the politics of nation-states that have done at least a respectable job of dealing with their objectively based biases, these subjective perspectives play an even larger role within those states' politics. I also suggest that their playing of this new, and even dominant, role in a nation-state's politics makes the development of a subatomic, subjectively based political theory imperative.

Let me also offer, by the way, that the conceptual separation of the objective and the subjective variables, though critical to a third-tier theory, is not at all difficult. As we know, for example, Senator Lieberman is not simply Jewish but is an Orthodox Jew. Conceding that heritage and the teaching of parents, clergy, and peers surely played some role in that orientation, I nonetheless suggest that the process of selection among Orthodox, Conservative, and Reform Judaism, not to mention the secular religious orientation of many who still maintain a Jewish identity, is far more a matter of subjective, or psychological, factors than is the objective religious identification itself.

Within Senator Lieberman's objective religious identification as a Jew, he has selected a subjective identification that keeps kosher food laws, the Jewish Sabbath and holidays, and a variety of other conventional religious practices. His appearances on television infomercials with the Reverend Jerry Falwell, Reverend Pat Robertson, Pat Boone, and Charles Colson evidence a fundamentalist bias. His politics, including his corporate-friendly restraining of the Securities and Exchange Commission chair Arthur Leavitt from looking into accounting companies' conflicts of interest in the late 1990s, mirror that same, subjective, identification. It is that psychologically based selection of an ideology, within and yet in some ways apart from the overriding, or objective, religious context, that forms the subatomic, subjective variable. For Senator Lieberman, recently a candidate for U. S. president in the 2004 election, that subjective orientation is far different than the orientation of, say, Senator Russ Feingold (D-WI) or Representative Bernard Sanders (I-VT), two politicians that I send an occasional, small check.

The Subatomic Impact

Why, specifically, does the third, psychologically based tier of political philosophy necessarily import what I am calling a subatomic theory? When I say that within every objectivity there is a subjectivity, what I mean, once more, is that within every objectively based grouping in the political society, a full range distribution of subjectivities, or psychologies, exists. I will talk more specifically about the nature of the linkages of particular psychologies with particular ideological orientations in Chapter Two. But let me begin modestly here, pointing out only that the kinds of personalities that prefer different ideological perspectives do not appear randomly within the objective groupings of which they are members. Over time, different personalities in fact appear in predictable places within the objective groupings of which they are part.

Put another way, if I were to take the objective grouping of Chicagoans of Czech descent and examine its involvement in politics, I would find that the full range of personalities that exists within the pool of Chicago Czechs would select themselves out and manifest different placements and roles within that objective grouping. Some members of the group would feel more comfortable, for example, marrying outside the ethnic community than would others. Some would feel comfortable moving into a neighborhood that is not primarily Czech, while others may continue to live within an old, ethnic neighborhood. Similarly, if I were to take an economically based grouping of Chicagoans, say a labor union, and examine its involvement in union affairs, I would find that certain personalities within that grouping would establish themselves as hardliners or softliners when it came to, for example, the willingness to settle for the typical "half a loaf" of so many labor-management negotiations.

Traditional research (cited below) reveals patterns of ideology within organizations, and within governments, and the psychologies that account for those patterns. In general, what that research shows is that particular personalities tend to rise to positions of influence at the top, or near the borders, of organizations. These same personalities not only lead the organization but also impact the internal "shape" of the organization—that is, the procedures that the organization uses both to deal with its internal business and to deal with the external world. When these personalities do such things subatomically, or within the organization, they do so in ways that manifest an ideological bias, almost regardless of the substantive goals of the group. When they impact how the organization interacts with other organizations, they manifest an ideology as well.

I will say a good deal more about the specific nature of these differentiated personalities in Chapter Two, and a good deal more about their specific placement within organizations, including governments in Chapter Five. What I wish to restate here are two simple notions: a) that there are differentiated personalities, or subjectivities, within all objective groupings of citizens; and b) those differentiated personalities can and do rearrange their placements and roles within objective groupings in such a way that some personalities both dominate the group itself and determine its structural shape and methods of interacting with other citizen groupings. When this happens, the objective grouping will become psychologically biased in the political arena, in addition to whatever objective bias it may already manifest.

In short, the group will be an ideologically biased political actor in two senses of the term because, after working out the relative subjectivities within the objectivity, the disproportionate influence of some psychologies over others within the objective groupings creates a bias that impacts the political system itself. This impact, again, goes beyond anything related to the attainment of the group's immediate goals. The very shape, or form, of a government's institutional arrangements can and has been altered by psychologically biased activity within and among those governmental institutions. It also impacts things like judicial opinions, and the deeper constitutional interpretations that lead to such opinions, which we will address later.

The reality, and importance, of these ideological biases within all political groupings requires a third-tier, psychologically based political philosophy to fully understand it. Such a philosophy is needed in order to describe the nature of political equity in a post-material, psychologically impacted political system. Put another way, because neither liberalism, nor Marxism, nor any of the Whole Group Equity theories contains a subatomic component, these theories cannot ensure that third, psychological level of political equity. Moreover, they cannot ensure the maintenance of what may have been won in objective terms, such as better pay, or better treatment of gays and lesbians, through liberal and Whole Group theory-directed activity. They cannot ensure such equity because they do not account for the subatomic, psychologically biased component of ideological bias that has resulted from the fact that certain psychologies within any objectivity speak disproportionately for the group.

Marx's Second Error

I have already scored Karl Marx for his rejection of the innateness of human psychology within Marxist political philosophy. His eschewing of the human essence, insisting on a purely existence-based, or objective, understanding of human reality, relegated his theoretical and real-world perspectives to a unique set of economic circumstances. I have conceded that Marxism continued to contribute to the popular understanding of how economic elites in the less developed world, and even to some degree in the developed world, took and in some places still take advantage of their citizenry. But Marxism has largely failed, both theoretically and practically, to gain favor, much less ensure post-material equity in a highly developed country like the United States.

Marx's error regarding the essence/existence or subjective/objective perspective was unfortunately accompanied by an additional significant error. That error not only debilitated Marx's theory but, like his first error, actually retarded the development of an effective, subjectively based political philosophy for the left. I speak here of Marx's dialectical Materialism, a concept borrowed from Ludwig Feuerbach and made central to Marx's overall theoretical position.[7]

In the generations immediately before Marx, many significant thinkers marked the German intellectual world. Among the most prominent was Immanuel Kant, whose responses to the overly optimistic French prescriptions of the *philosophes* (Voltaire, Diderot, Condorcet, etc.) made up the core of his skeptical view of humanity and humanity's capacity to alter the world. The immediate generation before Marx produced the intellectual who is still referred to as "The Philosopher" in Europe, George Wilhelm Friedrich Hegel. Our concern here is with what Marx did to Hegel, after what Hegel did to Kant; the former, in my view, leading to unfortunate consequences for Western political philosophy.

Both Kant and Hegel, along with various other significant German philosophers of the time, were known simply as Idealists. The Idealists dealt with the full panoply of philosophical issues including, of course, the notion of what is real. The Idealists focused on the historical flow, or the method of history, not the maintenance of a rosy worldview. Above all, the Idealists believed that the human mind was the principal engine of history. That is, they believed that what society envisioned for its future was the main force in bringing about, or at least trying to bring about, what comes next. Thus, as the consciousness of man expanded, the world progressed. Though Kant had a far more limited view of the possibility for deliberate human improvement than did Hegel (a matter that I will discuss in more detail in the following chapter), they both, again, placed mind before matter on the pathway of history.

Please know that this historical placing of the mind before matter was not anything like the everyday "mind over matter" usage that some people utilize to encourage a kind of rising above whatever calamity may have befallen them. It was a question, again, of a historical order, a "which comes first" kind of thing that philosophers have frequently concerned themselves with. Again, the German Idealists, in the tradition of the classical, Greek dialecticians, believed that the mind, which they referred to as the *geist* (to include both the mind and the spirit in a rather undifferentiated whole), propelled the progress of history.

Finally, the German Idealists had a reason for placing the human mind before the matter of the world within the historical order. Like the Greeks, they believed very much in the dialectic, the actual mechanism that drives the world forward. I will say more about the dialectic too in the second chapter, since Kant and Hegel had very different views of it. But for now all we need know is that the German Idealists created a vision of philosophy that included both the dialectical method of historical progress, again originally fostered by the Greeks, and the placing of the mind before real-world circumstances. This vision was sometimes called "dialectical Idealism" (Mao, e.g.), but is typically known as simply the classical dialectic.

Then came Marx. Marx's broad philosophical perspective, again, is known as "dialectical Materialism." Marx's prominence in philosophy is based in great part on his attempt to reverse the Hegelian, Idealist vision and place the material world ahead of the mind in the order of history. While adopting the method of the dialectic pretty much whole from Hegel, Marx, following again on Ludwig Feuerbach, merely reversed the order of historical change. The reality of the present world for Marx was materialistic. The reality of who owned the means of economic production, specifically, was what drove history. The "Idea", or the conceptualization of what the new historical order was all about, followed later.

This, I believe, was Marx's second great error, and my theory is in part based upon the belief that mind does precede matter in the progress of history. I think, in other words, that the ideal, the vision of a different and more complex world, precedes the material, or the existing characteristics within the real world, in pushing history along. The primacy of the mind in the historical progression is important to a psychologically based theory, of course. It is even more important if the psychological components of the theory include different minds.

But let us not get ahead of ourselves. It would be wrong to suggest that Hegel, and more certainly Kant, had any sense at all of how *individual* or *specific* minds played a role in the dialectically Idealist vision. For the Idealists, and particularly Hegel, the dialectical vision came from a collective consciousness, that consciousness being periodically elevated at various stages of the history of the mind. Before we are finished, we will burrow into that undifferentiated, objective whole and suggest that specific personalities, possessing very different visions of the future, in fact do play significant roles in the path of history. A psychologically based political philosophy separates these personalities out. It attempts to describe the root causes of the natural biases that occur when some psychologically based visions triumph over others. In short, the new Idealism builds on minds, plural, not a single mind.

For now, let us merely catalog Marx's Idealist/Materialist error with his essence/existence, or subjective/objective, error. Let us note that it was these two errors, concerning the core philosophical questions of a) how humankind should understand itself and b) how the path of human history should be understood, that underpinned Marx's theory of economic exploitation.

In sum, what I argue is nothing more than that Marxism, and all Whole Group Equity theories that are based solely on the objective condition of a grouping entire, are unable to bring about equitable outcomes in a post-material society. In my view, true political equity will only be possible when we a) place an understanding of human essences at the core of political philosophy and b) place understandings of the role of *different* human beings into the core of how we think about historical progress. Only then will we be able to create a psychologically relativistic notion of the dialectic.

The Twenty-First-Century Left

The political left in the United States remains what it has always been, a relatively weak force. But the American left is also, I suggest, in an important transitional stage. There is an evolution going on in left-of-center political thought, just as there is in the global political reality. Much of what has been written about the left in recent years, particularly in Europe, concerns the so-called Red-Green configuration. Rudolf Bahro, the principal European Green theoretician, has pulled away from the almost pure Marxism of his early writings, though he still allows that "(i)n any case, Red and Green, Green and Red, go well together."[8]

Inevitably, the need to think anew impacts left thinking. Theorists such as William Irwin Thompson write of the "Gaia", a kind of breakout from the purely rational, Western mode of thinking into something both more creative and more integrative of the many different kinds of worldly phenomena. Ironically, he argues, "it was the physicists ... who enabled us to break out of the grip of the positivity." Gaia, for Thompson, "hails a new friendship between art and science where the indeterminacy of Heisenberg and the relativity of Einstein, the imaginative qualities of the descriptions of science, began to be undeniable."[9] Thompson, I think, is expressing something very important for a psychologically based political theory. At a minimum, such a theory takes in the full range of human perspectives.

In the same vein as the Thompson commentary, the quality of Gaia is seen by others as evidencing a "reciprocity" of essence and environment in science. James Lovelock, for example, argues that organisms do not just "adapt to changes in their material environment. As per the Russian scientist Vernadsky, the environment (is) modified by the organisms themselves."[10] Essentialism, over the last years, has been slowly making a comeback in left-of-center thinking.

I confess that over those same years, I have become increasingly unconvinced by writers such as Kate Soper, who contends that "just as socialism can only hope to remain a radical and benign pressure for social change by assuming an ecological dimension, so the ecological concern will remain largely ineffective ... if it is not associated ... with key traditional socialist demands."

Soper speaks for a materially, or what Friedrich Engels sometimes called a "naturally," determined world. [11]

In distinction, I am more favorably disposed to the thinking of a contemporary left writer such as Mary Mellor, who properly recognizes that "essentialist idealism" is what Marx and Engels opposed most vigorously, and most tragically. Correctly deploring the excesses of sociobiology, Mellor is correct in saying that "the question of the relationship between the biological/ecological and the social remains."[12] Yes, the new vision will be both historically Idealist and essentialist, specifically including the role of differentiated personalities.[13]

The obligatory caveat applies. I am not suggesting that the twenty-first-century left can in any way ignore the real world or the very real impact of that world on the politics, as well as the people, of our time. Ultimately, I agree with those, like Lovelock, who are content with a warp and woof of essence-based, and existence-based, views of reality, although I believe the former must be the thicker thread. I still believe that the essence-based view of reality, and its corresponding Idealistic view of history, will provide the principal concept underlying a third tier, subatomic theory. Only this concept will permit the breaking away from the objectivist visions that still dominate so much of left-of-center political thinking.

Also, I suggest that the essentialist/Idealist view is stronger as an underpinning for a twenty-first-century left-of-center political ideology because this combination potentially provides a better bonding for the left's membership than any existence-based bonding. Above all else, an essence-based bonding insists on the recognizing of similar, psychologically grounded perspectives, not just the perspective that is generated by a common, or several common, external experiences.

Let me expand upon why I believe the essence/Idealist-based philosophical perspective is superior to that of Marxism or any other Whole Group Theory. Beyond the twin errors of Marxism, I suggest that all existence-based political philosophies rely on the kinds of identification among followers that are subject to change, sometimes substantial change. Whether someone is left of center politically because of economic condition, gender, sexual persuasion, or ethnicity, the friendly responsiveness of society to members of that aggrieved group will inevitably reduce the intensity of commitment to both that group and the left's overall political position.

I think it is generally recognized that Marxism's failure to receive any but the most cursory consideration in the United States comes from the rise, and what for a long time appeared to be the well-entrenched prosperity, of the American middle class. Therefore, to sustain a commitment to economic justice for the entire society when you have yourself achieved a fair level of economic prosperity must inevitably come from something far deeper than an objective condition. It must come from a deeply seated sense of justice, a sense that arises from something other than one's own circumstances. The commitment to justice must be sufficiently embedded within you so that you will continue your commitment to it, even after you have thrown off your own unjust burden.

Further, the contemporary weakness of Marxism also results from the schisms that seem to inevitably occur among objectively based, aggrieved groups on the left. The fragility of so many left coalitions has resulted from the very nature of the bonding among the component left groupings. That bonding was largely contractual, by which I mean that existence-based coalitions on the left have always relied on having each part of the coalition connected to another part of the coalition, merely by the attractiveness of some immediate, real-world goal that benefited all of the participating groupings. Labor and young people's movements, for example, have often come together and fallen apart. In much the same way as with individual, objectively based commitments to a left position, the goal of one or the other groups may change for some, or most, of the component groupings at any time. If that happens, the coalition will almost inevitably collapse.

Also, the political goal of one day may change for a variety of reasons. The fortunes of one component group may improve without similar improvement for other coalition members. An objective group such as the Teamsters Union, for example, may get what it wishes for in a single labor contract, or in a series of contracts over a period of time, and begin to shift its political loyalty. The Teamsters, for many years now, have increasingly become a Republican union.

Similarly, more than a few radical students have graduated from the schools in which they acted as political radicals, and after going on to attain gainful employment in, for instance, the insurance industry, they quickly lost their left perspective. Also, after a time, some components of a left coalition, built on external circumstances, may find themselves to be more in conflict than in a state of cooperation with the other alliance components when new issues arise, those issues appealing to one coalition partner but not the other.

In any case, the objectively based coalition is highly likely to be compromised at some point. As long as the alliances of any coalition are substantially based on the external, or objective, condition of the members of the alliance, and as long as a contractual form of relationship is what therefore bonds the alliance, I suggest that the coalition is fragile. I think such coalitions on the left have repeatedly been shown to be fragile, and to break.

Also, let us not forget that within any coalition that is based solely on an existential condition, there will, over time, be a subatomic sorting out of the personalities within each component group, as well as the overall coalition leadership. This sorting out alone will impact the structure of how the members of that left coalition interact with other members. I will speak, as I said, to the specifics of this "personality sort" subsequently, within organizations and within governments. All I reiterate here is that within every objectively-based group, a predictable distribution of subjectivities will occur over time. Once that happens, the new combination of personalities that inevitably comes to exist within the leadership and interactively significant positions of the component parts of the coalitions will enjoy a greater likelihood of a) fracturing the coalition or b) diverting the coalition from its original, transcendent purposes to the increasingly disparate goals of each subgroup.

In sum, what I suggest in closing is that a psychologically based political theory should assist the left in recognizing that its own best chance for permanent togetherness is a psychological coalescence. While Whole Group Equity theories have no foundation in psychology, what has been clear about the environmental movement, to use one example, is that it has nurtured citizens of a similar psychological predisposition to take environmental matters seriously.

Think of any environmental issue, whether it be global warming, the loss of species, General Electric's PCBs in the Hudson River, or clear-cut logging. In each case the pro-environment position extends the issue beyond the consideration of a simple business contract. What the corporations typically do, in contrast, is knock off the residual, environmentally sensitive consideration, thus preserving the naked business contract alone. Corporations consistently argue, and act, in such a way that the additional consideration—the untoward, perhaps sometimes unintentional, byproduct of their economic product—is simply not their concern.

There is a form to that kind of thinking. "We are an economic entity, and we seek only an economic result," they say. The response to that form of thinking, the environmental answer, is that the corporation, or failing that the public sector, must take other kinds of considerations, such as air quality, water quality, or species impact, into account. "You must look at all of what you do, beyond the economic," is the environmentalist response. The form of that response is psychologically different than the merely economic response, free of environmental concerns. There is one kind of mind, in other words, that more naturally thinks in the cognitive form, which includes environmental concerns. We will investigate that mind in the next chapter.

Although they are far from exhaustive, the above reasons make up a core of why the twenty-first-century left position will be more secure and more effective if it is based on what I call the Psychological or Natural Left. Of course, we can never forget, or deny, what we are, in terms of an economic condition, gender, sexual preference, ethnic identification, or whatever. But we of the Natural Left will hang together better, rather than surely hang separately, if we weave our similar subjective personalities through our objective identifications and base our theory on who we are. This makes up a subjectively based political philosophy. We will also succeed far better in appealing to subjectively left-of-center white, straight, reasonably prosperous males, successful females and other groupings who are objectively not discriminated against and whose subjective identification, once appealed to, can help our cause. And we can further energize minority, gay and lesbian, labor, and other objectively depreciated citizens if a subjective orientation is activated along with an objective orientation.

In reflecting again on that interesting group that made up the last session of the 2000 Illinois Green Party conference, I simply offer that it was something even beyond their common environmental concerns, and all of their other varied objective identifications, that held them together that night. What was going on in that hot top floor room on Lawrence Ave. was more than a contractual civility, or a waiting to hear what you have to say so I can say what I want to say. I detected a rather broad similarity of temperament among those in that room. The people there largely thought alike, structurally, just as they seemed to feel alike in their nuanced understandings of so many things. This group reflected a similarity of human essence that I think can be seen as a more promising bonding for the left side of the political continuum than any combination of existentially based positions on objective human problems.

By acknowledging that essential similarity and building on it, the political left, whether activated within a truly progressive Democratic Party, a Green Party, the Democratic Socialists, The United Citizens Party, or even the tiny, residual Lincoln feather (no longer a wing) of the Republican Party, can become a permanent part of American politics. In doing so, the left will surely be a more formidable political entity. It will contend effectively with America's conservative parties and corporations, and fight against an emerging global order that imperils democracy in the United States and throughout the world. It will also contribute to a different, I believe better, understanding of the American constitutional order itself, better ensuring that the very "game" of politics, now horribly distorted towards not only those of money but those of a particular cognitive bent, will more accurately reflect what the American citizenry at large truly wants in its politics.

The Six Hundredth Voter

Though I was born and raised in Evanston, Illinois, my parents, fortunately, were very fond of the city—Chicago. We went downtown frequently to plays, museums and restaurants and to generally be a part of a place that is still very special to me. As I grew into my teens, I would sometimes go into the City, by myself or with school buddies, to watch a baseball game or even a precinct on election day. My grandfather had been an alderman, a member of the great Bohemian club the Ceska Beseda, and an old friend of the Chicago machine's founder, Anton Cermak. My great uncle, on my mother's side of the family, was city auditor into the first two years of the elder Daley administration when Harry was 76 years of age. My father, in 1960, became the first president of the Chicago Police Board. He, and then Mayor Richard J. Daley, took the bold position that when citizens called police to tell them they were going on vacation, they had the right to have their homes watched so as to prevent burglary, rather than have Chicago's finest prying open the back door as the citizen was turning the key in the front.

Stories surrounding vote fraud, of course, are part of the Chicago political legend. Surely such fraud existed. The precinct captain's quick dip into the deceased's wallet in order to acquire the voter registration card, and the use of such devices as the chain ballot (one ballot being stolen at the beginning of the day and then properly marked by a precinct captain who handed it to an incoming voter in exchange for a blank ballot on the voter's way out) and the short pencil (a tally worker, usually a woman, finishing an uncompleted ballot with a half-inch of naked graphite jammed under a hearty middle fingernail) were fun to watch.

But what is often lost sight of, and what I want to dwell on for a moment in this period of sub-50 percent presidential voting, is that the Chicago Democratic machine usually scored laudably high voter percentages by altogether legal means. Of course, the person power was available in the precincts. The mayor's patronage list, bulging with 30,000 names, meant that there were roughly six Democratic job holders (need I say they had election day off?) for every precinct in the city. The president of the United States, incidentally, has roughly 3,000 available appointments. A precinct was a well-carved delineation in the Chicago of that time; the norm was 600 voters.

An election day's activity in those times revolved around what was known as a "hard card," an extended, usually taped-together collection of old shirt dry-cleaning cardboards. Each card hosted a large sheet of paper within the edging Scotch tape, the paper's lines highlighting the names, streets, and addresses of registered voters.

Long before election day, the faithful six precinct workers had canvassed their neighborhoods, not only informing people of the upcoming election but also querying each voter as to where he or she would be all day and when he or she would be coming to vote. Voting late in the day was not encouraged. Even Chicago precinct captains could get nervous, largely because their own employment depended on ward committeemen, who in turn had to hand over the entire ward's tallies to the mayor, in person, at the old Morrison Hotel.

And so, by knowing where everyone was going to be and when they could be expected to appear in the church basement, the school, the K. of C. Hall, or the funeral parlor, the workers easily managed a continued updating of the day's progress. Of course, the early canvass also permitted the captain and his crew to establish whether any voter required assistance in order to get to the polls. If Mrs. Moynihan had broken her hip, arrangements would be made for two largish gentlemen to carry her, usually still in her chair, down and then back up as many flights of stairs as necessary. With perhaps a little more difficulty, a precinct captain would arrange for a ride from the factory on, say, the West Side when the precinct was on the far South Side, even if his shift was over at 5:30 and the polls closed at 6:00. I witnessed a circumstance involving such a voter over forty years ago.

It was late on a primary election day and nearly all the hard card was checked off. The winner in primaries in Chicago city elections, I should say, always won the general election because the Republican Party barely existed in many parts of the city. The only true contests were almost invariably between the organization Democrats and the occasional reform Democrat who took a chance on bucking the machine. The machine took primaries very seriously for this reason but also as a kind of spring training for the November state wide elections when Democrats pitted the Chicago vote against the vote of the downstate Republicans.

Voters coming directly from work steadily trickled in the day I was there, as they were expected to do. The precinct captain seemed pleased, except for his worry about that one voter who worked on the other side of town and for whom he had sent a driver. Toward the end of the day, when the worker's shift was supposed to be over and a sense of a fair travel time had expired, the cross-town worker had still not appeared. Finally, with only about ten minutes remaining, a gigantic laborer almost fell through the church basement door. He was covered with dirt from his shoes to his large, Slavic forehead. He was still sweating and everything in his carriage indicated a state of advanced exhaustion. His driver and another precinct worker, with no small effort, assisted him to the Democratic voting table.

One of the little rules of Illinois primaries was that a voter had to declare his or her party before receiving a ballot. During the day no issue involving such a declaration had come up, the Democratic voters simply going over to the Democratic table and asking for a Democratic ballot, while the small handful of Republican voters did the same for their ballots, at a table just a few feet away. With this voter, however, there was a problem. It became clear that, standing at the De-

mocratic table with only moments left to vote, he did not speak English and seemingly could not, therefore, declare which ballot he wanted. The Democratic worker extended a ballot to him, but the Republican worker, not hearing a request and having endured a more than listless day (the Democrats had not spoken to him, even during the lulls), sprang from his chair, bolted to the Democratic table, and pointed out that the worker could not vote until he declared his party.

"Does anyone speak Polish?" the panicked captain asked, looking down at the voter's name on the hard card. Amazingly for a Chicago precinct in that neighborhood, no one presently there did. The captain, then the worker behind the table, then anyone else who thought he could make himself understood, entreated the Pole to speak. But the worker did not understand. In frustration, they shouted at him. He lurched back, the fatigue in his face now coupling with hurt, and anger. Finally, with hardly a minute left on the clock, someone pointed to his own mouth. Speak, speak, the precinct worker pleaded, and then pointed at the small cardboard sign taped to the front of the desk. The sign said "Democrats."

Suddenly the exhausted Polish worker's head snapped back. A look of recognition overcame his dirty face and the still deepening fatigue that had but a moment earlier almost overwhelmed him. After taking an incredibly long breath, he erected his frame, stretched back his shoulders, and lifted his chin above the sweat that still dappled his neck. Then he closed his feet, not clicking his heels but audibly bringing one shoe against the other from heel to toe. Finally, in perfect military manner, he made one full step backward, closed his feet again, opened his mouth for the first time since arriving at the poll, and bellowed, in broken English: "Democraat." I shall never forget it.

Lately, as I have witnessed the increasing nonvoting of more and more American citizens, particularly the young, I have come to think of the possibility that, as I am carried through my seventh decade, I may be one of the few remaining American citizens who has seen one of this country's full-size electoral districts vote 100 percent of its registered voters—legally.

CHAPTER TWO

Forms of Understanding

Roots

A psychologically based political philosophy, or a philosophy of the Natural Left, should be grounded in the richest possible intellectual tradition. The inequities of a post-material society are more subtle and less obvious than the kinds of inequities the real world of politics has experienced and the world of political philosophy has thus far considered. If the impact of subjective, psychological factors now outweighs the impact of objective factors, we need to reach inside the atom of objective political identifications and discover how to maintain the balances of subatomic, that is psychological, matter that alone will ensure twenty-first-century equity.

Each of the next three chapters contains one essential element of the theory's philosophical grounding, without which I do not think we can create much of lasting theoretical value. In this chapter, I will describe the precise nature of the psychological differentiation that, within its subatomic, subjective, context, accounts for the biases that only a third tier, that is a post-liberal, and a post-Whole Group Equity theory, can describe.

In Chapter Three, I will describe how the psychologically differentiated forms of knowledge described in Chapter Two impact the core intellectual questions surrounding a) the limits of knowledge and b) the dialectic, or the process of improving knowledge. We must have a good sense of the role of psychological differentiation in these two places. They are, again, the history and definition of knowledge limits, and the method of expanding those limits. Without this foundation, a psychologically based political philosophy will not be capable of explaining a third-tier standard of political equity.

In Chapter Four, I will briefly describe how the psychological differentiation that is central to a subatomic theory has worked its way through Western thought. I believe the psychological differentiation to have been a powerful intellectual force for a long time. Indeed, it has proven to be so powerful that it has emerged as the principal variable within the core intellectual disputes over a) the nature of knowledge and b) what should be included within intellectual arguments as seen by different schools of thought, within a variety of intellectual fields. I will limit my historical analysis in the fourth chapter to philosophy and jurisprudence, or legal theory, and economic theory. This brief intellectual history of cognitions is necessary to show how different psychological perspectives have manifested themselves in non-political as well as political environments.

The description of the psychological differentiation begins with a discussion of the single question that resides at the pinnacle of knowledge. That question concerns what are known as the "forms." As you know, there is a ladder of abstraction to knowledge. Some questions are more general, more encompassing, and ultimately more definitional than others. Specific, substantive kinds of questions depend, in the final analysis, for their answers on the understanding of higher principles of knowledge. An understanding of what makes up a good government, for example, rests on "higher" understandings of what democracy is, what freedom is, or what citizens can reasonably expect from public officials in terms of services and citizen participation.

At the highest intellectual level, the questions surrounding the forms deal with the shape, or the structure, of knowledge itself. Questions regarding the forms have been around since the works of Plato, specifically *The Symposium* and *Phaedo.*[1] We can think of them as the difference in shape between a bottle of Coke and a can of Coke, not the differences between a can of Coke and a can of Pepsi. Let me say clearly here that a fully elaborated psychological theory of politics will include a large variety of variables. But the questions of shape, or those concerning the forms of knowledge, are what exist, alone, at the top of the knowledge pyramid. They are, again, where our theory must begin.

To gain a better understanding of the psychological differentiation that underpins this political philosophy, I borrow from and to a small degree reinterpret two considerable philosophical figures. These are the German Idealists Immanuel Kant and G. W. F. Hegel. Kant and Hegel, whom I suggest differed greatly in their preferences for forms of knowledge. Understanding this difference, I believe, will lead to an understanding of the psychological differentiations that make up the subatomic theory, the theory based on subjective differences within objective groups.

As an examination of Kant and Hegel will show, much of the argument over the different forms of knowledge has centered around the distinction between what philosophers call "analytic knowledge" as opposed to "synthetic knowledge." Formally, an analytic statement is one in which the subject and the predicate are of the same class of information. "Blind people cannot see" would be an example. For our purposes, we can safely think of analytic statements that are, in everyday language, of the apples to apples form. Again, the variables of the subject and the predicate do not belong to a different classification of knowledge.

In a synthetic statement, in contrast, the subject and the predicate are of different classes of knowledge. The knowledge within each is of different kinds. For our purposes, synthetic knowledge can be thought of as knowledge of apples in relation to oranges. The purist synthetic example I give to my students is the mix of a primary number with a primary color. I ask them to think about 5 + blue.

Throughout the years, philosophers have argued over the two forms of knowledge. These scholars have generally argued that one or the other form is superior, or they have argued that the dividing line between them, or where analytic knowledge stops and synthetic knowledge begins, is at such and such a place. My concern is wholly different. I believe the issue is ultimately subjective, that is I think there is clear evidence of a very different preference for using one form of knowledge over the other when one contrasts the forms of thinking within Kant and Hegel. I think those preferences are identifiable, and that we can use the differentiations of those preferences to describe the core psychological relativity.

In their most abstract writings, both Kant and Hegel dealt with the question of the forms of knowledge. Kant, referring to the simple equation of $7 + 5 = 12$, argued that the equation was synthetic, or apples and oranges, in nature.[2] Kant reasoned that since there were two numbers on one side of the equality and only one number on the other side, there was in fact a real, qualitative difference within the simple mathematical statement. One side in its form was, for Kant, different from the form of the other side. For Kant, again, that made the equation $7 + 5 = 12$ a synthetic statement.

A generation later, Hegel returned to the equation of $5 + 7 = 12$, tweaking Kant a bit with the reversal of the 5 and the 7, and having a bit more fun with him by suggesting that Kant's mind simply could not get around a substantial synthetic cognition. In short, Hegel saw the $5 + 7 = 12$ equation far differently than Kant did. Hegel saw an equation he believed to contain such a tiny difference, particularly where all of the elements of the equation were whole numbers, that he would only label it as analytic, or apples and apples. Put another way, the slight cognitive difference that existed by having one number on one side of the equality and two numbers on the other was vastly outweighed, for Hegel, by the fact that all three elements of the equation were of the same quality; again, whole numbers. The similarity of one whole number to another was far more important to Hegel than the two-to-one imbalance of the numbers surrounding the equal sign.[3]

What does all of this mean for understanding how psychological differentiations impact political systems? What it means, I suggest, is that Kant and Hegel's differing perspectives on such a simple equation as 5 + 7 = 12 evidence very different kinds of minds. Put another way, I suggest that Kant and Hegel had clearly different subjective, or psychological, orientations. There were differences in perspectives that are essential to understanding the subatomic nature of our political philosophy. Neither the classical liberalism of the first tier nor the Whole Group Equity theories of the second tier deal with such psychologically differentiated preferences for one or the other of the principal (analytic and synthetic) cognitive forms.

Let me state it again. What I am saying is that for Kant, or for anyone with a mind similar to Kant's, even the minor difference of having the 5 and the 7 on one side of the equation and the 12 on the other side is sufficient to call the equation synthetic. So what kind of mind did Kant have? I think it is clear that he had an analytic, not a synthetic, kind of mind. He seemed to have a preference, all things equal, for similar, or apples and apples, kinds of knowledge. Even minute dissimilarities among variables led Kant to describe such variables as synthetic. For him, the variables were very different.

As for Hegel, the equation and Hegel's classification of it were precisely the opposite. If the contrast between 5 + 7 and 12 was not sufficient for Hegel to recognize a significant difference, then it is clear that Hegel's mind tolerated, or perhaps better to say required, a more substantial differentiation between variables before he would call them synthetic. I suggest that that position reveals Hegel's mind to have been synthetic in nature, in contrast to analytic. Once more, this is the psychological differentiation that will lie at the core of a psychologically based political philosophy. We need to examine it further.

The Rise of Subjectivity

The difference between the Kantian, or analytic, position and the Hegelian, synthetic, preferences for forms of knowledge should be central to any political philosophy based on human psychology. By itself, the distinction between the analytic and synthetic, or apples-and-apples as opposed to apples-and-oranges cognition, is important. But it alone is not sufficient for the theory. We must climb to another level of abstraction before the pure knowledge claims of Kant and Hegel are helpful to a psychologically based political theory.

The transition requires only that we take the ostensibly objective views of Kant and Hegel on the nature of the 5 + 7 = 12 equation and lift our vision toward a subjectively based description of why their very different kinds of minds arrived at the very separate conclusions they did regarding the equation's correct depiction. In short, all I am doing to Kant and Hegel is contrasting their different claims regarding the equation and then moving one step up the ladder of abstraction to suggest that the cause of their differentiation is subjective.

We are moving, in other words, to the level of taking Kant's and Hegel's ostensibly objective statements and using those very statements as examples of different kinds of minds. We are moving assumedly objective depictions into those of differentiated, subjective depictions.

There is, of course, supplementary evidence of the kinds of minds that Immanuel Kant and G. W. F. Hegel possessed. Their personalities were in fact very different. Roger Scruton, for example, noted that Kant evidenced "a remarkable self discipline" in such things as having his manservant wake him at five o'clock, taking his sole daily meal at one o'clock, and taking a post-meal walk "irrespective of the weather." Never convincing himself of the propriety of marriage, Kant saw it as little more than an agreement for the "reciprocal use of each other's sexual organs."[4]

A recent biography of Kant attempted to downplay those writings that found Kant to lead a mechanistic, even compulsive life. But even a favorable reader of the Prussian philosopher like Manfred Keuhn found Kant's life's purpose to be little more than "to compose character" ... "to compose ... order and tranquility in our conduct" and to "live appropriately."[5]

Hegel was a wholly different sort. From his rebellious days at the Tübingen seminary, where, as Terry Pinkard reports, he first "reacted to the strictness of (the) academic environment by forming bonds of camaraderie with (other students)," Hegel engaged in the outright disobedience of a variety of seminary rules. Hegel even spent time in the student jail, the soon to be philosopher being more than a bit of a rebel. Also, Hegel inclined to drink a bit too much, particularly with his friends, and he was remembered by his sister as a "jovial sort who loved both to dance and to visit the ladies." Along with his "cutting of lectures and his continual oversleeping," Hegel was truly a "gregarious soul" who spent a good bit of time in simple human interaction. In doing so, his hours and routines were irregular, his personal world disorderly.[6]

One can make too much of psycho-biography, to be sure. A Myers-Briggs test would more convincingly confirm the contrast between the personalities of Kant and Hegel that these giants' biographers typically report. But, in a general way, what we know about the lives of Kant and Hegel should not surprise us regarding the way they evaluated the $5 + 7 = 12$ equation as synthetic or analytic, respectively. The philosophers' very different personalities still shine through, and their very different inclinations toward order generally mirror their perspectives on the different forms of analytic and synthetic knowledge.

To repeat, I think it is clear that the kind of objectively based perspective (which Marx and other second-tier, Whole Group philosophers have typically offered) would simply not engage in the kind of interpretation that I have just outlined. The fact is that the dominance of the broader teachings of all Whole Group Equity theories, entirely apart from their substantive positions on economic exploitation, racial and gender bias and the like, have so dominated left-of-center thinking over the last 150 years that they have forestalled an understanding of the psychological differentiation that exists within any objective class. These teachings did not permit any essence-based notion of human psychology. They precluded differentiation within objective classes.

What I am suggesting, of course, is that a new political philosophy, based on differentiated human psychologies and the cognitions they prefer, is now possible. The differentiation between preferences for a kind of knowledge form, most pointedly references for analytic and synthetic forms of knowledge, should lie at the base of that theory.

As my reader has surely figured out, there never was an objectively correct answer to the question of whether 5 + 7 = 12 was analytic or synthetic. Though much has been written on the topic, my belief is that it was always a question of how one looked at it. Because Kant and Hegel had very different kinds of minds, their views of 5 + 7 = 12 resulted from that difference. In summation, close to one end of a spectrum the purely analytic mind has a greater difficulty with variation, or with complexity. It tends to find a bump in the intellectual road to be the Matterhorn. The purely synthetic mind, in contrast, is insufficiently stimulated by cognitive similarity, or even minute differentiation. It seeks greater differentiation, or the interplay between the world's apples and oranges. Neither kind of mind is inherently superior; these minds are simply different.

As I have already said, we should think of this subjective distinction of analytic versus synthetic as ranging along a continuum. Few of us, fortunately, are at one pole or the other. Also, I am sure that as others participate in the growth of this psychologically based theory, other psychological variables, beyond the simple analytic/synthetic spectrum, should be and will be added. But when this principal subjective range is placed, subatomically, within any whole group, I believe that those differences alone are important enough that they can underpin a twenty-first-century political theory for the left.

It goes almost without saying that only when we identify these core differences among differing personalities will we be able to consciously balance analytic and synthetic cognitions within the objective groupings of citizens. Only then can we reach the subtler and heretofore less obvious standards of equity that a twenty-first-century world will require. I will say a good deal more about how we achieve that standard of equity soon.

In Chapters Six and Seven, I will specifically suggest how the analytic and synthetic cognitions are reflected in the Constitution and the Bill of Rights, as well as in the decisions of the U. S. Supreme Court. When we get down to the analytic and synthetic cognitions, I think the errors of the Court, particularly in the campaign finance reform area, are damaging to America's constitutional democracy.

Nader v. Kreml

Henry Ford II did not call often, which was all right with my mother. She never liked him. But he did call occasionally, either about the Ford Motor Company or the automobile industry generally. Why wasn't my father home? Mr. Ford had tried the office, but my father wasn't in.

The history of my father and Mr. Ford was a long one. My father had created the first traffic division of a police department when he was on the Evanston, Illinois police force. He did this while attending Northwestern University. He received national recognition for what he did to bring Evanston's accident and death rate down. With the help of Northwestern and the City of Evanston, he founded the Northwestern University Traffic Institute, which was soon recognized nationally for its training of police, accident investigators, judges, prosecutors, and others who were concerned about the rising carnage on America's roads.

My father, while on the Evanston police force, had been deeply impacted by the death of a young woman whom he was carrying to his police car after an accident. He dedicated his career to reducing traffic fatalities. The Northwestern University Traffic Institute, over its lifetime, engaged in a variety of safety-related programs. It devised public education campaigns concerning traffic accidents, and researched such matters as the effects of drinking, speeding, and unsafe roads on safe driving.

The activities of the Traffic Institute inevitably involved the private sector as well as governmental agencies. The casualty insurance industry, the Kemper brothers in particular, were interested in saving lives and contributed generously to the Institute. The automobile industry, over time, saw that it too had some responsibility in this area and developed its own ties to the Institute. Though Studebaker's Paul Hoffman, the administrator of the Marshall Plan, was the most dedicated to safety of all automobile executives, the Ford Motor Company was the most ready among the major companies to make a commitment to doing something about traffic deaths and injuries. Ford was progressive for its time in recognizing that the automobile was part of the accident and injury problem. Senior readers and vintage car enthusiasts will recall the depressed steering columns of the 1956 Fords, an innovation Mr. Ford and my father created.

As time went on, my father became the head of the Transportation Center at Northwestern University and eventually vice president for planning and development there. He raised most of the money for the expansion of the campus into Lake Michigan in the 1960s. But my father never lost his interest in automobile safety, continuing to serve on the boards of the National Safety Council, the IACP, and other bodies.

By the end of the 1960s, that continued involvement would take an interesting turn. A young lawyer named Ralph Nader had published a book entitled Unsafe at Any Speed *in 1965. The book included a broad-ranging indictment of the Chevrolet Corvair, a car that was GM's rear-engine response to the need many citizens felt for a modest, economical automobile. Without question, the Corvair had been involved in an inordinate number of fatal accidents. The Corvair design was inherently faulty, although things may not have been so bad if GM had done a better job of instructing buyers on how a rear-engine car came out of a turn differently from a front-engine car. But the larger issue Ralph Nader raised concerned to what degree the public sector ought to be involved in the regulation of the automobile industry in matters of auto safety.*

Ralph Nader made a convincing case that there were many unsafe features in all American automobiles. From protruding hood ornaments, to bad sight lines, to potentially skewering dashboard instruments and steering columns that did to drivers what longbows did to the French at Agincourt, Nader scored point after point. But beyond his roll call of automobile perils was a unifying thread, one based on the notion of the "second accident," or what happened to the human body when the automobile it was riding in collided with another car, a telephone pole, or whatever.

Nader made it brutally clear that no matter what may or may not have happened to the automobile itself in any accident, it was what happened microseconds later, when the human driver and/or passenger hit something inside the passenger cabin, that caused the human carnage reflected in automobile injury and fatality rates. In brief, all Nader said was that an unsecured body within a car that had just sustained an accident was altogether too vulnerable to injury or death from the inside of the car itself, and not directly from the impact between two cars, or one car and an inert object.

Ralph Nader had successes in the 1960s. He convinced President Lyndon Johnson that the federal government had an obligation to step in and mandate certain regulations regarding automobiles, particularly the requiring of seat belts that would restrain drivers and passengers from careening around the cabin before the inevitable second accident. His argument was learned and convincing.

Not long after Unsafe at Any Speed *caught the public's attention and the Johnson administration had acceded to many of Ralph Nader's requests, Henry Ford II called our home again. Where was my father?*

As with all industries, the automobile companies have a trade association. The Automobile Manufacturer's Association, not surprisingly, is one of the more powerful lobbies in Washington. But, considering the size of the industry and its importance to the U. S. economy, it was not as powerful in the 1960s as one might have imagined. Although it was grudgingly prepared to live with the governmental regulations passed in the 1960s, it still held to the view that the government should only assist in what was basically a private-sector responsibility for the manufacture of safe automobiles. It was all right for the government to involve itself in things like the improved highway design quality that was evident in the building of the Eisenhower-inspired National Defense, or Interstate, Highway system, but not much beyond that.

Ralph Nader and his book had changed the thinking of many Americans about things. Detroit's executives needed someone to head up the AMA who was qualified to speak to the public, and Congress, on matters of traffic safety from the industry's perspective. I want to make clear that my father, even in his later life, remained deeply committed to automobile safety. He continued to fight for public safety programs throughout America, for driver education, for the development of a variety of accident investigation tools, and for the development of those law enforcement arrangements that would affix blame to drunken drivers, speeding drivers, unsafe drivers, or even drivers who did not maintain their automobiles in proper running, and stopping, condition. But over the years, as head of both NUTI and the Transportation Center, my father had become convinced that the casualty insurance companies, the automobile companies, and others within the private sector's industries were up to the task of solving the traffic safety problem. For him, the road to progress was that of an enlightened private sector, with the assist of only those public agencies who would deal with highway design, law enforcement, and so forth. My father accepted Henry Ford II's offer to become president of the Automobile Manufacturer's Association in 1970.

It was a tumultuous time in Washington, Watergate and the eventual resignation of the first president ever forced to leave office occurred at the close of my father's tenure. The years immediately before had been stressful throughout the country as well, with the anti-war demonstrations, the Civil Rights movement, and three dreadful assassinations. I disagreed with my father over some political issues, but I never doubted his deep commitment to improved traffic safety. And there is no question but that in speaking with him over the years I learned a good deal about the government and public life. Indirectly, I suppose I learned something from Ralph Nader too.

Maybe what I learned most importantly from Ralph Nader was what happens when the public and the private sectors meet in something of a dialectical confrontation. The substance of the conflict in this instance was about automobile safety regulation, but the form of the conflict, in retrospect, was typical of other important sectoral disputes. I also remember that my father's lawyer at the AMA was a noted Washington attorney/lobbyist named Lloyd Cutler, about whom I will also say more later. I met him, as I later met Nader, in a wholly different context.

CHAPTER THREE

Limits to Knowledge and How To Get There

How Much Can You Know?

In this chapter I will add two more blocks to the psychologically grounded theory. First, I will take the subjective differentiation between the Kantian and Hegelian perspectives on the 5 + 7 = 12 equation described above and apply that differentiation to the age-old philosophical question concerning the limits to knowledge. Philosophy has always been bedeviled by the conceptually rather simple but actually very difficult problem of discerning how much we can know.

It is my belief that to be useful, both as a theory and as a real-world guide to a more equitable polity, a subatomic, subjectively based perspective will expand the limits to knowledge. I will attempt to show how that can be done here by describing how a mutual, that is simultaneous, use of the analytic and the synthetic cognitions increases what we can know. Such an increase, particularly of the knowledge that the synthetic cognition contributes to the knowledge base generally, should help show the way to a truer, specific standard of political equity. Second, I believe that the subatomic perspective both alters and makes more powerful the very process of increasing philosophical knowledge. The dialectic, of course, has been used in a variety of ways over the centuries. I will focus originally on the ways that the German Idealists Immanuel Kant and G. W. F. Hegel perceived, and used, the dialectic. Then, I will suggest an altogether new way of putting this foundational concept to work.

Let us begin with the limits-to-knowledge question but let me do so with a caveat, that being that each of the next two chapters, though I believe them to be important, may be skimmed by the reader who is not primarily concerned with a) the impact of the cognitive differentiation on the limits to knowledge question and the English and American legal dialectics, and b) the impact of the cognitive differentiation on what I believe to be the patterns of intellectual history that cognitive differentiation accounted for. Though these are core intellectual questions, if the reader is solely concerned with the impact of the cognitive differentiation on a) America's governmental structures, and b) American law and particularly the *Buckley v. Valeo* ruling on campaign finance reform, she may well wish to concentrate on Chapters Five through Eight.

I would ask: at what point can you say that you know something with considerable certainty? Obviously, that question suggests a frontier. There is a border to knowledge, and as knowledge is extended into more and more difficult and/or contentious arenas, those who deal with the limits of knowledge are more prepared to say, and may be more accurate in saying, "you simply cannot know anything beyond this." We can reasonably well know a good bit of what goes on in nature, but we can only think that we know something about the supernatural, for example.

In short, the knowledge frontier is not difficult to define, particularly if one keeps two dichotomies in mind. The first dichotomy has to do with the forms of knowledge: the analytic and the synthetic, or the apples and apples as opposed to the apples and oranges forms that we discussed in the previous chapter. For the moment, I am suspending any discussion of the psychological differentiation between those who disagree over such things as the $5 + 7 = 12$ equation. I ask you merely to think of apples and apples as opposed to apples and oranges kinds of knowledge as they both exist, in an everyday kind of understanding.

But we do need to add a second dichotomy to the theoretical construct, a dichotomy that is as essential for the limits-of-knowledge question as are the analytic and synthetic forms. This dichotomy marks the difference between what is called a priori and a posteriori knowledge. A priori knowledge, put simply, is knowledge that comes through reasoning. A priori reasoning is nothing more than a coming to a conclusion about something without using empirical evidence. You do not find something to be the case because you have seen it, heard it, or touched it. It is true to you not because you know the relationship between, say, a light switch and the light that goes on when you push that switch from its "off" to its "on" position. You find something to be true because you have come to it by thinking about it.

A posteriori knowledge, unlike a priori knowledge, relies on empirical evidence. An example is the two pencils that your first grade teacher placed next to the two pencils that were already on the table to show you that two and two add up to four. She wanted to teach you how to see things in a certain way, an additive way in this case. In the early years, and still to a good degree throughout your life, empirical demonstrations are helpful for increasing knowledge, as well as fortifying old knowledge.

What should be obvious by now, I hope, is that in most cases a priori or reasoned knowledge is a more speculative kind of reasoning than is a posteriori or empirically based knowledge. You are surer of things when you can see them or hear them, for instance. There is also a greater likelihood that other people will see them in the same way that you do, although even that is never certain. But there is a better chance, all things being equal, for what philosophers call trans-subjectivity when things are empirically known. There's a better chance that you and I will see the same thing than that we will reason to the same thing.

There are exceptions, of course, to the general notion of the more certain nature of a posteriori thought. Kant's a posteriori knowledge, gained only by induction (the most speculative of a posteriori statements), was surely less certain than his a priori knowledge in the domain of mathematics.

The speculative side of a priori knowledge has always been the bugaboo of philosophy. What kind of reasoning are you using? Are you merely speculating? Or are you perhaps engaging in wishful thinking, your biases being much a part, as is so often the case, of what you claim to know by reason? In fact, it was the highly speculative reasoning of the French *philosophes* in the pre-Revolutionary period, again, that so riled, and inspired, Kant. "How could these French take the underlying reasoning of something like mathematics, and claim that they possess the same certainty regarding their so-called laws of politics?" is what Kant, in effect, was asking. Kant thought that such extended claims by Voltaire and the Legislationists for knowledge about the laws of politics, for example, were what led to the tragic excesses of the French Revolution and the rise of Napoleon.

So, using the two origins of knowledge (a priori and a posteriori), combined with the two forms, or shapes, of knowledge (analytic and synthetic), permit me briefly to describe how the limits to knowledge have been expanded over the last three hundred years of Western thought. There is a pattern to this expansion of what could be known, and I believe psychological differentiation has played a significant part in the development of that pattern. If we can correctly identify the pattern, we can make progress toward developing the subatomic, psychologically based theory we are aiming for. That theory will depend on a broader notion of what the limits to knowledge are in general. Let us begin with a prominent philosopher who spoke clearly to the issue of how much we can know.

Sometimes political scientists are not as aware as they should be that John Locke was far more than a political philosopher. Locke wrote broadly on a range of philosophical matters, and specifically on the nature of knowledge. To be sure, his conservatism there was reflected in his political thinking. As we have already reviewed in our discussion of Marx, the key to understanding Locke's general philosophy was his notion of the tabula rasa or the idea that the human mind is originally a blank. All that that mind eventually contains, therefore, came from the outside.

Once understood, Locke's notion of the tabula rasa makes his view on the limits of knowledge predictable. In discussing the limits of knowledge in his *Essay Concerning Human Understanding*, Locke did marginally address the differentiations that existed between different kinds of knowledge.[1] But he did not get to the specific differences between analytic and synthetic forms of understanding. He relied, principally, on the differences between a priori and a posteriori knowledge.

But here, Locke's distrust of speculation could not have been clearer. Locke maintained that a posteriori knowledge, or knowledge of what has been proven empirically, was the only knowledge claim one could reasonably make. No knowledge existed beyond a posteriori knowledge. Again, he never mentioned analytic or synthetic knowledge or the role that these forms might play in defining the limits to knowledge.

Soon, Locke's restrictive position on the limits to knowledge was challenged by Gottfried Leibniz. Leibniz was a German mathematician who went beyond Locke regarding the limits of knowledge by arguing that a priori knowledge, or knowledge gained by mere reason, was in fact possible. You could, at least, know some things by thinking intelligently about them.

But Leibniz's mind was indeed that of the mathematician. Unlike Locke, he did utilize the analytic to synthetic distinction of knowledge forms, but he only allowed analytic knowledge, not synthetic knowledge, to be known a priori. What did mathematics rely on? For math, you had to reason, and as long as one was only talking about numbers, you could put a great deal of faith in that reason. Beyond numbers, one would not want to venture speculatively. And so, we were up to permitting a priori knowledge, but only sometimes.

Then, Immanuel Kant made his contribution to the expansion of knowledge's limits. Kant was a philosophical skeptic, again doubting the bold knowledge claims of all speculative thinkers. He confirmed Leibniz's position on the possibility of a priori knowledge, and then went a little, but only a little, beyond it. Recall that Kant had argued that the equation $5 + 7 = 12$ exemplified a synthetic cognition. With that sense of the synthetic cognition, and only that sense, he agreed that synthetic knowledge could be known by a priori reasoning. Because he had limited what he believed to be synthetic knowledge to mathematics and the physical sciences, the higher questions of philosophy would not be included as permissible synthetic a priori knowledge. For Kant, much of philosophy was just too speculative, and too often biased. Since it did not import sound reasoning, the synthetic form could not be used in the philosophical endeavor.

To continue, the lineage of Western notions of the limits to knowledge, so far, ends precisely where we might think it would: with G. W. F. Hegel. Hegel was anything but a skeptical philosopher. He was very much a speculative philosopher, believing that gathering levels of insight could accumulate within the human collective consciousness. For Hegel, consequently, even synthetic a priori knowledge within the domain of philosophy was possible.

Of course, it was appropriate for Hegel to believe that synthetic a priori knowledge was attainable because, as an Idealist, he believed that humankind could again reach the level of Absolute understanding that he searched for in a less secular context at Tübingen. All that was lost in the Judeo-Christian Garden after the Creation, according to the Biblical teaching, but Hegel was energized by the notion of getting it all back. Being able to use synthetic, apples and oranges reasoning, within the arena of philosophical questions, would help immeasurably, Hegel thought, in regaining Absolute understanding. That was heady stuff, and a good many philosophers, and real world figures, have thought not only that Hegel went too far but also that in going too far he developed a theory that could, and has been, sorely twisted. His later writings that highlighted the role of Germany in the final stage of political development brought the wrath of those like Karl Popper, Karl Friedrich, and Søren Kierkegaard. What I suggest is that we can go, and should go, one step further, while at the same time not creating something that will be used improperly by either dictators, or extreme moralists.

A psychologically based, relativistic political philosophy, one that is based on psychological differentiation, goes beyond Hegel regarding the limits of knowledge by suggesting one new thing. As I have said, the ostensibly objective, but differentiated, perspectives held by Kant and Hegel on the equation $5 + 7 = 12$ were in fact divined from their particular and very different subjective perspectives. I suggest that the *simultaneous* incorporation of the analytic and synthetic cognitive forms ensures a better philosophical and political perspective than does the solitary use of either the analytic or the synthetic cognition. I think that this simultaneity of differentiated perspectives is the key to a psychologically relativistic theory. Further, I believe that it can only come from a subatomic understanding of the subjective variable within all Whole Group objectivities.

Put another way, the simultaneous inclusion of both the analytic and synthetic cognition, once we have inserted the subjective (psychological) preference for one or the other cognitions, permits an immediate improvement of all understanding, including a priori, speculative understanding. If I know how two cognitively different minds speculate on the same philosophical problem, just as if I know how two individuals measure the distance across a river from different points on one side of the river, I will have a far better sense of the reality of that philosophical problem than if I utilize but one perspective.

In short, whereas Hegel greatly favored the synthetic cognition within his philosophical perspective, arguing that it alone was responsible for the great improvements in human understanding, I argue that if we combine an analytic form of cognition with a synthetic form of cognition, the synthetic being the cognition that I believe is too often minimized in America's legal and political argument, we will far better gauge a standard of political equity. The essence-based, Idealistically grounded philosophy that I offer to the twenty-first-century left shows that synthetic and analytic cognitions are something far more than intellectual abstractions. These forms of knowledge come from someplace. They are not only natural in their origin and in their form, but they are absolutely essential for the advancement of the understanding of, and the equitable solution of, a variety of issues in the real world of politics.

What I suggest here, in short, is that a twenty-first-century left must argue that the synthetically generated perspective, like any analytically generated perspective concerning a grouping of individuals, is entitled to its full political consideration. In the twenty-first century we must consciously include the synthetic cognition, and of course the kind of mind that produces the synthetic cognition, as an equal political partner with the analytic cognition and its psychological hosts. This must be accomplished in the worlds of both political philosophy and political reality. Only this new subatomic standard of equity will ensure equitable treatment for objective groups and individual citizens. To guarantee this equity, the very argument over equity in a post-material society, and the very structures of government that deal with public policy, must be placed into cognitive balance.

Of course, the biases of American politics continue to evidence imbalances that exist between and among whole political groups. But even here, I believe those biases are in great part the result of subatomic arrangements within all political groups, and within the government that allocates goods and services among groups and individuals. Thus, only a theoretical elevation to a wholly different, third-tier political theory that purposefully incorporates understandings of the subatomic, subjective differentiation, will restore political equity. Grounding that theory within the fundamental philosophical questions regarding the limits of knowledge is a necessary part of those understandings.

The Method of New Knowledge

The notion of the dialectic has been with us since the Greeks, if not earlier. Plato believed in the value of the contested conversation, the dialogue, which promised that both participants to the argument would come away with something better than what each of them brought to the discussion. Indeed, they should come away with something even better than the summed knowledge of the two discussants. They should come away with an improved *form* of understanding. A dialectical argument over political positions or political candidates, for example, should illuminate how the political system should work and perhaps does not work.

Not unexpectedly, Kant and Hegel differed notably in the form of the dialectic each utilized. For Kant, the dialectic was primarily a categorization device. Kant was much concerned with the proper placement of knowledge into configurations that made a general sense. Kant's dialectic, in other words, did not have much to do with history; it was certainly not the engine of change that brought about human progress. For Kant, changes in the world's realities would always be the work of Providence.[2]

But for Hegel, as you might imagine, the dialectic was very different; the dialectic was the principal engine of improved knowledge, and thus of real world improvement. For Hegel, the dialectic propelled each stage of history onto another level, moving humankind from one set of understandings to another, ever more complex, level of understanding. Hegel's *Phenomenology* did nothing less than trace a path of human progress from a simple consciousness of the senses to an Absolute comprehension of all knowledge.[3]

Not surprisingly, Hegel's preference for the synthetic cognition meant that he viewed the entire cognitive form of the dialectic as synthetic. Many who have heard of the dialectic learned that the three-stage historical process of a) thesis, b) antithesis, and c) synthesis marked the essential substructure of the concept. In fact, Hegel never used these terms. For Hegel, the dialectic moved from the stage wherein a pattern of knowledge was known only "in itself," to a second stage wherein knowledge was known "for itself," and then to a stage wherein knowledge was known "in and for itself."

In the first dialectical stage, the "in itself" stage, meant that at some early point in the process of moving to a new and better level of historical understanding, the new level still existed outside of the context of the collective conscience. The new, more complex understanding, in other words, was still outside the great hall of contemporary knowledge and therefore existed alone, within its own rationale, and not yet in conflict with the old pattern of understanding.

The second stage, the "for itself" stage, occurs when the new complex of understanding comes into conflict with the old understanding. It is this stage, most often called the "contradiction," that does what the ancient Greek dialogues promised. The new level of understanding triumphs over and transforms the old understandings by introducing something that is both more complex and more explanatory than the old understanding. Not all of what the old explanation contributed is lost, to be sure. But the paradigm changes after the contradiction, the best of the old understanding assuming its place, if in a reconfigured form, within the new vision. Subatomic physics simply subsumes atomic, Newtonian physics.

The third stage, the "in and for itself" stage, is the period of reconciliation. The battle, the contradiction, is over. The new, more complex vision, having achieved its victory, now fully rationalizes the new understanding. A degree of homeostasis, or intellectual equilibrium, sets in and, for a while, the progress of history is less tumultuous, mostly finding newer and better applications for the novel paradigm, or at most making minor adjustments to it. Inevitably, of course, history marches toward what will be the next dialectical contradiction, challenging the formerly new paradigm.

All of the above is the standard understanding of the dialectic. With Hegel, again, it was a vital concept, ever pushing forward the frontiers not just of substantive knowledge but also of deep complexes of understanding that embraced mind first and then the real world. Only vulgar Hegelianism, do not forget, saw Hegel as exclusively concerned with the mind. Nonetheless, I think there is more to the story. For just as I have argued that the limits of knowledge could be pushed beyond Hegel with the simultaneous use of the analytic and the synthetic cognitions, so too I have suggested that the dialectical method is more powerful when it includes both cognitions, and not just one. That leads to the next question: in what order do the two cognitions exist within the dialectic?

Judith Shklar, the late political theorist at Harvard, once said about Hegel's dialectic that it pushed history along as "a single ordered whole."[4] For Hegel, in other words, the dialectic was all of a cognitive piece, a synthetic piece, with no substantial cognitive differentiation existing among the three dialectical stages. I disagree, with Hegel, not with Shklar's depiction of his dialectic.

Just as I think Hegel to have been wrong in restricting the limits of knowledge to the a priori synthetic cognition, with no recognition of the complementary and simultaneous role of the analytic cognition, I also think Hegel to have been wrong in saying that the stages of the dialectic were cognitively undifferentiated. I think the stages of the dialectic *are* cognitively differentiated, in fact very clearly so.

Again, the "in itself" stage of the dialectic does not yet contain a contradiction. A rationalized, internally consistent set of understandings is not challenging anything that is cognitively differentiated. I believe this stage is of the analytic form. The dominant complex of understanding is still as well rationalized as it was at the conclusion of the last dialectical stage.

But then there is a conflict. In the "for itself" stage, or the contradictory stage, the two incompatible understandings collide. As the fray brings together things of an entirely different form, the contradiction moves to its cognitively synthetic state. Again, the rationalized form of one understanding and the rationalized, but more powerful and complex form of the emerging understanding, are not of the same shape or form. The act of their interfacing brings a conflict not just of substance but also, very importantly, of that form. History's succession of apples, in other words, eventually runs into an orange. The can of Coke meets the bottle of Coke.

Finally, I argue that as the "in and for itself" stage takes over, and as it restores intellectual order once the conflict has been sorted out, that new order is again analytic. The discordances of the contradiction have been harmonized and quiescence rules. That is, it rules until there is some even newer vision with its second-stage, synthetically formed, contradiction.

Why would a mind as extraordinary as Hegel's not see that the dialectic was not an aggregate, and that each stage of the aggregation was in fact made up of different cognitions? I think Hegel did not see the psychology behind the differentiated cognitive forms of the analytic and the synthetic because Hegel, after all, lived in an earlier time. Psychology, at least the personal psychology of Freud, Jung, Adler, etc. was not yet a part of the intellectual story. Thus Hegel could never imagine the dialectic as the sequenced alternation of psychologically differentiated forms that I think it clearly is.

I truly believe that if G. W. F. Hegel were with us today, and if he were aware of the psychology that underlies the different preferences for different cognitions, as he surely would be, he would see the cognitively alternated depiction of the dialectic's stages quite clearly. Further, regarding the extension of the limits of knowledge beyond the synthetic a priori (with the simultaneous use of the analytic and the synthetic cognitions), he might well have found the alternated cognition dialectic to be even more powerful than what he envisioned for the dialectic in his time.

The English Legal Dialectic

Changing the form of the dialectic to one made up of alternated cognitions is, of course, an intellectual abstraction. Therefore, in part to illustrate the alternated cognition dialectic but in part as well to introduce some real-world applications that should be of value later, let us examine two concrete examples of how I believe the cognitively alternating form of the dialectic actually worked. The examples I have chosen occurred in two significant periods of

Anglo-American legal and political development. The first stretched from the late sixteenth century to the early seventeenth century in England, a birth time for English democracy. The second occurred in the early latter half of the American twentieth century, covering but not exclusively existing during the one time when the United States Supreme Court clearly made new law. This was the period of the late chief justice Earl Warren. Hopefully, these examples will appropriately introduce the legal issues we will ultimately be concerned with within the cognitively based constitutionally perspective we are building.

What I hope to show here is that during these two very rich periods of Anglo-American legal and political development, the alternated cognition dialectic was in fact quite important to the development of both the law and the politics of the time. The analytic-synthetic-analytic dialectical sequence will be outlined in both examples. These are not legal or political explanations, but mere descriptions of the sequence of the cognitive forms that existed during the different stages of these two dialectical periods.

The first example portrays the significant legal and political triumphs of the great English jurist Sir Edward Coke. Coke began his distinguished career as a private lawyer, and yet, by the close of his illustrious life, he had made major contributions to English public law. While still a young lawyer, Coke tried the famous *Shelley's Case* (1584), a matter involving a dispute over a land title.[5] The details of *Shelley* depict a rather routine fight over title between two branches of a family. The question of whether one brother could legally sell the land and the manor they were living in relied on how the title to the land they owned had been passed down to them.

Under one interpretation—the one of the old feudal land law, although there were cases before *Shelley* that had begun to change it—the law still included a clear differentiation between the life estate, or the right to live somewhere for the rest of one's years without directing to whom it should pass upon that person's demise, and what was called the remainder interest, which was simply the interest after the life estate ended. Again, the old land law kept these two interests separate, even when the life estate and the remainder interest were given to the same person. Thus, the remainder interest prevented a clear, or fee simple, title to the land to any buyer.

With regard to the alternating cognitive nature of the dialectic, *Shelley's Case* is important for one reason. The separation of the two interests, the life and remainder interests, made it more difficult to sell the property to someone than if the interests were merged. Coke's legal argument in favor of permitting the title to be transferred convinced the court that the life estate and the remainder interests should be merged, allowing a current occupant to sell the property without any encumbrance on its title. As a result of such a merger, the good-faith purchaser in the normal course of trade could assume full ownership and possess the whole, or fee simple, title to the land. This notion of the rights of the good-faith purchaser for value continues in the law today.

Coming when it did in English history, that is during the Elizabethan period when England was successfully challenging several contenders for mercantile primacy, the ruling in *Shelley's Case* made it easier to sell real property, and even personal property, in a way that facilitated business among the rising commercial class. In a significant way, it went a long way toward liberating that class's wealth-creating activities from feudal impediments.

Once more, it is the cognitive form of *Shelley's Case* that is important for the theory we are building. What seems clear is that the cognitive form of *Shelley's Case* is unmistakably analytic. The case's ruling facilitated a bilateral contract—that is, it facilitated that core commercial interaction that essentially homogenizes two variables, the product or service on one hand and the price on the other, and makes them qualitatively interchangeable. It facilitated that kind of contract by removing a potential encumbrance to the transaction. That encumbrance, cognitively synthetic of course, no longer impaired the *Shelley* contract.

From the perspective of *Shelley*, we can look back on legal history and see that this case and similar cases were the first stage, the dialectically analytic stage, which marked the beginning of a new historical era. It is the first, or "in itself," stage of the new dialectic, and what happened next, with hindsight, just as clearly fulfilled more of the dialectical progress.

Recall again that at this, still early stage in Coke's considerable career, he was but a private lawyer. His immediate, or objective, purpose, the furtherance of his client's position, led to the above key case that helped free up titles and thereby play its part in the Elizabethan mercantile ascendancy. But the death of the "Virgin Queen," the Tudor Elizabeth I in 1603, and the resultant ascendance of the Stuart King James I, signaled a substantial reversal in both the political fortunes of the English commercial class and the continuance of that evolutionary political progress toward democracy that the Tudors had tolerated, if not assisted. More would need to be done to continue the commercial age's historical progress.

The short of it is that the Stuarts, unlike the Tudors, saw the new commercial classes as a threat to their traditional prerogatives, largely wrapped up in the notion of the divine right of kings. They were unsympathetic, particularly, to what they considered to be the intrusions on government that the new middle class and its allied parliamentarians had engaged in during the previous century. Nonetheless, the common law continued to grow, in spite of the Stuarts. To chronicle that progress, let us briefly examine three legal cases that responded to the Stuart anti-common law, and anti-statutory law, position. I believe that these cases were cognitively synthetic in their nature and that they all were representative of the contradiction, or the "for itself," stage of the English legal dialectic.

In 1610, a case arose in London concerning a licensed physician. The heart of the matter was that the London College of Physicians, who had an interest in having Dr. Bonham decertified as a doctor, took just such action.[6] Coke took the doctor's case, arguing that the judgment should be overturned because of the age-old principle that no one should be a judge in a matter in which that person has an interest. Coke was successful; Dr. Bonham was reinstated, and this important principle became a bulwark of the common law.

Note that in *Dr. Bonham's Case* the public sector, the Stuart monarchy's institution of the College of Physicians, is being held to a new standard, one borrowed from a rule of adjudication that had long existed within the private law. Just as a common-law judge should not rule on, say, a property case when the judge owns part of the property, so too a body should not be allowed to rule on a matter when the members of that public body would gain from their decision. I suggest that represents an expansion, in this case a healthy, cognitively synthetic expansion, of the public sector.

Dr. Bonham's Case, of course, is legendary in the study of constitutional law within the United States. James Madison referred to it in the #10 *Federalist*, and its use of private, common-law reason underpinned the notion of judicial review. In short, the rule of *Bonham*, governing a simple confrontation between a physician and his governing board, was transported well outside its immediate context into one of the great axioms of public law. The rule, in other words, was cognitively, as well as substantively, transformed.

If one thing is clear about *Bonham*, it is that, unlike *Shelley's Case*, it is cognitively synthetic in its form. It did not homogenize the variables in order to facilitate a contract, as *Shelley's Case* did. Rather, it transformed a judicially centered principle concerning any legal claim into a grand public principle that still rests at the core of the American political arrangement. There is a cognitive mutation here, a mutation that qualitatively moves from private adjudication to public adjudication and at the same time stretches the meaning of the common-law principle into something far more robust. The apple has morphed; it has become an orange. The second, or contradictory, stage of the dialectic clearly was at work.

Briefly, I will describe two additional matters in which Coke played a key role, the first being more of an ecclesiastical confrontation than a legal case. In 1616, James I announced the appointment of a cleric who was unpopular with the constituency he was appointed to serve. Coke vigorously opposed the appointment, that opposition costing him the judgeship he had gained by that time as a result, and almost costing him his head in the bargain.[7] It was not only what he argued but how he argued that placed him in such peril.

In this dispute, Coke had the temerity to suggest that the standard practice of buying and selling clerical appointments (a contractually formed practice, or one reflecting the analytic cognition, incidentally) should give way to a requirement that the king consult with those over whom his appointees would minister. Substantively, the notion is a precursor of representative government. But I also suggest that the form of the reasoning is easy to discern. The movement to the democratic notion of requiring consultation before an appointment is clearly synthetic. There is an encumbrance to all of this after all, an encumbrance on what otherwise might have been a simple, unimpeded appointment. Down a long and winding road, that encumbrance turned out to be something very important to democracy.

Note that here again we are at the middle, contradictory, or "for itself" stage of the dialectic. There is conflict going on, not only between James I and Edward Coke, but also between the forms of doing political things that are either analytic on the one hand, or encompassing a heretofore aberrant variable that imports a synthetic cognition on the other. That Coke's principle of representative participation, along with many other contributions, evolved into a general notion like representative government, is but one more piece of evidence of the contradiction's role in historical progress.

Coke's last confrontation with the Stuarts occurred in 1628. Then, in a battle with James I's successor Charles I, whose dread of democracy was yet stronger than his predecessor's, Coke insisted on the king's acceptance of the "Petition of Right." This Petition, essentially, asked for the liberty of complaint, the freedom of the citizenry to grieve to their king, and the right to hold the king's attention to a citizenry's pleas of injustice. These grievances were based, as Coke would have it, on rights originating in the common law.[8]

The Petition of Right is universally recognized as a further step in the development of Anglo-American constitutional government. Once more, I suggest that the cognitive form of Coke's argument is synthetic, embracing the notion of the citizenry, collectively, bringing their public grievances to the king's attention in a further step toward democracy. This notion is, therefore, cognitively similar to *Dr. Bonham's Case* and the 1616 clerical appointment controversy. Again, it marks a further synthetic form-based growth within English law and politics.

The freedom of petition, of course, now rests in the American Bill of Rights, as well as other significant places. The inclusion of a protesting citizenry into the decision process of a democratic government, obviously, adds an additional variable, a cognitively synthetic variable, to the historical contradiction. The second, or contradictory, historical stage is once again at hand.

If the first two stages of our alternated cognition example have been examined adequately, let us then briefly review what I think to be the final, or the "in and for itself" stage, of the English legal dialectic. What the dialectic tell us is that once the contradictory, or "for itself" stage of the dialectic is completed—that is, once the battle has been won for the new vision—a reconciliation sets in that calms the dialectical waters until the next historical wave comes along. In fact, that is what happened in the English law.

By the middle of the eighteenth century, well after William and Mary and their supporters had ousted the Stuarts in the 1688 Glorious Revolution, a politically confident parliament had become far more vigorous in the enactment of statutory laws than it had ever been. As a result, common-law purists became alarmed, not only at the quantity of the new laws but also at what they considered to be a disturbing of the delicate legal balances that were at least ostensibly regulated by common-law judges in the centuries since Magna Carta, if not Alfred and the Domesday Book.

Let us look briefly at the most significant eighteenth-century common-law advocate, Sir William Blackstone, the most prominent figure among those who sought to preserve a largely unadulterated common law in his *Commentaries.* Declaring boldly that he did not wish for the common law to be "further tinkered with," Blackstone hoped that his encyclopedic recounting and defense of common law principles would forestall additional statutory meddling. Claiming that the common law was a "science" that possessed all of its needed equilibriums within it, Blackstone decried an English statute book that had "swelled to ten times a larger bulk over what it was but a short time earlier."[9]

Blackstone clearly tried to forestall any further legislative activity that would abuse the common law, bolstered by the dual claims that the common law inherently contained both a high level of internal consistency and a mirror of the great Natural Law principles. Such an argument, even at the highest levels of abstraction, was clearly of the analytic form. The things the common law addressed were held to be sufficient for the private business of owning real and personal property, selling that property, making loans, engaging in bailments (borrowings), and things of that kind. No more could possibly be needed.

For Blackstone, to put it another way, the private, legal world was better left in its largely voluntary, contractual form. The intrusions of the public sector, the laws that were made to deal with public concerns, only made his law more complex, more confounding, and less predictable. Blackstone, above all, wanted to return his beloved common law to the simple verities, or to what, from our perspective, is the analytic cognition. This is a good example of the third, "in and for itself," or rationalizing stage of the dialectic. For nearly a century, aspiring lawyers throughout the Anglo-American world used Blackstone as their principal text, and were thus taught the core principles of the English-speaking world's legal systems.

Thus, from the cognitively analytic *Shelley's Case*, through Coke's cognitively synthetic battles with the Stuarts that brought the common law's reason into the public world of an emerging democracy, and then into the cognitively analytic conservatism of Blackstone, who deplored any meddling with the common law he saw as inherently perfected and self-regulated, the English dialectic ran its full course. Through this dialectical process, the law progressed. So too English democracy progressed, and of course the American colonies were soon to borrow most of what that law and that politics had to offer, on their own terms.

Again, the sequence of that dialectic was unmistakably analytic-synthetic-analytic, the alternation of the grand cognitions being quite evident. A significant period of historical change demonstrated what I believe to be the correct way of thinking about the forms of all significant historical change: the psychological, or cognitively alternating, dialectic.

The American Legal Dialectic

In order to demonstrate that the United States, like England, has undergone a legal dialectic of its own, I offer our example of what I believe to be a meaningful, alternating cognition in a judicial context. I suggest that the period directly preceding the Earl Warren era of the Supreme Court, the Warren Court era itself, which I am defining to include *Roe v. Wade* (1973) although Warren retired in 1969 and some conservative cases intervened, along with the period directly following the Warren era, are clearly dialectical when taken together. I believe that only a dialectical understanding of what happened in this period of American legal history gives hope of overcoming a great threat to the American political system. I am referring to the outrageous scandal that is America's campaign finance system, and particularly the case of *Buckley v. Valeo* (1976), which has until now impeded attempts to reform that system. I will say more about all of this later. For now, let us examine America's legal dialectic.

To begin, I suggest that, in a form not unlike the Coke/Blackstone span of years, the pre-Warren, Warren, and post-Warren periods of judicial decision-making evidenced alternating cognitions within the dialectical improvement of American constitutional law during the post-middle twentieth century. The fact that the Supreme Court decision makers themselves almost certainly did not understand what they were doing during this period in dialectical, much less cognitive terms, should not in any way negate the fact that what they did was indeed dialectical. There is a clear alternation of cognitions here, much like what happened in England from three hundred to two hundred years earlier.

The conservative John Hart Ely and other traditional constitutional scholars have written that the best argument for the kind of judicial law making that the Warren Court engaged in during the 1950s and 1960s revolved around the notion that the political branches of the government (the legislature and the executive) had failed to come to grips with significant issues such as racial equity, reapportionment, and women's rights. Ely, quite naturally, was not sympathetic to the Warren Court's legal expansions, arguing for judicial intrusion only when the processes of the government were obstructed. But in my judgment, what happened during the Warren Court from a subjectively balanced perspective, and from the perspective of legal and political equity, was fully justified. Yes, there were objective, non-cognitively related, matters that needed to be dealt with by that Court, and surely the obstructions, or at best the laxity, of the legislative and executive branches in not dealing with these matters is part of the Warren Court story. But I suggest that an entirely non-objective explanation for what the Warren Court did is equally, if not more, valid than the traditional, objective explanations. I believe that a dialectical, cognitively based understanding of the Earl Warren era is the best way to look at this.[10]

Recall that more than anything else, what the great English jurist Edward Coke did was transport the common law, and its private-sector reasoning, into a more cognitively complex, and more democratically advanced, setting within the public sector. In so doing, Coke utilized the largely private common law's grand principles and synthetically interjected them into the workings of a government that had stopped, if not reversed, the evolution toward democracy of the Tudor period when the Stuarts took over in 1603.

Within the history of the United States Supreme Court, the Warren Court, not unlike Coke alone, existed during a period in political history when major claims for fair treatment went largely unfulfilled. I argue that in dealing with such claims, the Warren Court engaged in a Coke-like infusion of an altogether different form of legal reasoning into American jurisprudence. That form, I believe, was unmistakably synthetic.

As I did with Coke and the English, I will describe but three examples of that synthetic form. The first deals with the African-American citizen's claim to an integrated education. The second deals with the reapportionment issue. The third deals with women's rights, particularly the right of a woman to choose whether or not to carry her pregnancy to term. Note that I am skipping the first stage of the dialectic, the analytic or the English *Shelley's Case* stage, at the outset of this discussion. I am doing that for a reason. I will return to the first dialectical stage when we have reviewed the second and third dialectical stages because I believe it is the most difficult, and the most important, for an understanding of the American dialectic and its potential contribution to overturning *Buckley*.

From a psychological perspective, the *Brown v. Board of Education* case is one of the most cognitively synthetic in all of American jurisprudence. The case relies on the Fourteenth Amendment, that horror of political conservatives which, without question, has been broadly used to expand American civil liberties. The Fourteenth Amendment's original intent was to ensure the new African-American citizen, the former slave, of certain federal protections: the right to equal protection of the law, the right to due process, and the right to enjoy the same privileges and immunities (often business accesses) as other citizens.[11]

Though it was far more broadly interpreted by the Warren Court, the blanket of the Fourteenth Amendment of the U. S. Constitution had always been more passive than active. That is to say, it prevented what had historically been hostile state authorities from discriminating against the new, and vulnerable, African-American citizen. It was hoped that the equal protection of the laws, and protection from the discriminatory harassment of legal authorities who held deeply prejudicial views about Blacks, would permit these new citizens to live fuller, more unimpeded lives.

Once more, the original notion of the Fourteenth Amendment protection was largely one of shields, not swords. It was a major step to move from the essentially passive protections of the Fourteenth Amendment to active protections—that is, to move from a prohibition on states from discriminating against its citizens in a narrow legal sense, to assigning a state the affirmative duty to provide some particular service such as integrated schools. Recall as well that early post-Civil War statutory law, such as the 1866 Civil Rights Act, exclusively protected the liberally generated guarantees of civil rights, specifically the right to own real and personal property, the right to alienate, or sell, real and personal property, and the right to sue and be sued, in tort.

To speak as the Warren Court did about the purpose of such legal activism, that being the full integration of the African-American citizen into the mainstream of American society, makes the case even more synthetic in its form.

The Warren Court wanted no less than a fully integrated society, and said so. Decisions such as *Brown* clearly envisaged a richer, more heterogeneous social and economic America, not just a color-blind legal, or even political, system. I suggest that this is undeniably synthetic in its cognitive form.

My second illustration of the second-stage, cognitively synthetic nature of the Warren Court deals with that Court's decisions on reapportionment. The 1946 case of *Colegrove v. Green* had declared questions of reapportionment to be "political questions."[12] The Supreme Court, in other words, prevented judicial involvement in how states allocated federal, and state, legislative representation. What had happened throughout the twentieth century was that many state legislatures, dominated by small-town and rural interests, had ceased to engage in the decennial redistrictings that most states' constitutions required. This was more likely to be the case, of course, if a state possessed a large, growing, and therefore threatening city within it.

They had also made their public incorporation laws more generous, permitting citizens to be hemmed in by newly chartered suburbs. And, if these two devices were not enough to stifle city growth, state legislatures also tightened annexation laws to make it more difficult for the central city to grow, even when there was adjacent unincorporated land.

Even in southern or other rural states, farm and small-town populations feared the political power of their growing cities, and that was so even if many of the urban residents had only just left the rural area nearby. In the state of Tennessee, where the *Colegrove* challenging case of *Baker v. Carr* (1962) originated, even mid-size cities like Knoxville and Chattanooga felt discriminated against by rural and small town interests.

By the time of the 1960 census, the above inequities had increased even beyond the distortions that political science Professor Kenneth Colegrove had sued over in the 1940s. In 1962, the Warren Court reversed *Colegrove*, first deciding that the issue of reapportionment was open to judicial consideration and then later proceeding to strike down a) unfair national representation in the House of Representatives, b) the rural favoritism of the Georgia County unit system, and even c) the representational disproportions that existed within the forty-nine bicameral states' upper houses.

These opinions certainly stretched the letter of constitutional authority. They were also clear reversals of the precedents of prior Court decisions. But such legal reversals were not altogether different from those that Edward Coke faced in his disagreement with James I over the notion of constituent representation in clerical appointments. The idea of consulting with those whom one is to govern was extended, by the Warren Court, to the need for equality in representation in cases such as *Baker* (above) and *Reynolds v. Sims* (1964).[13] In *Reynolds*, the notion of democracy was further extended, a synthetic cognition incorporating the right to roughly equal representation within the upper state legislative house (as above).

Substantively, where did that extension lead? Did it not lead to establishing the urban polyglot of America, the heterogeneous concoction of an American city as a full partner within the larger political system? And is this not a synthetic formed alteration, a reach beyond the solitary, northern European, almost invariably Protestant America to something far more varied and complex? I think so.

Finally, what of the rights of women regarding their most personal choices? Did the second dialectical stage, the cognitively synthetic, contradictory stage, evidence itself here as well? Moving beyond the *Griswold v. Connecticut* case of 1965, wherein the Court assured full access to birth control information for women by using fully half of the Bill of Rights, the far more controversial *Roe v. Wade* (1973) case assured women the right to choose whether or not to carry a fetus to term.[13] This case, of course, is still controversial and may even be reversed, or at least trimmed, by recently appointed justices on the Supreme Court.

Though I will be speaking in more detail about the private and public sectors shortly, let me say that this so-called "privacy" case is really only private in the everyday, or substantive, sense of that term. Yes, the pregnant woman maintains her right to speak only with her physician, her partner, or whomever else she alone chooses. But what were the anti-choice or pro-life advocates doing? Actually, the anti-choice or pro-life, citizens were trying to prohibit private choice, and to do so by promoting a public, but singular and universally applicable, position on the issue of pregnancy and its termination.

The rejection of a singular, publicly enforced position in *Roe* is really the crux of the case. The core of Nixon appointee Justice Blackmun's argument, was that since "medicine, philosophy, and theology are unable to arrive at any consensus," it would surely be inappropriate for the Supreme Court to impose a universal, that is singular, rule on the citizenry. *Roe,* contrary to everyday understanding, speaks for and indeed protects the public sector. It is a victory for the public sector's role as the protector of private-sector choices. From a cognitive perspective, *Roe* speaks for complexity, or for the differentiation that resides only in the synthetic cognition. It was the other side that wanted a universal rule, and that rule would dominate the public sector.[14]

So far I have done no more than illustrate what I believe to be the clearly synthetic cognitive nature of three prominent Warren Court era holdings. In a rough sense, I think these cases cognitively parallel the three cases or conflicts of *Bonham*, James I's 1616 clerical appointment, and Charles I's petition controversy, which were at the heart of Edward Coke's jurisprudential battles with the Stuarts. The Warren Court era marked the greatest dialectical period of American jurisprudence, just as Coke marked the grand jurisprudential dialectic in England. I don't think John Hart Ely saw this.

Of course, we know what happened after several Warren Court members retired from the Supreme Court and their seats were filled with Nixon appointments. I suggest that one American Supreme Court case illustrates better than any other the analytically formed withdrawal from the dialectical expansions of the Warren Court. The case was decided by the Warren Burger Court and, like many Earl Warren Court cases, was highly political in both its tone and its impact. Specifically, it reduced the arena for affirmative action, restricting it to only those instances wherein a record of racial discrimination in the immediate jurisdiction that sought affirmative action relief would be permitted.

This case grew out of Richmond, Virginia, where a recently empowered black majority government had granted itself "minority set-asides" as a promoter of black contractors' looking for public sector work. What the Burger Court held regarding that plan in *Richmond v. Croson* Co. (1989) was that a general and long-standing pattern of discrimination against the African-American community did not justify a specific, affirmative action form of redress in that jurisdiction.[15]

By insisting on an immediate and direct linkage of the place of injury to the place of restitution, reducing the importance of the general and long standing racial discrimination practiced so broadly throughout American society, *Richmond* unmistakably rejected the synthetic cognitive form. After the unprecedented period of cognitively synthetic judicial activism that occurred in the Warren Court, the *Richmond* ruling, I suggest, returns to the analytic cognition. The third dialectical stage's analytic cognition had taken over the Supreme Court under the conservatives. And there it still remains, at least most of the time, today.

What I have written so far on the American example of the alternating cognition dialectic includes both the synthetic growth of the law that took place in the second, cognitively synthetic, or "for itself," dialectical stage Warren Court, as well as the third, "in and for itself," cognitively analytic or third dialectical stage, Burger Court. Let us return now to the first stage of that American legal dialectic, for I do not believe there to be any doubt that there was, indeed, one defining, analytic, or "in itself" case that marked the introduction of the dialectical period. This first-stage case dealt with a controversial issue and, again, signaled the initiation of the Warren Court's dialectically formed transformations of the law.

As the pressure for equal treatment for America's African-American citizens grew, the courts, as Professor Ely and others have suggested, became the outlet for those citizens who could not achieve their goals within their state legislatures or the United States Congress. The first cases that dealt with the political position of blacks were voting-rights cases. A case like *Smith v. Allwright* in 1944 trumped highly inventive southern-state, Democratic Party schemes to keep African Americans out of state electoral primaries.[16] Blacks, from then on, were at least legally entitled to participate in state, local, and national elections, although it was not until the Voting Rights Act of 1965 that the federal government put teeth into the enforcement of *Smith.*

Shortly after *Smith*, the case that brought forth what I believe to be the most important theoretical ruling of the twentieth century substantively spoke to an even more delicate, racially charged matter: private-sector housing. So-called restrictive covenants had existed in the English and American common law for a very long time. They still exist, and are enforceable, when a real estate development, for example, mandates a setback (a uniform distance from a street) for all houses, or minimum square footages within a development's homes, or bans mobile homes in fixed-foundation communities. All such devices, of course, are based on the wishes of the larger community and constitute legitimate attempts to maintain overall property values.

Unfortunately, the history of real property arrangements in this country has included other forms of restrictive covenants, these regarding the exclusion of various ethnic groups. Whether against African Americans, Jews, Asians, or some other "out-group," these provisions, lodged in many land titles and neighborhood association charters, had been enforceable for a long time. Before 1948, in other words, ethnically based restrictive covenants were held to be enforceable because they did not run afoul of the Constitution's Fourteenth Amendment prohibition against state action. If it was only a court that was upholding the ethnicity-based exclusion, rather than a legislature passing such a restriction, then the state or local government was found not to be involved in the discrimination.

In 1948, all of that changed. It changed when Chief Justice Carl Vinson's Supreme Court issued its ruling in the case of *Shelley v. Kraemer.* The *Shelley* case collapsed several similar contests into one, but the title case came from St. Louis, wherein a white woman, Ms. Sophie Fitzgerald, contracted to sell her home to a Negro family in spite of covenants in the deeds of most homes in that neighborhood against such sales.[17] Though Ms. Fitzgerald had not joined the neighborhood association, the group had attempted to void her contract of sale to the Shelley family.

The Supreme Court seized this opportunity to rule on ethnically based restrictive covenants generally. *Shelley v. Kraemer* is not only an important case;

it is also a case that has been wholly misunderstood and improperly taught even at the best law schools. *Shelley v. Kraemer,* above all, did two things that are significant for understanding how the American constitutional dialectic advanced the legal and political fortunes of our country.

First, *Shelley* substantively marks an early point in the civil rights struggle, a point at which the analytic cognition could still, and I think clearly did, make a contribution. At the same time, it is a prime example of the limits of the analytic cognition, or an example of why the analytic cognition can only contribute to the first stage of that three-stage, alternating cognition, dialectical transformation. After *Shelley,* only the synthetic cognition could make the kind of progress that the Warren Court made in cases such as *Brown* and the others we have looked at.

Conservatives, of course, railed against *Shelley* from the outset. They had long been content with legal protections against those who would racially integrate neighborhoods. The theme of their complaint was predictable. Specifically, they maintained that the privilege to discriminate in the sales of private property resided in the private sector. Such discrimination, as I said earlier, was therefore not an example of state action, even when it was enforced by a court.

The conservative jurisprudential scholar Robert Bork, a onetime federal judge and George H. W. Bush controversial nominee for the Supreme Court, wrote in 1971 that *Shelley* ruled on "a private, racially restrictive covenant." For Bork, Shelley "converts an amendment whose text and history clearly show it to be aimed only at governmental discrimination into a sweeping prohibition of private discrimination."[18] He argued, in other words, that the case was a victory for the public jurisdiction. I differ.

What are the sectoral positions of the parties in the *Shelley* case? First, let's ask whether all contracts are of an equally private-sector character. I think they are not, and I think this is where the error of *Buckley* can best be laid bare. There is a spectrum to all inter-actional activity, that spectrum running all the way from the most private to the most public kind of contract. In the context of *Shelley v. Kraemer,* I find it obvious that the act of selling a house is far more private than is the action of a neighborhood association, which is a collective, quasi-public organization that sought to restrict that sale. Judge Bork misunderstood that Ms. Fitzgerald and her African-American buyer were acting far more in the private sector than were the neighbors who wanted to keep black families out, and were willing to use the courts to do so. Why did Bork make such a mistake?

To be sure, there is a sectoral differentiation within *Shelley.* But it is, I suggest, exactly the opposite of what Judge Bork claims it to be. Remember, the court used the fourteenth amendment to extend *Buchanan v. Worley* (1917),[19] wherein a city ordinance barring Black home purchases had been held to violate the amendment. Well, sure, compared to a legislated law, the covenant is the more private. But the *Shelley* court, again, did not think about the fact that the full spectrum of private-to-public sectors runs all the way from a public law, through a quasi-public neighborhood association, to a purely private contract for the alienation of land. Yes, the case was argued as a constitutional case, invoking the fourteenth amendment and the notion of "state action." But, largely as a result of the use of that theme, the court did not recognize that it was in fact ruling in favor of a bilateral contract between a buyer and a seller, and against what was at best a multilateral contract that a) included a large segment of the community (not Ms. Fitzgerald) and b) attempted to enforce a public policy-like notion of segregation on the neighborhood. By focusing on the contrast of *Shelley* with the rule of the public ordinance case of *Buchanan,* at one end of the spectrum, the court never realized they were handing victory to the private contract over the quasi-public covenant. If I had argued the case, I would have argued it as a private contract matter, and I would have cited *Shelley's Case* of 1584 as precedent.

Even beyond the sectoral considerations I have just discussed, I suggest that a further examination of the case, that is a subjectively-based examination of the cognitive forms of the case's two positions, is even more illuminating. What is more of the analytic form than a purely bilateral, or one-to-one, contract? That, again, is a win for Ms. Fitzgerald and the Shelley family's side of the case. There were no encumbrances, no oranges with the apple, and there were no third parties, according to them. In contrast, the neighborhood association's position was the position of the encumbrance, adding what was clearly a synthetic variable. The neighborhood, wanting in affect to be a third party to the contract, was in effect saying, "You must observe this encumbrance on your common law-based, civil right to alienate property." Is this not the synthetic form? Is not the neighborhood trying to complicate a pure contract? I think the answer to that question has to be "yes."

In candor, I believe the above sectoral and cognitive analyses are far deeper than the analysis of Judge Bork, and even that of the best law schools and the practicing attorneys and judges who teach, cite, and rule on the basis of the *Shelley* case without ever reaching the sectoral or cognitive realities of the case that exist, whether we choose to acknowledge them or not, at a higher level of abstraction. I merely suggest that we look at this case at not one but two levels of abstraction beyond what the justices of the *Shelley* Supreme Court utilized. I shall say a good deal more about sectors and cognitions in the Constitution in Chapter Six. All I point out here is that the cognitive nature of this case lies appropriately within the first stage of the historical dialectic that judicially altered America's law as it has never before or since been altered.

Just as Coke was doing in *Shelley's Case,* when he unencumbered a title in order to facilitate a sale and thus help to accommodate all sales to good-faith purchasers in a way that helped open the door to the commercial age, so too *Shelley v. Kraemer*'s less renown counsel facilitated a sale in a way that opened real estate to all without a synthetically formed, public-sector-sanctioned encumbrance. What *Shelley* v. *Kraemer* did in 1948, from a cognitive and sectoral perspective, was almost precisely what *Shelley's Case* did centuries earlier. Within the context of the dialectical trilogy's first stage, the two analytic, first-stage decisions in *Shelley's Case* and *Shelley v. Kraemer*, I submit, are structurally on all fours.

I have noted here Supreme Court nominee Robert Bork's misunderstanding of *Shelley v. Kraemer* within the context of what I believe to be the alternating cognition of the dialectical form. I should also point out that in *Moose Lodge No. 17 v. Irvis*, the case of the African American who was refused admittance to the fraternal order's dining hall, then Associate Supreme Court Justice and later Chief Justice William Rehnquist revealed his own misunderstanding of *Shelley v. Kraemer*. In that opinion, Rehnquist cited *Shelley v. Kraemer* in precisely the same context as Bork had earlier, calling the neighborhood association's activity a matter of "private conduct 'however discriminatory or wrong'...."[20]

Not only did the late Chief Justice Rehnquist, like Bork, fail to recognize that *Shelley v. Kraemer* contained a far more private act than the covenant on the other side of the case, but, more importantly, Rehnquist's argument nicely revealed his own biases. Without consciously dealing with cognitions, of course, both Rehnquist and Bork clearly considered Ms. Fitzgerald's position to be the one of encumbrance, or of the cognitively synthetic cognition. That position is clearly wrong, and, once more, self revelatory at the same time. The pure contract is of the analytic, not the synthetic, cognition. It is the encumbrance of the contract, argued for by the neighborhood association, like the feudal encumbrance on the separated life estate and remainder interest in *Shelley's Case*, that attempted to confront the apple to create the synthetic cognition. Like Kant, Bork and Rehnquist's $5 + 7 = 12$, although all numbers, was called synthetic.

Of course, neither Judge Bork nor Justice Rehnquist ever addressed the cognitive nature of *Shelley v. Kraemer,* or of any other case in any of their writings. Perhaps not surprisingly, neither Bork nor Rehnquist ever wrote anything that is very far up the ladder of abstraction. But we have now addressed the cognitive nature of *Shelley v. Kraemer*. This case, though neither Bork nor Rehnquist has or had the kind of mind that can readily understand it, marked the beginning of America's only significant legal dialectic. Again, that dialectic began with an analytically decided case but, once more, it was a case that tells us what we need to know about the limits to analytically assisted legal progress. *Shelley v. Kraemer,* like *Shelley's Case* before it, tells us how the analytic cognition only moves history so far. Hegel understood that and so should we. The contradictory stage, the dialectic's second or "for itself" stage, is invariably synthetic, and it is invariably necessary in order for history to move beyond a simple, analytically-based, introduction.

Though we will talk more about the Constitution and the ideological, sectoral and, of course, cognitive properties of the Constitution later, permit me to point out that nearly all conservative jurisprudential writers read the Constitution in a way that does not permit much use of the synthetic cognitive form. Their protests over "activism," though the first four stages of Supreme Court activism were all conservative as I will discuss later, would have the Court never engage in synthetically formed legal rulings. Though there surely can be synthetic excesses, and for the record I would never have been a part of the orgy of synthetic confusion found in the two *Griswold v. Connecticut* opinions of Justices William O. Douglas and Arthur Goldberg, I still maintain that a sub-atomic, cognitively-based jurisprudential theory mandates the balanced use of both cognitions, analytic and synthetic, on the Supreme Court.

To review, what I have attempted to do in this chapter is place two core theoretical groundings under the framework of a psychologically based, subatomic political philosophy. I say without reservation that the issues surrounding a method for the expansion of knowledge are only thoroughly understood when the cognitive variable within human psychology is included. The simultaneous perspective of both the analytic and the synthetic cognition expands the limits of knowledge beyond the a priori, exclusively synthetic vision that Hegel argued for. That is the next border of knowledge, going beyond Locke, Leibniz, Kant, and Hegel.

Similarly, the conscious use of an alternating cognition dialectic better illuminates what the dialectic can do, and in many real-world historical situations has done. I hope it is now apparent why the first stage needs to be cognitively analytic; the second, or contradictory, stage synthetic; and the final, third stage analytic again. With the greatest respect for the Philosopher, who surely understood the power of the synthetic cognition, I believe this alternating cognition dialectic is an even more powerful explanatory tool than the "single, ordered whole" of Hegel's exclusively synthetic dialectic, as Harvard's wonderful, late theorist Judith Shklar properly described it.

We will revisit such foundational concepts as the cognitive nature of the dialectic, principally in the context of my explanation of the philosophical position of the Natural Left in regard to Constitutional Law. This one concept, I assure you, is the key to an understanding of the synthetic cognitive perspective within a psychologically based, subatomic political philosophy. It is what I will continue to build on.

The Democratic Party Charter

I began to teach political science at the University of South Carolina in the fall of 1971. Only a few weeks into my first semester, the South Carolina Democratic Party chair, who was an adjunct professor in our department, came into my office.

Donald L. Fowler was later to become the National Democratic Party chair, playing a significant role in Bill Clinton's 1996 presidential election victory. But in 1971 Don had recently stepped away from a tenure-track position in our department to be the Democratic state chair and begin his own public relations firm. He served also as the national committeeman for the South Carolina Democrats for many years and went on to become co-chair of the national party during a good bit of the Clinton administration.

On that day Don introduced himself, said that he had heard of my earlier involvement in politics, and asked if I would be interested in helping him with what he considered to be a significant project. The 1968 Chicago Democratic Convention riot had led to the creation of the so-called McGovern-Fraser Commission, a panel charged with opening up party procedures in a number of ways. The Democratic Party sorely needed it, but Fowler was not convinced it needed all that the Commission was advocating.

In our discussion, Don specifically focused on those McGovernite Party reforms that dealt with a Party constitution. The Democratic Party had never had a charter—neither did the Republicans for that matter—and Party reformers, perhaps justifiably, felt that the writing of a set of ground rules for the National Democratic Party was long overdue.

Within the McGovern-Fraser Commission, the chief responsibility for bringing a draft charter to the 1972 Miami Beach Convention fell to the Minneapolis Congressman Donald Fraser. By 1971 Congressman Fraser and others on the committee brought a draft of their charter to a meeting of the Democratic National Committee. This was the draft that Professor Fowler plopped onto my desk and asked me to look over while he spoke to some of the specifics.

Something curious was going on. Although my own politics were probably more liberal than Don's, and though I was truly outraged at what had gone on at the Chicago Convention, the more I saw of Congressman Fraser's draft and the more I listened to Don, the more disturbed I became. A Democratic National Committee of fully two thousand members, an executive committee on which no regular members of the DNC could sit, along with a variety of other jurisdictional dispersions and procedural labyrinths led me to at least the tentative conclusion that the reformers might actually do more harm than good. A still too unrepresentative Democratic Party would not be improved by becoming a fractured, weakened Democratic Party. After further discussion with Don, I agreed to write an alternative constitutional draft.

Over the next months, I tinkered with that draft, showing versions to Don periodically, who in turn shopped them around among members of the DNC and others. By the time of the 1972 Miami Convention, Don had arranged a meeting with Congressman Fraser that was to be held at the Fontainebleau Hotel, just before the beginning of the convention. As the principal drafter of the alternative document, I was invited to attend that meeting, along with Don, Congressman Jim O'Hara (D-MI) and a labor leader whose name that for the life of me I cannot remember. Two or three people who had worked with Congressman Fraser on the reformers' draft were there as well.

The meeting began amicably, with a review of our general positions followed by a clarification of the principal differences between our two documents. But inevitably, as time wore on, the meeting became more contentious. At the outset I said nothing, assuming the position of a staff person rather than a full-fledged participant. By the end, however, I confess that I restrained myself less well, at one point getting into a shouting match with a U.S. Congressman for the first and only time in my life.

I told Congressman Fraser that I thought he had overshot the mark, and that the institutional and procedural filigree that the Fraser draft contained would be counterproductive to the Democrats' remaining competitive. In a less than scholarly way, I'm sure, I broached the abstract notion of something known as the trichotomous variable, the three-part spectrum. There were dangers, I said, to too much <u>de</u>centralization, just as there were dangers to too much centralization.

At the end our side, mostly Don Fowler, summed up our position and pleaded for consideration of the counter-productivity argument. Although Congressman Fraser surely had the votes in what was after all the McGovern convention, he called within a few hours of our meeting and announced that he would pull charter ratification from the convention agenda and support the regulars' principal request. What we had requested was that a national party commission be formed which represented both the part of the Democratic Party that made up so much of the McGovern-Fraser Commission, and the more traditional party members who, admittedly, had long exercised too much influence in the Democratic National Committee. That commission would prepare a document that could be submitted to the next convention. Because the regulars had agreed as part of the bargain to the holding of mid-term conventions, that convention was scheduled to be held in Kansas City in the summer of 1974.

Later in that 1972 convention, two party commissions were formed. The first, dealing with the charter, was to be chaired by the former North Carolina governor (later U. S. senator) Terry Sanford. The second commission, dealing with delegate selection to national party conventions, was to be chaired by the then Mary-

land Representative, and now U. S. Senator, Barbara Mikulski. That commission was properly charged with developing a set of delegate selection rules that would end the all-too-frequent minimization of African-American, female, and youth participation in the Party.

The next two years were taken up with the hearings and conferences that the commissions held around the country. I had been asked to serve as the drafter for the regulars' caucus of the charter commission, which was informally led by Don Fowler and Congressman (eventually Speaker of the House) Thomas "Tim" Foley of Washington state. The "reform" caucus was led by Fraser, when he was available, as well as the journalist Hodding Carter III and the party activist and lobbyist Ann Wexler. The Sanford Commission, which used my draft as its principal working document, eventually ground out a charter for the Democratic Party. It was brought to Kansas City in 1974 and, with some further amendment, ratified.

I have often asked myself why I worked for what seemed to be the ideologically more conservative of the two sides in the Democratic Charter battle. There was no question but that I shared the view of the reformers on a variety of contemporary political issues such as civil rights, women's rights, and opposition to the Viet Nam War. Further, the reformers' core argument concerning the exclusiveness of the Democratic Party well into the 1960s was more than credible. Even without the riot in the streets the 1968 convention would have been a disgrace, with the McCarthy floor convention phones being shut off, with significant players not being given a chance to speak, with the exclusion of some non-Humphrey delegates, and with the Chicago mayor at one point shouting anti-Semitic epithets at Senator Abraham Ribicoff of Connecticut. No, in their basic charge, the reformers were correct. With regard to representation in the Party, there was no question but that minorities, women, and young people needed specific protections for enhanced party representation.

And yet, having granted all of that, I still sensed two things about the reformers that I think made me less comfortable with them than ideological positioning alone would have predicted. First, though this all took place in the early 1970s, and my searchings into philosophers such as Kant and Hegel were still not mature, I already possessed at least a gut feeling that the excessive decentralization which the reformers seemed obsessed with would ultimately hurt the party. In the main, I don't think it was a question of bad faith. It was, in most cases, little more than a matter of unintended consequences, a group of people who had suffered the slings and arrows of exclusion grasping for openness in the form of radical structural decentralization.

Somehow, I just didn't get the sense that an effective party synthesis, a synthesis of liberal proposals, could ever come out of the structures and processes that the reformers were offering the party. Although I'm sure I was not con-

scious of all the reasons behind it, I had a sense that highly centrifugal structures such as the ones the reformers were proposing would not only divide the party so that it would be less not more able to compete with the Republicans, but also ironically lead the party into more conservative, interest group directed positions over time.

But beyond my sense of how the proposed structures might vitiate a necessary quality of synthesis within the Democratic Party, I sensed something else, something about at least some of the people who were on the reform side. At one level, these individuals were cordial, even friendly, and I'm happy to say that most of what went on in the Sanford Commission, with a good bit of the credit due to the able former North Carolina governor, was civil if not engaging. But there was still a tone to the arguments among some of the reformers, a tone that evidenced a stridency or an overbearing righteousness that I found myself uncomfortable with. Hodding Carter III at one point screamed that Don Fowler was a Nixon Democrat, an appellation that was as gratuitous as it was inaccurate. Finally, that unmistakable singularity of concern, that single-issue tunnel vision that surely existed among some who represented one outgroup or another, struck me as not only obstructive to a liberal synthesis but as not coming from the kinds of personalities that were naturally synthetic in their own cognitive preferences. Maybe, as strange as it seemed, I was beginning to let myself think that the reformers were not really the liberals in the group after all. Maybe their seemingly liberal perspectives were merely the objectively-based visions of those who came from various groups. Maybe those who wanted to keep the party together were cognitively more synthetic than the reformers. At the time, just a thought.

In any case, the problem of the singularity of concern complemented the over-centrifugal structural concern I held regarding the reformers. I sensed that if the Party structures were over-decentralized, then very specific interests within the Party, with very limited agendas, could capture segments of the Party and make those segments their own. Though various groupings and interests, without question, carried legitimate claims into the commission's discussions, many of the individuals who did the carrying, I felt, were too often too narrow themselves.

To close, I should immodestly report that although there were compromises on both sides, my draft of the National Democratic Party charter remained the basis for the first constitution of a major political party in this country's history. America's Democratic Party is the world's oldest political party. Its charter, I must say, is an unremarkable document, providing as it does for a rather conventional arrangement of the Democratic Party's institutions. Its core framework, designed to maintain some measure of structural cohesiveness within a very diverse political party, is not dissimilar from what a variety of other constitutions or by-laws provide in many political and nonpolitical institutions. All in all, however, I'd like to think that the Charter has made at least a small contribution to the well-being of the Democratic Party over the last thirty years.

CHAPTER FOUR

The Cognitive Triumph—Fission and Fusion

From the Objective to the Subjective

Obviously, I believe the cognitive differentiation between the analytic and the synthetic forms that I have been describing is a powerful thing. When I say that this cognitive differentiation is a part of the forms, sitting at the very top of the knowledge pyramid or the ladder of abstraction, I do not refer to the forms as some esoteric, intellectual abstraction. No, the forms are in all knowledge, grand to mean. They are at the center of all meaning, the shape of all understanding being the single greatest harbinger of the understanding's substance. This is the principal epistemological differentiation, with no other dichotomy approaching the impact of the forms, and so this is where a psychologically based, essentially cognitive, third-tier theory must begin.

Again, in the simplest possible framework, there is a difference between the comparison of a can of Coke and a can of Pepsi, and the comparison of a can of Coke and a bottle of Coke. As I will review in this chapter, I think the forms are significant within philosophical considerations, even beyond their role in defining the limits of knowledge, and defining their role in the dialectical improvement of knowledge, and the dialectical improvement of politics and law that I reviewed in Chapter Three.

I will relate here what I believe to be convincing evidence that the single most important cognitive differentiation inherent in the forms has been so strong throughout Western intellectual history that it has actually transformed the principal intellectual arguments of Western thought. As the reader knows, there are schools of thought about everything. Such schools are handy, simply because they take a variety of at least partially linked and frequently overlapping perspectives on a topic and organize them into reasonably cohesive, and reasonably understandable, aggregations. All of us understand a lot of what we know by the informational family of which each knowledge particle is a member.

In the broadest sense, the two grand schools of thought that the Greeks gave to us were the rational school and the skeptical school. The rational school, at its root, believes that there is a kind of order to the world and that, to at least some degree, the human community is able to understand that order. There are differences within the rational school, of course, particularly over just how orderly the world is and how much of it we can understand. We will examine these differences shortly.

On the other side of the Greek ledger lay the skeptics. The skeptics essentially believed that the world has no order or, at a minimum, that humankind cannot know that order. Truth, the parameters of a just society, and even a code of interpersonal behavior therefore can never be well defined, much less enforced.

There is not much doubt that these two grand schools of thought, the rationalist and the skeptical, continued to be the dominant intellectual aggregations for centuries after the Greeks. In the modern age, major thinkers such as Descartes and Montaigne still represented the rational and skeptical positions reasonably well.

And yet, I suggest that these two grand philosophical schools no longer make up the dominant aggregations of Western thought. The powerful workings of the cognitive differentiation, the differentiation between the analytic cognition and the synthetic cognition that I believe is best illustrated by the Kantian versus Hegelian depiction of the $5 + 7 = 12$ equation, has created a new alignment of Western thought. The cognitive differentiation, in other words, brought about two new intellectual schools, which now supersede the non-psychologically differentiated, classical rationalist and skeptical schools.

The Fission-Fusion Path

What follows is a shorthand review of the cognitively based, historical pattern of development that I believe replaced the rational and skeptical schools of Western philosophical thought as the principal bodies of knowledge with a spectrum that reflects the cognitive differentiation we have been examining. Two themes dominate. Just as there was a fission, or a breaking up of the two classical intellectual aggregations just described, so too there was a subsequent fusion, or a rejoining of the parts that broke off from the grand schools of rationalism and skepticism. That rejoining marked a wholly new configuration of the old parts.

Specifically, each of the rationalist and skeptical schools broke into two subschools, along lines that reflect the cognitive differentiation between the analytic and the synthetic cognitions. In other words, each of the two original grand schools of rationalism and skepticism developed a fissure along what I believe is a clearly cognitive fault line.

Then what became for a while the four sub-schools, once they were separated from their two original schools, realigned so as to create two new, cognitively compatible grand schools. In short, I believe that the cognitive differentiation between the two classical schools, the rational and the skeptical, was so powerful that it broke apart and realigned the principal Western intellectual configuration. I suggest that an understanding of the new configuration will greatly assist an understanding of a subatomic, cognitively based political theory. If a new standard of political equity is to be achieved, this understanding should be a part of it.

To repeat, I believe that a cognitive differentiation existed within both grand philosophical schools from the outset. For the rationalists, in broad gauge, the cognitive differentiation between Plato and Aristotle contrasts the somewhat more organic worldview of Plato's *Republic* and the somewhat more mechanistic worldview of Aristotle. The Platonic view, in short, is more differentiated. The Gold, Silver, and Bronze or Tin man, along with the vertical gradations of authority starting with the philosopher king and running from the guardians all the way down to the slave, bespeaks the synthetic cognition.

Also, the roles within the Platonic society are complementary; the parts are not interchangeable because of a clear, qualitative differentiation among those parts. The warrior and the priest could not perform the same duties, simply because they are qualitatively different kinds of people. I think this Platonic position, again, is cognitively synthetic. It is cognitively differentiated, as with the apple and the orange.

I find the Aristotelian perspective to be cognitively different from the Platonic perspective, Aristotle believing in the participation of all Greek citizens in government. He believed this because each citizen was held to have a similar capability to at least be a part of the polity. Aristotle also believed in the rotation of leadership within a polity. Though surely not everyone would be qualified for governance, there was less differentiation in leadership qualities among citizens with Aristotle, a good number of whom could manage an authoritative public position.

Plato's *Republic*, as many writers have suggested, describes something of a totalitarian left position. It almost surely, from my perspective, constitutes an excess of the synthetic cognition. Aristotle's position, in contrast, is more cognitively inclined toward the analytic, although Aristotle certainly envisioned a closely knit, ultimately cooperative society. I do not talk of polar positions here, only positions that are sufficiently differentiated and that in a way not so different from the Kantian and Hegelian positions on the 5 + 7 = 12 equation, are sufficient to serve as exemplars. So much for the cognitive differentiation that existed inherently within the rationalist philosophical school and that eventually, in my view, sustained a fission along the differentiation.

On the skeptical side of the original divide between rationalists and skeptics, or on the side challenging those who believe in a rational world order, I believe there was also an inherent differentiation from the outset. Essentially, that fission occurred because there are two very different avenues of challenge to rationalism available. The first is to argue that the order claimed by the rationalist is not sufficiently orderly. This position holds, that is, that the rationalists' world is not sufficiently consistent and internally coherent, either in the mind of the polity or in the real-world political arrangements of the polity, to enforce the order. This, I submit, is an analytically based criticism of rationalism.

Within skeptical thought, the above anti-rationalist position is clearly evidenced by, for example, Thrasymachus. I find his position to be cognitively analytic because it recognizes no qualitative differentiations among citizens save the singular difference of strength. There is no political currency available except a kind of Machiavellian, or social Darwinist, sense of power. All political interaction, therefore, trades in that same currency. I find that to be analytic.

The second form of skepticism is quite different from that of Thrasymachus. It is the relativistic position of, for example, Protagoras, who is best known for his notion that man is the measure of all things. Here, there is not only a recognition of qualitative differentiations among humanity, differentiations that are far more complex than the sole quality of strength, but also an understanding of the differentiations that exist among perspectives on humanity. This vision, I think, is clearly of a more synthetic nature. It is relativistic. Unlike the Thrasymachan position, it argues that rationality is claiming too much order for itself, or too much certainty about how the world works. This position contrasts, of course, with that of those who find a lack of sufficient order within classical rationalism.

Now imagine the progress through history of four quite separate lines, two each from the two original, or grand, positions. From the organically rationalist position of Plato and from the mechanistically rationalist position of Aristotle, I suggest two lines flowed that eventually separated along the schism of their cognitive differentiation. Then, eventually, each married its cognitively compatible partner as it progressed down the two cognitive lines that simultaneously flowed from Thrasymachus's and Protagoras's cognitively distinct skeptical positions.

In skeletal outline, therefore, I suggest that the cognitively analytic position of the rationalist Aristotle descends into the analytic positions of, for example, the Nicaean Christians, and Augustine, and Aquinas's reconciliation of Aristotle and other Greek thought with the beliefs of the Roman Catholic faith. This line carried through the Enlightenment scientists Newton, Copernicus, and Galileo, all of whom were Cartesians in their own way. Ultimately, the line led to Kant, to whom I shall return shortly.

On the skeptically originated, cognitively analytic side, I shall be even briefer. The Thrasymachan rejection of order and inherency came down through the Roman Epicureans and found its way into modernity with the method (not the substance) of John Locke. Locke was substantively of the rationalist position, being part of the evolution of natural law into natural rights that I will speak of in the jurisprudential section of this chapter. But methodologically, Locke was a utilitarian, providing methodological fodder for his successor David Hume, who, in the latter's *Treatise on Human Nature,* wished to create a science of man.That science of man was not to be based on a priori knowledge, of course, but was to be centered on a study of the behavioral rather than the inherent reality, the empirical rather than the contemplative niceties. It was Hume who separated the observer from the observed, or the mind from what the mind perceived, arguing in the best skeptical tradition that the twain could never meet.[1]

Now, enter Kant. Kant, I suggest, is not only the best exemplar of the analytic cognition (recall his position on the 7 + 5 = 12 equation) but also the intellectual figure who marks that extraordinary philosophical moment when the two sets of cognitive streams that originated in the opposing headwaters of rationalism and skepticism merged. With Kant, the cognitively analytic position that came down from the skeptic Thrasymachus and the cognitively analytic position that came down from the rationalist Aristotle finally joined.

Kant, recall, had restricted a priori thought to mathematics, the natural sciences, and individual morality. Though he labeled almost all of mathematics synthetic, I do not believe it, and far more importantly, neither did Hegel. In *The Science of Logic,* as noted, Hegel had a little fun with Kant, arguing that the 5 + 7 = 12 equation was merely analytic, being made up of "something *already complete* in the object" (emphasis his). In a dialectical context, he further contended that the equation "did not pass through any further *middle term*" (emphasis his).[2] Kant, as we have seen, would have nothing of speculative reasoning, particularly of the metaphysical kind. Again, Kant's writings mark one of the two great philosophical confluences around a cognitive similarity. He was part skeptic and part rationalist, but from a cognitive perspective, he was a pure-blooded analytic.

What, then, of the other cognitive side? Coming down from the synthetic side of the rationalists, that is from Plato, I find the Roman Stoics and then, into modernity, the outspokenly relativistic Montesquieu as key to the other confluence. Montesquieu's *Spirit of the Laws* is a clear rebuttal of Cicero's notions of one law, universal, for all times and for all peoples. For Montesquieu, different cultures could be expected to have different constitutions, whether written or unwritten. The laws of different places, for Montesquieu, could and even should be different.[3] One step beyond the relativism of Protagoras, it was Montesquieu who talked of man as both the master and the perceiver of reality. It was Montesquieu who embraced a reflexive, self-defined, and essentially introspective view of humankind. But he did so with the understanding that different peoples would no doubt see different things. This cognitive position, I suggest, is clearly synthetic.

One more thing needs to be said about Montesquieu. Hegel liked him. The philosopher who had openly chided Kant over the latter's synthetic depiction of the 5 + 7 = 12 equation, and who thought little of so many of his philosophical predecessors, warmly embraced Montesquieu's relativism. Although Hegel's relativism was historical rather than cultural, metaphysically directed rather than legal, relativism as a philosophical concept would never be better promoted than it was with Hegel's dialectical Idealism, or the classical dialectic of historical stages within the mind. Much of this followed from Montesquieu.

And so, where does Hegel fit in the fission-fusion path? The answer to that is not difficult, for just as Kant marked the confluence of the rationally and skeptically generated analytic position, I suggest that Hegel marked the other grand, synthetic, cognitive confluence. It is Hegel's Protagoran relativism, in sync with a traditional rationalism that was kept flexible and organic by Montesquieu above anyone else in the modern era, that furthered Enlightenment notions of human progress. Although the claims for rationalism were surely muted by the excesses of the French Revolution, the synthetic side of rationalism and the synthetic side of skepticism still met within Hegel. And, I suggest, that is where they remain today.

Together, therefore, Kant and Hegel are important for more than being the German Idealists whose ostensibly objective depictions of the 5 + 7 = 12 equation are the best exemplars of the differentiated subjectivities that underpin a psychologically based political philosophy. In part because of where they happened to come along in history, but also because of where they stood in their cognitive preferences, they are also the two grand intellectual figures who marked that extraordinary completion of a historical fission-fusion process which in turn demonstrated the cognitive spectrum that dethroned the rationalist and the skeptical schools as the dominant Western intellectual differentiation. The cognitive differentiation was that powerful. It worked its way through the classical schools of rationalism and skepticism, and eventually reconfigured them.

After a while, of course, the Kantian line led to the philosophical positivism of Bertrand Russell and the early Ludwig Wittgenstein, with these two figures' reliance on empirical, a posteriori knowledge, logical positivism, and the analytical philosophy that has long dominated the American academy. The deductivism of these philosophic positions, of course, largely utilized qualitatively similar, cognitively analytic variables. The Hegelian, cognitively synthetic, line led to that relativism which was perhaps best illustrated by the relativism of Einstein in physics, and insights such as Heisenberg's indeterminacy. The cognitive division, from this perspective as well as across the epistemological divide, proved to be dominant.

And yet, if the cognitive division in fact marked the principal intellectual divide in so many areas, why is it not yet recognized as the principal political divide in politics? Why have the two cognitions not received fair treatment in the world of political theory and, more importantly, within the American polity and the emerging global community? To help answer these questions, I ask you to bear with me for two brief reviews of how the fission-fusion path marked two other academic fields: jurisprudence, or legal theory; and economic theory. Each of these portrayals will be far briefer than the prior philosophic review, but they should serve as further evidence of the cognitive differentiation's strength, and as a talisman for reform of the American political and judicial systems' imbalances. Most specifically, they should point the way to a thoroughgoing reform of the most heinous imbalance within America's political system, the oligopoly creating campaign finance laws.

Natural and Positive Law

In most jurisprudential, that is legal-theory, textbooks the greatest divide is depicted as the separation between the natural-law and the positive-law. The natural-law position, of course, is derivative of the rationalist philosophical tradition. The idea that there is an innate order to the world, and that that order imports certain norms and rules, as well as the rights of a citizenry to enforce these norms and rules for the good of society, is the nub of the natural-law position.

Positive law is derivative of the skeptical philosophical position. If the world has no innate order, or at least if that order cannot be known, then some individual or group must impose an order, and its resultant law, on society. Some would argue for a Thrasymachan law, or for that social Darwinian notion of survival of the fittest that we visited earlier. But most in the positive tradition have argued that since no natural law existed, humankind must create and enforce its own law, in order to prevent the law of the jungle.

I suggest that the above two grand schools of jurisprudence, the natural-law school and the positive-law school, went through the same pattern of fission and fusion that the two grand schools of philosophy did. Each divided themselves along the lines of the cognitive differentiation that existed between them. Then the four sub schools realigned themselves into two new grand schools, each made up of the cognitively compatible sub-schools as they grew out of the previous grand divide. A brief look at how this happened is in order.

The natural-law position came down roughly from the rationalists' notions of an innate order and flowed through the writers of the Roman and Byzantine period in the works of Cicero, Seneca, and Justinian. The universality of law and law's accessibility are clear in these writings, although the degrees of certainty of such knowing surely vary.

Into modernity, the natural law became more individualistic and more cognitively analytic, with the English, and particularly the cleric Richard Hooker, mutating the natural law into natural rights, although Hooker would still have those rights belong to the citizenry entire. Hooker greatly influenced John Locke, who went on to rest natural rights within the individual, not the citizenry entire. Predictably, the Lockean form of contract was even more unfettered than Coke's, the post-Stuart commercial contractor freer to do business than ever before.[4]

In turn, Locke greatly influenced Voltaire, who fathered the so-called "Legislationist" perspective, Voltaire's claim for legal certainty drawing on the scientific certainties that the French philosopher extended to law and politics. "We are equipped to calculate, weigh, measure, and observe" Voltaire confidently told Frederick the Great. It was just such hubris that the skeptical Kant so abhorred.[5]

Finally, the cognitively analytic jurisprudential line progresses to the English Sir William Blackstone, who feared, as we reviewed earlier, that a statute book "swelled to ten times a larger bulk" would contaminate his pure notions of the common law.[6] For Blackstone, the common law had become a science and was already in perfect sync with the natural law. It was just such reliance on the internal, and secretive, calculus of a science that the late Daniel Boorstin, soon to be Librarian of Congress, attacked in his incisive *Mysterious Science of the Law*.[7] In sum, the analytic side of the original natural-law position came to signal a cognitive preference for a well-ordered, internally consistent, and almost purely static vision of the law.

The cognitively analytic strain that grows from the skeptical side of the original grand divide comes into modernity with Hobbes's notion of the so-called legal imperative. The legal imperative is the law of command, the law that must be obeyed because there are assured consequences otherwise. There is no necessary grounding in morality undergirding the law of command, although the good order of the society is thought to be enhanced by those who advocate their brand of public order. Hobbes's notion of society is clearly Thrasymachan, the Leviathan of government being essential to avert the survivalist, king-of-the-hill world.

After Hobbes came Kant who, though never as much the legal thinker as he was the philosopher, is hardly irrelevant to the law. Legally, Kant's classically liberal view of society would generate an open system, one that regulates itself under categorically defined principles. This substantive position squares with Kant's reflection that "completeness (is) my chief aim in the law."[8] Such a need for the law's perfection reflected the influence of the mathematician Pufendorf, in much the same way that the latter had also influenced the natural-law derivative thinking of Locke.[9]

The immediate cognitively analytic successor to Kant was Jeremy Bentham, the English utilitarian whose tightness of common-law reasoning mirrored his legislative calculus. They were both designed to make the law impervious to the aberrant, external variable. Bentham is well known for his attack on Blackstone, an attack that much is made of in the jurisprudential literature but which I suggest is directed solely toward the substance and not the form of Blackstone's natural-law position.[10] Bentham, after all, created a tight calculus of logically unchallengeable legalisms himself. Cognitively, and methodologically, he and Blackstone were far more similar than Bentham wanted to admit.

Overall, the intellectual fusion on the cognitively analytic side had pretty well taken place by the early nineteenth century, with Admiral John Austin's refinements carrying that fusion further toward legal, and cognitive, purity. Austin believed that "With the goodness or the badness of laws ... it (the grander principle of law) has no immediate concern."[11] Like his predecessors, the cognitively analytic internal consistency of the law, and completeness of the law, occupied his mind.

And so it was for the "analytics." They reign, not surprisingly, with impunity today in the jurisprudential writings of someone like Judge Robert Bork whose work, in tune with his mistaken understanding of the sectoral positions of *Shelley v. Kraemer*, reflects a great need for legal completeness and internal consistency, rather than a search for justice. The arguments of Herbert Weschler and the late Alexander Bickel at Yale, as further examples, reflected what they both liked to call "Neutral Principles,"a code term for the non-inclusion of the synthetic, equity-based concerns of those who found themselves outside the law's pure calculus.[12] The appearance of neutrality is hardly convincing when such writers' cognitive imbalances are taken into account. They are and were analytics, and they wanted the law to be analytic. Let us look now at the synthetics.

First, let us ask if the synthetics have come to their fusion point on the other side of the new, cognitive divide rather than the natural-law/positive-law divide. I think that they have come to that point, the post-Revolution notion of a natural law recovering, not unexpectedly, from the Philosopher through those who either immediately preceded or were influenced by Hegel. Though Hegel chided Frederick von Savigny for his simplicity, there is no question that Savigny's eighteenth-century commitment to historicism anticipated Hegel, and added life to the law.

In the nineteenth century, G. F. Puchta continued the German historicist tradition in jurisprudence by rejecting the lack of relativity he found in the Marxist, materialistic legal theories of the mid-century. Like Montesquieu, he embraced a moderate relativism, one based on the differences and the diversity of Right among the people in the law.[13] The German Rudolf Stammler's early twentieth-century writings also reflected the richness of the folk spirit. That spirit added a further flexibility to the law, Stammler decrying those who would "still ones' philosophic conscience," and go too far "in the generalization of concrete legal material" that they do not "distinguish between pure forms of conceiving and judging and the material treated according to those forms."[14]

In short, the German historicists built a legally flexible road back from the latter-day Enlightenment's overstated preciseness. The often pessimistic, romantic response to brittle rationalism in literature and art was inevitable. But the intellectual historicists provided a more optimistic response to those who saw no hope for the world. They did so within a jurisprudential context that was at the same time rich in its philosophical tradition and accepting of the historical imperative to be flexible, and growing.

Later, others contributed to a synthetic tradition in the law. In France, Léon Duguit wrote of different aptitudes and diverse needs. The sociological school would prosper in Europe under Duguit and his notion of the solidarity of a populace.[15] Then a more flexible view of the law came to The United States with Roscoe Pound's championing of the multiplicity of social interests and the need for an ever-changing law. The Supreme Court's associate justice Oliver Wendell Holmes Jr., though surely not of the sociological school, would admonish the readers of his *Common Law* that the life of the law was rich and varied because of experience, not logic.[16]

Perhaps the coming together of the synthetic thread is best illustrated by the writings of two distinguished modern scholars, Lon Fuller and H. L. A. Hart. Fuller, the long time, mid-twentieth-century chair of jurisprudence at Harvard, was an incomparable figure in the development of a new, that is post-Revolution, natural law. Fuller's call for the suspension of conflict between what he called the upper side of the law, or the actual rulings of cases, with the under side of law, or the law's internal reasoning and principles, along with his critique of those who would "never let the green fields of life lure them from the gray path of logic" in the law, mirrored his recognition that oughts rather than mechanical reasonings are what give the law vitality. This marked the synthetic vision at its richest.[17] With Fuller, the law was vibrant, changing, but hardly arbitrary, and it unashamedly placed justice above methodological purity, equity above internal consistency and completeness and legal progress above small-minded stability.

It was the writings of Professor Fuller, when combined with the work of one whose intellectual parentage comes from the skeptically grounded, positive-law jurisprudential strain that completed the synthetically cognitive side. Intellectually following Hobbes, Kant, Bentham, Austin, and Hans Kelsen, Professor H. L. A. Hart, held the chair of jurisprudence at Oxford at the same time Fuller sat at Harvard. A brief, intermediate look at Kelsen is needed to fully understand Hart.

Hans Kelsen was a firm adherent to the positive law, creating what he labeled the "pure theory" of law. The pure theory eschewed a focus on the specifics of legal mandates and concentrated instead on a variety of legal contexts. In defining his perspective in such a way, Kelsen offered a flexible brand of positivism that provided for both an incorporation of a variety of different, again contextual, approaches to law, and an inclusion of the oughts of law in a limited but nonetheless path-breaking way, for the positivists. From Kelsen, it was therefore not a giant leap to the last great figure on the cognitively synthetic side that came from the positivistic grand school.[18]

When did the fusion come on the cognitively synthetic side? I suggest that it came exactly in 1958, and specifically in the *Harvard Law Review*, where Professors Fuller and Hart engaged in one of the greatest dialogues of modern Anglo-American jurisprudence. Vigorously disagreeing with the natural law's claims for inherency within Fuller's position described above, Professor Hart nonetheless mimicked the cognitive form of his cross-Atlantic colleague.

For Hart, the key jurisprudential distinction between morality and the law was bridged by his agreeing with d'Entreves that there was an essential connection between law and morals. At the same time, Hart noted that Admiral

Austin's jurisprudential examples were always a confusion between law as it is and as morality would require it to be.

Hart went on to note that even Bentham, acting as an anxious spectator of the French Revolution, foresaw the time in any society when the law's commands were so evil that the question of resistance had to be forced. Importantly, Hart's thinking was holistic; he argued that "in considering the law we needed to widen our point of view and ask, not whether every particular rule of law must satisfy a moral minimum ... but whether a system of rules which altogether failed to do this could be a legal system."[19]

For Hart, even laws other than criminal laws provide facilities more or less elaborate for individuals to create structures of rights and duties for the conduct of life within the coercive framework of law. These rules provide facilities for the realization of (human) wishes and choices, a position that I suggest is close to Fuller's warm embrace of the oughts of morality necessary for just law. Hart is the writer, after all, who mightily dueled with Lord Devlin over the legal status of homosexual behavior, affirming the broadest tolerance of human conduct consistent with the social bond.

Though the epistemological coming together on this side of the cognitive ledger, from the grand rational and skeptical positions, took longer than it did on the cognitively analytic side, Professors Fuller and Hart clearly brought the cognitively synthetic side of the modern jurisprudential argument together as it never had been melded before. The traditional view of the Harvard-Oxford duel has highlighted the conflict of very different jurisprudential perspectives. I suggest that those who saw their meeting in 1958 as conflict were using an old paradigm. In fact, the two Harvard articles marked a reconciliation. As in philosophy, the cognitively distinct positions eventually supplanted the non-cognitive, classical schools of natural and positive law as the principal intellectual distinction in jurisprudential thought. This, I suggest, was the fission and fusion within jurisprudential thought, and from that perspective, Hart and Fuller were far closer than most observers believed. Let us look, even more briefly, at the cognitive evolution of economic theory. Though its history is far shorter, and thought it is not directly linked to law or political ideology, the breakout of cognitive differentiation in economic thought does bear on the equity issues that unquestionably lie at the heart of the Constitution.

From the rationalist side, the physiocrats, such as François Quesnay, Robert Turgot, and Pierre Du Pont, represented the beginning of modern economic thought. Their pre-classical position veered off to the synthetic cognitive side with Adam Smith, who was hardly a pure capitalist as is so broadly misunderstood, but rather an economist who conditioned his approval of the market with the expectation that markets would yield results approximating rationalist standards like natural price and natural value. [20] Smith's intellectual tradition was the Scottish Enlightenment, with its profound sense of proportion; he, for example, specifically embraced contract counterbalancing economic devices such as antitrust law and labor unions to ensure justice in the economic realm.

Like Smith, David Ricardo's theories of rent, wages, and value evidenced a substantive concern with the distributive side as well as the productive side of economics. But Ricardo was less certain than Smith about the natural equilibration of markets, and thus their fairness. His core notion of labor embodied retained a rationalistic inherency to it, as opposed to the automaticity of later economic approaches.[21]

The latter-day work of John Stuart Mill, once he had freed himself from the utilitarian constraints of his father, James, and his down-the-street tutor Jeremy Bentham, approached democratic socialism. The last edition of his *Principles of Political Economy*, published in 1871, surely contrast with the first edition, published in 1848, in its concern for distributive result and in its generous inclusion of political factors within the distributive equation.[22]

The pinnacle of modern synthetic classicism is perhaps best represented in the work of John Maynard Keynes. Keynes's approval of conscious public sector intervention in order to ameliorate economic boom and bust cycles contrasted with Joseph Schumpeter's notion of booms possessing their own calculus of length and strength, without the encumbrance of human intervention.[23]

On the more analytic, classically rationalist side, figures such as Thomas Malthus, with his notion of labor commanded, surrendered to what were perceived to be the inevitable dictates of markets, including labor markets.[24] His contemporary on the continent, Jean Baptiste Say, is most noted for Say's Law, which remains a much reinterpreted proposition, but one that at a minimum predicts an automatic relationship between production and demand.[25] The analytics have always loved it.

Thus, it is the automaticity of rationalist thinkers such as Malthus and Say that links up on the analytic side of the cognitive equation. Utilitarian economists such as James Mill, Bentham, and later the so-called Austrian school and its marginal utility economists William Jevons, Carl Menger, and Leon Walrus, meet there. This is the linkage that led to the even more purely analytic writings of Friedrich von Hayek, Ludwig von Mises, and those of the monetarist Chicago school who have been concerned with price theory and microeconomics generally, like Milton Friedman.[26]

In contrast, the synthetic, non classical epistemological side was initiated by the writings of de Sismondi, who, much in the early nineteenth-century romantic tradition, was the first economist to question the natural equilibriums of the classical economists and call for governmental intervention. More recently, the synthesis of classical and skeptical precognitive positions is probably best represented by the writings, for example, of John Kenneth Galbraith, who continued the call for equity-based governmental intervention in the economy.[27]

Philosophically, the cognitively synthetic position is also well represented by an economic theorist such as Daniel Fusfeld, who has argued that conceptual issues have arisen (in economics) that challenge the scientific claims of logical empiricism, general equilibrium theory, and mathematical models. Perhaps not surprisingly, Fusfeld reached beyond the boundaries of economics, arguing that psychology contributes broader and more complex foundations for an understanding of behavior than the economists' assumptions of utilitarian optimizing. [28]

In review, I contend nothing more, nor less, than that the grand cognitive divide that we have examined all along, that is the epistemologically relevant divide between the analytic and the synthetic cognitions, turned out to be so powerful in so many fields that it supplanted the grand rationalist versus skeptical separation that began with the Greeks and continued to serve as the principal Western intellectual divide for a considerable time. Put another way, the classical intellectual divide was eventually replaced by a sorting out of the different cognitive preferences of different human psychologies in ways that now give us a cognitively directed grand divide. The cognitive forms, that is, the patterns of thought that the greatest intellectuals of their respective periods used, greatly impacted the substance of what they taught. I think that eventually these cognitive forms created an entirely new epistemological configuration, or spectrum, within those intellectual fields.

The cognitively structured historical exercise is over. I think that the rigor that I have imposed here is essential to an understanding of the cognitive divide that I find not only to be important in its own right but also because the cognitive divide lies at the core of a subatomic, psychologically based political philosophy. I hope I have made it clear that the limits to knowledge question and the dialectical attainment of new knowledge question are dependent on a subjectivist, moderately relativistic view of the principal forms of human cognition. I hope I have also been convincing that different human cognitions have already carved a considerable path through something as important as Western intellectual history. To ensure political equity in the twenty-first century, we will need to understand how the balance of these cognitions, as they exist within a new political philosophy and the real world, necessarily guide us to a new way of thinking about the American constitutional order.

The First Campaign

I was proud of what I had contributed regarding the threatened excessive decentralization of the National Democratic Party in the early 1970's. But what a number of us who worked on the Charter accomplished there could not be repeated within the general government, particularly the U. S. Congress. The late 1960s and early 1970s penchant for organizational decentralization infected the Congress, particularly after the post-Watergate triumph of the Democratic Party class of 1974. The coming to Congress of a younger generation that had only contempt for the folkways of two legislative institutions that were still largely centralized in their structures meant that structural change would move almost exclusively in one direction. It did so with a vengeance.

To be sure, the movement away from centralized leadership in the Congress began with the reining in of the powerful Speaker of the House Joe Cannon in 1910 and 1911. The development of a full-fledged committee system in 1946 dispersed power still more. But the sub-constitutional reforms of the mid-1970s and beyond dispersed power in ways that greatly extended the constitutional dispersion of powers that were at the heart of America's original institutional arrangement.

The reduction in the number of chairships that any congressional member could hold, the continued increase in the number of committees, the increase in legislative staffs and the increase in the autonomy of committees from core congressional leadership, worked the Washington disassembling. Then subcommittees felt left out. They wanted autonomy from their full committees, and of course, they required more staff, and more money, for their micro legislatures. These new arrangements gave more authority to more people. But nobody seemed to care that the core institutional leadership suffered. This was participatory democracy with a vengeance, as the 1960s New Left had prescribed.

The young Congressional reformers were in part rebelling against the unwillingness of committee chairs, and often the House and Senate leadership, to promote civil rights, Medicare, federal aid to Education, and a host of other initiatives that had lain fallow since the times of the Roosevelt's New Deal and Truman Fair Deal. But these reformers didn't want either the baby or the bath. Though they had won the legislative battle, they still insisted on structural reforms within the Congress.

As with the McGovern Democratic Charter proposals, I had my doubts. Civil rights, Medicare, aid to education, and other progressive initiatives had been passed by the early 1970s, and the structural changes that the congressional reformers were still arguing for seemed potentially counterproductive to the maintenance of viable public structures within Congress.

Sadly, thinking about it is where my concern had to end. Unlike with the Charter Commission, where I like to think I contributed to the forestalling of overly *centrifugal excesses, I held no governmental position and the Congress, with its sub-constitutional alterations, became an increasingly weaker institution. By the end of the decade it was having difficulty harnessing the federal budget. There was overwhelming evidence that the dispersions of power within the Congress, and the ability of each member to protect pet projects in a way that busted the budget, were at the root of why the fiscal 1980 budget, a pre-Ronald Reagan budget remember, was already $63 billion dollars in the red. By the end of the 1980's, what had begun the decade as a $942 billion national debt was three and one-half billion dollars. Yes, I believe that Senator Patrick Moynihan (D-NY) was correct when he said that Ronald Reagan willfully promoted that debt in order to defund the federal government. The deficits, and debt have continued to climb since then, even the Clinton presidency running a surplus for only one year when the trust fund using "unified budget" scam is properly taken into account.*

But let us return to 1980. Having had the experience with the Democratic Charter Commission that I did, and having been an observer of Chicago politics in my early life, I decided to do what I could to bring attention to the underlying structural reasons for the growth of the national debt. I was so convinced that the national debt would begin to skyrocket after fiscal 1980 that I announced my candidacy for the Democratic U. S. Senate nomination in South Carolina in order to discuss this issue. I had lived in South Carolina for only eight years when I offered for the Senate there, running against the well-regarded incumbent, Senator Ernest "Fritz" Hollings in the primary. I called attention to the structural reasons for why I thought the national debt would almost surely increase. I also called for the formation of a national commission that would study the American constitutional, and sub-constitutional structures.

To run, I took leave without pay from the University and, after making two speeches at the end of 1979, campaigned throughout the first five months of 1980. I received over 27,000 votes, roughly 8 1/2% of the vote in a three-person race. Far more importantly, I attracted the attention of the dean of American journalists, Richard Strout, who wrote about our campaign in the TRB column in The New Republic *and also wrote an article on it for* The Christian Science Monitor. *Strout had been concerned with the excessive dispersion of our government's institutions for a long time and wrote favorably on what we were doing. He relayed our call for the convening of a national commission on America's governmental structures.*

To shorten a long story, my call was answered first by a wonderful gentleman, Prof. Charles M. Hardin of The University of California—Davis. Hardin asked if he could reference my name and the Strout articles when attempting to organize a constitutional study group. He heartily began the task of putting together a conference, held at the Dupont-Plaza Hotel in Washington, D.C., January 17-

18, 1981. Soon, the leadership of the group fell to the noted Washington lawyer Lloyd Cutler, who had served as Counsel to the President under Jimmy Carter, and was my father's lawyer when my father was president of the Automobile Manufacturer's Association.

Cutler solidified what became known as The Committee on the Constitutional System, serving as co-chair with former secretary of the Treasury and undersecretary of state C. Douglas Dillon, and the then Republican Senator from Kansas, Nancy Kassebaum. The committee met with some regularity, mostly in Washington, D.C., although it did in a few instances hold hearings at various locations around the country. By January of 1987 the committee had completed a package of constitutional and sub-constitutional structural proposals, Cutler personally delivering our work to the president while others submitted it to the congressional leadership.

Lloyd Cutler knew me through my father but considered me to be a bit of a radical and never encouraged me to play much of a role in the Committee, even though it had grown out of my 1980 campaign. To be fair, there were probably few people in the country who could have assembled such a prominent group of participants as Lloyd Cutler. Among them were the former Arkansas Senator J. William Fulbright; former chair of the Joint Economic Committee of the Congress, Henry Reuss; then University of Chicago Law School Dean, later Stanford University President Gerhard Casper; Burkett Professor of Law at The University of Virginia A. E. Dick Howard, and other prominent political, academic, and private sector figures. In spite of the horsepower represented, there were quirks in Cutler-led discussions of constitutional change. Two in particular illustrate, I think, the cognitive imbalance of Cutler's, and I'm afraid Greater Washington's, thinking about its government.

At the start of each meeting, Lloyd Cutler would summarize what we had done before, leading off with the most salient of our Constitutional proposals, the extension of the House of Representatives term from two to four years. There was virtually unanimous consent that the already apparent problems of campaign funding, in concert with the problems attending the length of time needed to campaign, made the two-year congressional term increasingly unworkable. Members of the Congress's lower house now spent less time on legislation and, at the same time, were subject to increasing influence from wealthy contributors.

Beyond the four-year House term, we went on to endorse the abolition of Section Six of the Constitution's Article One. This change would permit members of the Congress to simultaneously serve in the executive branch, ostensibly as cabinet or sub-cabinet members. We also endorsed what James MacGregor Burns, a distinguished political science professor at Williams College and a supporter of my 1980 campaign, had long argued for: the "team ticket." This innovation would permit the presidential/vice presidential, congressional, and senatorial (if running) candidates of each political party to be selected with the pull of a single lever.

All three of the above constitutional proposals are structurally centralizing, or centripetal. They were designed to counterbalance both an originally centrifugal constitutional framework, and the centrifugal reforms that the previous decade's office holders had visited on America's political institutions. I should point out, incidentally, that though the idea of converting to a full-fledged, European-style parliamentary system was discussed, there never was much support for it. Most of us felt that in a nation as large and diverse as ours, a parliamentary political system would simply not work.

At the sub-constitutional level, we made proposals as well. Appropriately, they had to do with remedying the excessive structural dispersions in the Congress that the 1970s reforms had brought about. To restore party leadership in the two houses of Congress, to restore party-based funding to congressional candidates, to restore cohesion in committee and subcommittee structures, staffs, and responsibilities—all were part of what the Committee on the Constitutional System found important. Our sub-constitutional proposals were as centripetal as our constitutional proposals.

But two rather remarkable things happened within our group, both of which provided revealing insights into how Lloyd Cutler thought about constitutional change, and perhaps how he thought about government generally. Recall, please, my mention of the review of the four-year House term at the beginning of each CCS meeting. It did help to get people back into the discussion after the gaps between our meetings. And yet, without fail, Lloyd Cutler would invariably end his four-year-term soliloquy with the briefest of statements that linked our four year term for the House proposal with an endorsement for an eight-year term for the Senate. And then Cutler would go to the next topic.

I went to the full commission meetings in Washington, although not all of the regional meetings that were held around the country. The eight-year-term proposal for the Senate was barely discussed in Washington, with brief mention of the abolition of the mid-term election altogether being the only rationale ever given. And yet, Cutler always mentioned it and it was a part of our final proposal. Again, that proposal went to the president, the Congress, and the press, although, unlike the four year proposal for the president and the Congress, I have never heard of a single politician, academic, or even member of the political press who has ever expressed an interest in having the senate term be double that of the president.

To me, an eight-year Senate term would be an anachronism, a rider attached to our most salient, and most likely to be successful, proposal. What kind of mind,

I wondered, would run so automatically from the four to the eight? What kind of mind would so unquestioningly assume the latter proposal to be a necessary partner to the former? I wasn't sure—that is, until sometime later, or until the time that we discussed the proposal concerning the possible dissolution of the government under a European-style vote of "no confidence" if a deadlock within the government should occur.

In contrast to the eight-year Senate term proposal, the question of whether or not CCS would endorse something like the English parliament's vote of no confidence and its attendant dissolution of the entire government, was much discussed in CCS. Cutler himself was most enthusiastic about the idea, and in our final, late 1986 meeting, a large block of time was allotted to the issue.

For the first time in our meetings, a team leader was appointed for each side of this issue and, with our champions, the battle was truly joined. The proponents argued the classical centralizing position, claiming that the no-confidence vote would help America's political parties to be more responsible. The proponents argued that a political system that allowed for governmental dissolution would enhance party solidarity, as parties could sanction those who would not follow a party proposal by putting their positions, presidential or congressional, at risk.

The antis argued the opposite, of course, suggesting that the centralizing thrust of a vote of no confidence and the attendant dissolution of a government would not fit well with a government that was as decentralized as ours. This notion of party responsibility would conflict with the decentralization of the American government by having more centralized parties traumatize institutions that ordinarily worked by comity, or mutual give and take. But note that both sides assumed the no confidence vote to be centralizing, their sole difference being whether or not such a centralizing element would fit into our decentralized system.

After a while, something began to dawn on me. It became increasingly clear that neither Lloyd Cutler, nor anyone else who had spoken to the issue, considered the possibility that the relationship between the vote of no confidence in the British system was not directly related to the other parts of the U. K.'s centripetal system but was, in fact, inversely related to the other parts of that system. I slowly came to understand, in other words, that the vote of no confidence mechanism, taken by itself, was in fact centrifugal, although no one seemed to recognize it.

What I think I understood, to be specific, was that the dissolution aspect of the British system was the necessary, complementary escape valve that was so badly needed by an otherwise very centralized governmental form such as that of the British. I also began to understand that the keeping of the six-year Senate term, without changing it to eight years in the American system, was inversely related to the moving of the House term to four years too, while moving the time to eight years was directly related. By not being changed, that is by maintaining the six-

year Senate term, roughly sixty-six senators would remain in the Congress after each election, something I considered necessary if we were to move to the four-year House term. In retrospect, I think I should have argued about the no confidence proposal with Lloyd Cutler, just as I should have argued about the eight-year term. But I did not.

What became clear to me as I thought more about it afterward was that Lloyd Cutler never considered the possibility of the inverse relationship, either with regard to the eight-year Senate term or with regard to the proposal for the vote of no confidence. In fact, Cutler, as I think back on it now, never utilized the inverse relationship in any of his considerations. For him, there was only direct reasoning, variables moving linearly, or in the same direction. That was the kind of mind Lloyd Cutler had, and that was the way he thought about things. And the late Lloyd Cutler was a very intelligent man.

Interestingly, the outcome on the vote of no-confidence proposal was twenty-two votes against adoption, and twenty-one in favor. Again, all of the other forty-two votes in the room seemed from the discussion to believe that the no confidence vote would be centripetal in nature. The only remaining question for them was how well the assumedly centripetal no-confidence mechanism would fit into our system. As the reader, I'm sure, has discerned, I voted with the twenty-two votes against the no confidence proposal, but I voted that way for a reason that was cognitively the opposite to at least all the other CCS members who spoke. I voted against it because I believed that such a decentralizing device within our already highly centrifugal, weak party, weak congressional, and highly federalized system would put our government up with the Weimar. You can't reconstitute a disassembling government with the analytic cognition.

CCS' dissolution discussion, and the eight-year Senate term proposal, helped me to understand something I had never fully comprehended before. Lloyd Cutler helped me greatly with that understanding. I would go on to other political campaigns, about which more will be said later. Not long after CCS, Lloyd Cutler went on briefly to become Counsel to a second President of the United States: Bill Clinton. More on Mr. Clinton later as well. In the next chapter I will explore the relationship of the relative centrifugal-to-centripetal nature of governmental institutions to the cognitions and public policies that different governments tend to generate. Different political structures both grow out of and in turn promote the use of different cognitions. Getting this straight is fundamental to an understanding of a psychologically based political philosophy, and to the reform of the highly decentralized political system that we will examine more closely in the next chapter.

CHAPTER FIVE

Aristotle and America

The End of the Pyramid

The first four chapters of this work have been largely descriptive. I have attempted to lay a philosophical groundwork for a psychologically based, subatomic political theory by demonstrating the linkage of a psychological, cognitively based proclivity for a way of thinking with differentiated perspectives on both intellectual and real-world political issues, as well as political structures and processes.

In sum, what I have described so far is how the core of a psychologically based theory should be made up of a) the psychological linkage to the classical knowledge forms of the analytic and the synthetic cognition; b) the psychological variable's impact on the limits-to-knowledge question, specifically the importance of a simultaneous use of differentiated cognitions to achieve full understanding; c) the cognitively alternating nature of the dialectic, that is the analytic-synthetic-analytic sequence in historical progression, as well as its use in understanding the ideology of historical progress in the law, and d) the impact of the cognitive divide within philosophy, jurisprudence, and economic theory (revealing a fission within both the rationalist and skeptical positions in their intellectual evolution, and a subsequent fusion into the analytic/synthetic cognitive spectrum).

We should now place the psychological variable into political philosophy, and at the same time continue our analysis of political reality. All in all, the subjectively dictated, cognitive differentiations between those who find the equation $5 + 7 = 12$ to be an analytic statement and those who think it to be a synthetic statement are still key. We must remind ourselves, again, that in the real world of human psychologies, the analytic to synthetic distinction is represented by a range, or a spectrum, rather than by two discrete points. Let us begin to build on what has been laid down so far.

I begin with Aristotle. I do so because Aristotle categorized governmental forms that I think can and must be associated with their corresponding cognitive forms in order to build an equitable political philosophy, and government. In the *Politics,* Aristotle described the principal forms of government as a) by the one, b) by the few, and c) by the many. When these governments were healthy, they worked for society's benefit and were labeled, respectively, as a) monarchy, or the generous public ministration of one individual (such as Pericles); b) aristocracy, or the beneficent rule of an elite; and c) constitutional democracy, or the rule of the citizenry as a whole. When these forms served only themselves, they were labeled again respectively as a) tyranny, or the subjugation of the citizenry by a single dictator; b) oligarchy, or the dividing of the spoils by a handful of selfish collaborators; and c) pure democracy, or mob rule.[1] Of course, Aristotle recognized, as did America's Founders, that all governments possess some of each of the three elements.

Typically, political philosophers, and those who teach political theory, have arranged the three Aristotelian political forms into the shape of a pyramid. They have done so because, from a pre-psychological perspective, a pyramid conveniently ranks the governmental forms according to the number of participants that are permitted in that government. Among the good governments, therefore, constitutional democracy, or the government of the many, is placed at the base of the pyramid, with aristocracy and monarchy resting respectively above. From an objective perspective, there is not much to argue about with that arrangement. The degree to which more or fewer people are included in public decision-making has been, and to a degree remains, a legitimate political consideration.

But numbers alone do not tell us much about what cognitive forms are used within the various governmental forms. They do not tell us much that would be useful to a psychologically based political philosophy. Most assuredly, they do not lead to a subatomic standard of political equity.

What, then, would a subjectively oriented arrangement of Aristotle's governmental trichotomy look like? I think a subjective, that is psychologically based, perspective on the arrangement of government places the aristocratic form at one pole on the continuum of cognitive forms, the monarchical arrangement at the other cognitive pole, and constitutional democracy, among the healthy governmental arrangements, at the center. In other words, though the aristocratic form has objectively been considered to be in a middle position, at the center of the pyramid, I suggest that a cognitive analysis reveals a horizontal, cognitively based spectrum with aristocracy at one end and monarchy at the other. Why do I propose this?

By definition, a political aristocracy reflects the power of certain significant subparts within the whole. Important to a cognitive perspective, it is clear that any political subpart is invariably more homogeneous than its political whole. This is true with attributes such as geography, language, culture, history, ethnicity, and the like. Cognitively, therefore, the subpart is more analytic than the larger political system, the conflating of many subparts inclining the whole toward the synthetic cognitive form, all things equal.

For example, even in the relatively homogeneous entirety of early modern England, for example, each of the Dukedoms of Northumberland and Kent represented a greater homogeneity than did the entirety of England. In each of the subdivisions, in other words, the subpart was somewhat differentiated from the whole, even though it was not as differentiated from the whole (of England) than were, say, the various parts of continental Europe.

The Roman Empire, the Carolingian Empire, and the various European leagues and alliances always encompassed a rich variety of nationalities, cultures, languages, etc. that in many cases made the differentiation between part and whole greater even than, say, the latter-day British experience that included Celtic Wales, Scotland, and alas, all and now still part of Ireland. Even today, the European Union habitually argues over the degree to which its association of nation-states should be deepened—that is, brought to a greater level of unification—or broadened, that is, maintained as a highly diverse confederacy with only a growing list of national members. The two are not mutually exclusive, of course, although those who argue about them sometimes make it seem so.

This European argument is but one exemplar of the kinds of disparities that exist between parts and wholes in all political arrangements. Again, the subparts of the whole are almost always more homogeneous, or cognitively analytic, than the whole. But, more important, we should recognize that there is a great range in the *degree* of cognitive differentiation that exists between the subparts and the whole within any political unit. The subparts may be only a little more homogeneous, or cognitively analytic, than the whole, or they may be a great deal more homogeneous than the whole. The key question is: to what degree does the cognitive difference between the subpart and the whole impact the cognitive nature of the whole?

Part of the answer to that question, I think, lies in the fact that the greater the cognitive difference between the subpart and the whole, the more the subpart will attempt to draw the cognitive nature of the whole into the analytic form. The more differentiated the subparts are as a collection, in other words, the more those subparts will succeed in forcing the whole to embrace the analytic cognitive mode within the interactions among the subparts and the whole. Only a subatomic, subjective perspective reveals this relationship, but I think once the subatomic perspective is utilized, the relationship becomes quite clear.

Put another way, if political subparts are highly homogeneous, that is if the subparts of any political system are highly analytic from a cognitive perspective, their impact on the entirety will be greater, or they will pull the whole into a more analytic procedural mode, than if the subparts are less homogeneous, or more cognitively synthetic, from the outset. In a modern nation-state, an aristocracy exists if the subparts are very powerful from an objective standpoint, and from a subjective standpoint if they are highly analytic in their cognitive nature and in the way that they interact with the political entirety.

This is why I believe that aristocracy, or its corruption oligarchy, is more clearly analytic within the Aristotelian trilogy than it has been in a vertically understood configuration. Today, aristocracy is made up interest groups, the most powerful of which is the modern corporation. That corporation is surely just as economic in its essence as the traditional landed aristocracy. And, to be sure, there are powerful liberal interest groups as well, including civil rights groups, women's groups, gay and lesbian groups etc. that are not only undeniably left of center ideologically but, because of the sub-atomic "personality sort" within all groups, also ratify the essentially contractual nature of dealing with the government.

Thus, whereas a pure monarchy over-aggregates the citizenry by integrating potentially synthetic differentiations within any systemic subpart into a single whole, and whereas a constitutional democracy aggregates the citizenry moderately, permitting a balance between individual and group interests, a modern aristocracy, or oligarchy, evidences the cognitive impact of the subpart's internal homogeneity, again because of the solitary goal of engaging in the profitable business contract and because of the form of its interaction with the government. That form, quite naturally, is analytic. The American political system can be referenced as an example of what I believe to be an increasingly aristocratic, if not oligarchic, arrangement, with its attendant, increasing dominance of the analytical cognitive form, again with the interaction of interest groups and their campaign contributions.

I suggest that in the twenty-first century, the United States evidences a form of interaction between interest groups and the core public unit that is altogether different from what has gone on throughout most nations in most of Western history. The form of the interaction between, say, the American federal government and the now fifty state governments in the still relatively young United States, with the painful exception of the Civil War and surrounding period, may not have changed much over the last two hundred plus years. For all of their distinctiveness from each other, the American states have always possessed at least a fair portion of the public sector's quality of heterogeneity. Public entities, after all, are essentially microcosms of the nation of which they are parts and there is, therefore, a measure of cognitive similarity between the fifty states, and their aggregate populations, and the federal government and the larger national population.

But what about the modern form of private-sector subunit or interest, particularly the modern corporation? How great is the cognitive contrast between the natural interactions of the modern corporation and the central government? The answer, I think, is obvious. I believe there is a vast difference between a) the relative cognitive similarity between America's political states and the national government on the one hand, and b) the lack of cognitive similarity between the modern corporation, a banking corporation, for example, and the federal government on the other.

To put it another way, the state of, say, South Carolina is nowhere near as cognitively differentiated from the American federal government as the New York bank Citigroup is from the American federal government. Similarly with the preferences for cognitive forms of interaction, there is nowhere near as much cognitive difference between the preferred forms of interaction that a state would prefer to engage in vis-à-vis the American federal government as compared to the preferred forms of interaction that Citigroup would prefer to engage in vis-à-vis the federal government.

After all, many states' problems are not so different from the federal government's problems. As a result, there is a measure of cooperation, as well as cognitive similarity, in how these entities deal with education, housing, health care, the aged, etc., even if one entity is only dealing with those problems within a relatively restricted geographical area. Cooperative interaction such as that between an American state and the federal government is also cognitively synthetic. It embraces the disparate variables and, to at least some degree, commingles them politically.

But what the biggest American bank, Citigroup, prefers to do vis-à-vis the federal government is very different cognitively from what a state does with the federal government. Citigroup is concerned, almost exclusively concerned, with making money. Vis-à-vis the federal government, it is concerned with reducing its tax burden, warding off antitrust intervention, avoiding labor problems, avoiding prosecution for predatory lending in a small state, and even avoiding environmental enforcement regarding its disposal of reams of paper. Citigroup does not want to cooperate with the federal government; it wants to get the best deal it can from the federal government. Not only is its own business of the contractual, or analytic, cognitive form, but it also, more quietly, wishes to place the important decision-making centers within the government into a contractual, or a cognitively analytic, relationship to it.

Thinking of it somewhat differently, just as Citigroup wishes to have as few governmental encumbrances on its work as possible, thus not having to worry about antitrust, excessive lending regulations, labor unions, and the like, it also wishes to have as few encumbrances as possible on the contractual relationships that develop over time with individual public officeholders and institutions such as congressional committees. All things equal, a corporation like Citigroup does not wish to share governmental attention with other lobbying groups or even with a political intermediary institution such as a political party. It wants direct access, again a contractual form of relationship, with those it interacts with in the government. It gets that, of course, by contributing to political candidates, meeting directly with successful candidates, and bargaining from there. Because Citigroup is a far more cognitively homogeneous subpart of the overall American system than is a state, Citigroup has a far different preference for the forms of interactions that it wishes to engage in vis-à-vis the central government than does a state.

I now ask you to consider the possibility that in America's federalist, separated powers government, as well as in the sub-constitutional arrangements that we have at least in part reviewed already, the American political system has come to what I believe is the historic, subatomic moment. We are at the point, I suggest, when the subjective, that is the psychological, differentiation among significant political players has begun to supersede the objective differentiation in America's ideological identifications in such a way that the government's core structural arrangements need to be understood very differently from the way they have been in the past. Accordingly, they will also need to be retrofitted to achieve subatomic equity in the future.

What do I mean by this? In the next subsection, I will attempt to describe how the over-weighted imposition of the analytic *form* of interaction on the American government by large private interests has progressed to such a point that the sub-constitutional nature of the American government has changed significantly. In the context of the subatomic, psychologically based political philosophy I am describing, I will label this condition "undemocratic decentralization." I suggest that a subjectively derived understanding of an undemocratically decentralized government should now replace those political understandings that have so far dealt only with "whole group" interest groups or with "whole group" understandings of America's political institutions.

Institution-To-Institution Interactions— Undemocratic Decentralization

The Aristotelean, trichotomous description of governmental arrangements I have referenced above is as useful today as it was to the Greeks twenty-five hundred years ago. In this subsection I will make a simple point: that what Aristotle called constitutional democracy can be destroyed in not one but two ways. If constitutional democracy, and its corruption, pure, or mob democracy, lie in the middle of the horizontal spectrum of governmental arrangements, as I think they do, and if monarchy, or its corrupt form tyranny, are dangers to constitutional democracy on one pole of the spectrum, then I think it undeniable that aristocracy, and its corruption oligarchy, poses every bit as much a danger to constitutional democracy at the spectrum's other pole. Is there a structural arrangement that is roughly the other extreme from Platonic, cognitively synthetic totalitarianism, or from something like Rousseau's notion of a populace forced to be free? I think so. And I think America is very close to it, if we do not already have it.

The way I suggest that we examine the distortions of constitutional democracy that are on the other end of the spectrum from monarchy's corruption, tyranny, is quite simple. It is to look at the Constitution and make what I believe to be the most reasonable breakdown of America's core political document. I believe that the Constitution can be broken down into three clear layers. The first includes institution-to-institution interactions. Essentially, I speak of the core federal institutions, although I will certainly include the internal, or "sub-constitutional" components within the Congress, the Presidency, etc. within what I am describing, as well as the relation between the federal and state governments. I suggest that there have been significant changes in the ways that our public institutions interact with each other, particularly at the federal level, over the last thirty years.

I refer to the second constitutional layer as the citizen-to-institution layer, that being nothing more than the electoral processes that the Constitution prescribes, including the terms of office, and things like the Electoral College, the indirect election of Senators that was done away with in 1913, the highly indirect selection of judges, etc. The third layer, which I believe has been very largely ignored in constitutional scholarship, includes the interactions of private citizens with each other. I am suggesting here, of course, that the Constitution is not exclusively a public sector document. It does, as a matter of fact, have a fair amount to say about private sector interaction, specifically with regard to the principal common law document of the contract. As a byproduct of my suggestion that the Constitution is not exclusively a public sector instrument, I also suggest that the Constitution is not exclusively a procedural document. Although I am hardly the first to argue that the Constitution does have a substantive side to it, it is still the traditional view that the Constitution does no more than set out the rules for the political contest. I hope to spell out in a way that no one has so far what I believe to be a clear private sector balance in the constitutional arrangement, suggesting as I will with the two previous constitutional layers, that that balance has been largely betrayed.

Let us then look at the first imbalance, that existing within institution-to-institution interactions. Recall what I said earlier regarding the 1970s reforms of America's sub-constitutional order. Congressional committees grew in number, as did the gap between them and the legislative leadership of the two congressional houses. Subcommittees similarly grew in number and similarly distanced themselves from their committees entire. Staffs grew. Home offices grew. Transportation subsidies back to the district grew. At the same time, the importance of seniority declined, and members in both houses were restricted in the number of committees and subcommittees they could chair. In short, Congress both fractured itself and distanced itself from both its own leadership and, I would argue, the citizenry.[2]

As a result, the availability of subcommittee chairships, almost immediately upon arrival for new members of the centurion Senate, meant instant access to political power. But it also meant instant accessibility to a rookie senator or a still junior House member by that permanent and experienced Washington lobbyist cadre whose sole task is to promote private, singular interests. But even apart from the easy lay-up of prostituting the new member, incumbency has proven to be no guarantee of interest group invulnerability. Incumbencies have grown enormously over the last three decades, with election after election assuring certain victory for over 90 percent of House members and almost that percentage in the Senate.

Over time, lobbyists, not unlike what went on in the late nineteenth century, could get to know a congressional member at, say, the Metropolitan Club, develop a working relationship with her at, for example, the Mayflower Hotel, and seal a deal with her at the antebellum restaurant Harvey's, where the Oysters Rockefeller were very good even though the sign commemorating Senator Abraham Lincoln betrayed an unfortunate lack of historical understanding.

Americans, indeed informed citizens everywhere, know the dangers of concentrated power. Lord Acton's "power corrupts and absolute power corrupts absolutely" is part of the political science canon. But Acton and his citers were referring to a condition of over-centralization occurring in the public sector. Indeed, throughout recent history, and throughout even the most recent writings of political theory, the threat to power has nearly always been the threat of concentration in the public sector. Whether it was a military junta (Chile's Pinochet), a family (Haiti's Duvaliers), a ruthless dictator (Hitler and Stalin), or whoever else, the autocratic entities of the recent past were whole and singular. A polity was oversynthesized into the will of the one.

But if I am right about the horizontal arrangement of Aristotle's trilogy, history now begins to yield examples of the other end of the structural spectrum's danger. Look to pre-democratic political history first, with periods such as those of the warlords during times of weak Chinese emperors or the Holy Roman Empire with its German princelings, as times when decentralized government may have been more arbitrary with its citizenry than a beneficent, more centralized ruler might have been. Weak European kings, or even an inordinate delay in attaining statehood, as in the case of the pre-Bismarck German states, frequently permitted a harsher rule in the subparts than what might have been the case in a consolidated nation-state. Can excessive decentralization similarly impede equitable rule in a fully constituted, modern state? I think so.

What kind of dynamic might bring undemocratic decentralization to an existing democracy? As I have already discussed, part of the American dynamic toward undemocratic decentralization was the unwise 1970s fragmenting of America's sub-constitutional order that, along with the original, constitutional decentralization of federalism and the separation of powers that the Federalists gave us, left a surplus of access points available to those who "contract" with the government for very specific benefits. This phenomenon, I think, has already been written about from an objective, pre-cognitive perspective by first rate political scientists like Theodore Lowi and Grant McConnell.[3]

But contract is the right word, cognitively speaking, for the form of interaction within the federal government now. Of course, there will always be interests, and interests will invariably attempt to influence governments. But what is the form of that influence in an overly decentralized government? I don't think it is arguable that it is the analytic form. It is the form of the contract between, say, a bank lobbyist and the Senate committee on banking, unlike the form of influence that takes place in a less decentralized polity or even a monarchy, wherein the path of influence is at least somewhat encumbered by the claims of other interests.

Rather than lose constitutional democracy to a concentrated form, or to an overthrowing of the whole government by a singular dissident group, what I have come to call undemocratic decentralization clearly happens much more insidiously than does, say, a military coup. Again, it happens on the other end of the structural spectrum from the over-concentration of public power in both its form and its method. Did Jack Welch, the recently retired CEO of America's granddaddy corporation General Electric, ever wish to take over the American government? There is no evidence of it. All Jack Welch ever wanted was to dominate an increasing number of private markets, achieve what Wall

Street types now call "pricing power," that is, the ability to increase profit margins through administered or imperfectly competitive markets, and either keep the government out of the way or, even better, enlist the government in a variety of corporate welfare schemes and tax avoidances.

To ask an absurd question: does Travelers Insurance, now integrated with the bank Citigroup and the investment company Merrill Lynch, wish to have its chief lobbyist take over the government? Of course not. Why would it want to? All the insurance industry wants is the continuation of long-standing policies that keep the federal government from having any regulatory role whatever in the insurance industry and as little as possible in the other two industries. In the main, they have succeeded in doing that to date, at the same time that individual states do what is at best an uneven job of protecting their citizenries from the huge insurance industry.

To put it simply, undemocratic decentralization is the death of a thousand contracts. It is the double locking the front door while the burglar, not unlike some 1950s Chicago patrolmen, picks the lock on the back door. What I offer is the theoretical challenge to that long-standing and for too long unchallenged notion that a polity, a limited democracy, dies only from a concentration of power. Undemocratic decentralization is a wholly different kind of public sector corruption. With the deepest respect for those who, like McConnell and Lowi, surely had a sense of this, I suggest it is time that we describe decentralization's political abuses in their most robust, that is subatomic, cognitively theorized and dialectically Idealistic, clothing.

Beyond the specific sub-constitutional alterations of government that I have already mentioned, let us now turn to the question of how it happened that the American federal government came to have its parts so greatly distended from the center. How have we become so compromised, in a way that we not been since at least the 1880s? Let us ask first what psychology or, better, what cognition instigated what occurred here. I believe that what occurred was caused, apart from the objective desire for gain among larger and larger private institutions, by an increasing subjective dominance of one psychologically housed cognitive form over another within the halls of the American government, and within the groups that impact the government.

To understand undemocratic decentralization fully, let us first briefly review two sets of writings, both without apparent political or ideological overtones but, I suggest, with clear political and ideological implications. The first deals with organization theory, the second with cultural and historical cycles. Both organization theory and cyclical theories of history have a pattern to them. These patterns, without question, reflect a psychological bias that gathers momentum over time. The calculus ultimately reveals the triumph of one personality over another, and, accordingly, the triumph of one cognitive form, the analytic form, over the synthetic form. A well formed organization or institution becomes unformed, or distorted, in favor of one cognition to the detriment of another.

In the organization theory literature, I believe researchers such as Anthony Downs confirmed the theoretical notions of earlier writers such as Robert Michels, who wrote of the "iron law of oligarchy" and the destiny of all organizations. In his research, Downs demonstrated that what he called the "rigidity cycle" or the "ossification syndrome" as he also labeled it, resulted from something he named "bureaucratic free enterprise." What he meant was that as the more competitive and calculating personalities within any organization rise to the top to form an oligarchy, they also transform the very shape of the organization, in order to further their own personality preferences. That personality, and his or her institutional byproduct, typically breaks the organization into smaller, more functionally homogeneous, and more manageable parts.[3]

Howard Aldrich confirmed Downs's notions concerning institutional decentralization, at the same time that he labeled the catalyst of such change as those he called "boundary personnel." Downs felt that boundary personnel demonstrated a need for a "large volume of standardized transactions" (note the analytic cognition here) over the heterogeneity of a larger, more inclusive (I would argue cognitively synthetic) organization's transactions. Aldrich demonstrated that the psychology which preferred "streams of homogeneous elements" would triumph inside organizations and that the organizations, again over time, would reflect that victory. I think his insights were largely psychological, with their appropriate cognitive biases.[4]

Much like the research of organizational theorists, a similar phenomenon, that is the ascendance of one cognition over another, is also evident in the writings of those who have studied cultural and historical cycles. Pitirim Sorokin described how all societies seemed to have inevitably moved from what he called ideational cultures to sensate cultures. The ideational culture promotes the life of the mind, or of the arts. Such cultures favor what Sorokin called "the great symphony of life," the coalescence that moves in "both a quantitative and qualitative spatial direction."

The sensate culture, in contrast, naturally prefers "reality,"or a worldview that, as Sorokin put it, "seek[s] power over inorganic, organic and psychological nature." This, naturally, is a monotonic vision, not unlike the view of political power that Thrasymachus held or that Hobbes insisted on in order to maintain the order of society. Occasionally, there is a balance between the ideational and the sensate, Periclean Greece finding what Sorokin called the "idealistic" center. Sorokin's idealistic state, quite naturally I believe, contains a nice equity between analytic and synthetic forms.[5]

In the large sweep of political history, similar themes are available. Arnold Toynbee's tracing of civilizations revealed a movement from a "variety and elasticity, experimentation and creativeness" to a "mimesis" or a kind of "drill"that is characterized by a "mechanization of human life and movement." Toynbee noted that the powerful interests of the latter stage "check and sterilize each other" as they fragment the political institutions they work through. The declining society becomes "deaf to the unearthly music of Orpheus' lyre."I suggest that the analytic-to-synthetic contrast, and imbalance, could not have been portrayed more clearly.[6]

Similarly, even in the conservative Oswald Spengler's *Decline of the West*, this student of historical cycles finds that "the ripest and deepest forms and images" that exist within a society's "infinitely-varied external culture" almost inevitably fall to the "spiritually dead man of the autumnal cities—Hammurabi's Babylon, Ptolemaic Alexandria, Islamic Baghdad [and] Paris and Berlin to-day." Spengler contrasted the "evocative" creations of a nation demonstrated by "Plato, Rembrandt, Goethe and Beethoven" with the thinking of the "spiritually dead" works of "Parmenides, Descartes, Kant and Newton." [7]

Finally, similar themes to those cited above can be found in the writings of Edward Gibbon on the decline and fall of the Roman Empire, and, in works of other grand historians as well. My suggestion, again, is that there are psychological, ultimately cognitive patterns to the movements of history. A cognitive pattern takes over, and that pattern reflects one psychology in favor of another and in turn minimizes one cognitive form's contribution in that same, biased, direction.[8]

The phenomenon that I have described above, in its organizational, cultural, and historical settings, best explains what has happened to our government. The dramatic shift to the analytic cognition within congressional committees and subcommittees, congressional staffs, and individual governmental agencies, as well as within the vastly increased number of electoral incumbencies, is part of what has led to the increased and cognitively biased fragmentation of our government. The decline of parties and the increase in campaign expenditures are two of the principal causes of the fragmentation.

As with structure, so too with process. Now, the influence of powerful, cognitively analytic institutions finds its way through ever narrower, and less generally accessible, arteries that serve only the most powerful interest groups. I believe that the subatomic cognitive perspective reveals this bias more than any other perspective does. Only when the internal distortions of whole systems are revealed is the increasingly contractual, increasingly analytic nature of private-to-public-sector interaction so obvious. I believe that this perspective results in a better understanding of what I call undemocratic decentralization.

In short, just as we have always been taught to fear the over-concentration of power, we must now learn that the excessive fragmentation of power is an equal threat to democracy. In passing, I would point out that the U. S. delegation of national election authority to counties, beyond even state-level subsovereigns, seems to have done no less than alter the outcome of a recent American presidential election. This is undemocratic decentralization in a context I never expected to witness, even in the already constitutionally centrifugal United States.

Citizens and Institutions— Type 2 Undemocratic Elections and the Compressed Distribution

Imagine that you, my reader, have recently become a candidate for a significant public office. I come to your home one evening soon thereafter to brief you regarding the rules of campaigning in the mythical jurisdiction you will be running in. I begin by telling you that you may not publicly speak or appear before the media more than seven days in advance of the election. No, you may not ring your neighbor's doorbell tonight. I then inform you that you may not spend more than five thousand dollars in your quest for office. That means you cannot bring your message to more than a few. Oh, and one more thing. You may not hire anyone else to help you in your campaign. You are on your own.

Absurd? Not really. In fact, these kinds of restrictions are common in the ersatz elections that dictators around the world have commonly laid before their publics, all in order to legitimate their undemocratic rule. The last prohibition I mentioned, the no-staff restriction, comes with the second. No money, no people. We would agree, I should hope, that the above set of rules prevents democratic elections.

But there are two extremes on the continuum of electoral arrangements, just as I believe that there are two structural and procedural extremes of political arrangements. What if I were to visit you in your home tonight, for the purpose of explaining the realities of modern elections to you as a first-time office seeker, just as in the example above? But instead of telling you about a seven-day campaigning restriction, or some money and staff restrictions, I shout at you, "What are you doing sitting at home tonight?" What if I said, in the early evening, that I had you scheduled to speak to the American Legion at 8:00, the League of Women Voters at 9:30, and then that you needed to return to your home, or use your cell, to make sixteen phone calls that needed to be returned by 11:00, all to important funding sources.

Would you like to go to bed after that? Sorry. You have to work on your speech for the union breakfast tomorrow morning, before flying to the other end of your jurisdiction to meet with a media consultant who is just too busy (and important) to come to you. Then you need to fly back for the prayer lunch and the afternoon of walking another six miles as part of your promise to walk the length of your district by election day.

And what if it went on like that, day after day, month after month, so that you are campaigning, and raising money, and campaigning, and raising money as far as your eye, or anybody else's, could see? Would that be an onerous schedule for any office seeker? Undeniably. Would it be like many political campaigns today? Without question. Would it be undemocratic? Until now, I did not think that most citizens would have thought of it that way. But I think they should. I suggest that what I have just described is undemocratic, and I suggest that it is undemocratic for the exact opposite reason that our mythical potentate's restraining electoral rules on your campaigning in a banana republic would have been undemocratic. In recent years, American citizens have begun to witness the other end of the continuum, the non-tyranny but equally undemocratic end, of the electoral as well as the governmental realm.

The sad fact is that the 2000 election year saw the expenditure of over $3 billion on federal election campaigns. This figure exceeded by a full 50 percent the expenditures of just four years earlier and then was substantially exceeded again in 2004. In the 2000 campaign, President Bill Clinton, not a candidate, had dinner with one group of contributors for which the fee was $500,000 a guest. Rhode Island Democratic representative Patrick Kennedy, son of Senator Ted and chair of the Democratic Congressional Campaign Committee, has recently created a club for $100,000 congressional contributors. And these figures, recall, are Democrats. These are the leaders of what used to be called "the party of the people." The 2002 campaign only continued the graph's upward movement, and the 2004 campaign was off the charts.

What, specifically, is wrong with such expenditures? We will deal with the legal issues surrounding the campaign finance scandal and campaign finance reform matter in Chapter Six. There, I will discuss what I consider to be the gross misreading of the Bill of Rights by the Warren Burger Supreme Court, along with the palpable incorrectness of the campaign finance reform case of *Buckley v. Valeo* and its progeny.

In this chapter I write solely of the formal and informal structures of our elections. To explain our mythically frantic and money-soliciting candidacies, I focus on what has happened to the *form* of our overfinanced electoral system that makes it less democratic than it was even a few years ago. Once more, I first separate the objective from the subjective, for it has been well said already that many citizens who want to run for office no longer feel they can. Others simply do not want to. Many good citizens and even respected officeholders have said that the grind of the money grubbing, on top of the campaign, is just too much.

Regarding the subjective consideration, the undemocratic decentralization of the electoral process has caused every bit as much harm to the American polity as has the undemocratic centralization of the government's core structures discussed above. The highly centrifugal arrangements of the Congress that took place in the 1970s not only hampered the ability of the federal legislature to do what it should for the citizenry. It also turned the individual candidate for America's national legislature into more of an independent contractor, far more beholden to the singular interests who buoy her increasingly more onerous campaigns than at any time since the late nineteenth century.

The Congress's new structural arrangements have drastically reduced the role of the potentially synthesizing political party, and not only in the day-to-day operation of America's federal legislature. They have also reduced the party's traditional ability to aggregate political interests and apportion both money and favor in ways that were not invariably fair but were, in the aggregate, at least more broadly representative of the public interest than what the political contractor can do.

Is this new arrangement undemocratic? You bet it is. It is undemocratic in great part because the very cognitive form of the $100,000 contribution, or the $500,000 contribution, is not at all the same as the cognitive form of the $100 contribution. It is almost a truism, and I am not the first to say it, that the $100,000 of one contribution is not just one thousand different hundred-dollar contributions. That amount from one source is far more than a quantitative multiplier of the contribution that each typical American can afford to make. It denotes an interest, in fact it may better be said a demand, for a very specific governmental result. It is qualitatively different from one hundred thousand dollar contributions.

Whereas the $100 contribution, for a Democrat let us say, might signify a pro-choice position on abortion, the protection of Social Security from the private securities industry, or the staring down of the pharmaceutical companies on prescription drugs for seniors, this small contribution has virtually no impact whatever on a specific policy. The contributor already knows that it has no impact on policy. Her contribution merely falls in with a large number of other, similarly small contributions in its general endorsement of a variety of more or less ideologically consistent goals. The contribution, in other words, is cognitively synthetic, as it should be within the public-sector election process and within the broad-based umbrella parties that the United States purports to have.

Oh, to be sure, that small contribution may be generated by a heightened interest in but one of the issues of the day. Yet, by itself it does not generate the kind of relationship nor the expectation of a relationship with an office-holder or office seeker that a large contribution, with its inevitably contractual implication, almost always does. Thus, the large contribution is far more likely to be cognitively analytic. It evidences the form of a contract, much like making a purchase. And think for a moment beyond where the money comes from. Think where it goes.

A large part of that outrageous sum of money goes to the media, which has done very well over the last years, increasing their prices along with their campaign-related volume, and thus a candidate's campaign costs. Of course, the media has also weighed in against campaign finance reform. And much of the money goes to the exploding army of underlings who work in political campaigns, whether as consultants, pollsters, phone bank operators, focus group coordinators, and, of course, fund-raisers. To put it simply, there is a second layer of oligarchy in America today, an electoral oligarchy that protects the corporate oligarchy it serves and makes America's political system even more difficult to reform.

The campaign business is a well-paid business now, and it is surely a full-time occupation, as its practitioners very much want it to be. But it is still just that: a business. Its dealings with campaigns are highly contractual in form. They, like all they protect, are cognitively analytic, and they further what I label as undemocratic decentralization. The Toynbee-like "drill," within the context of what were once democratic political campaigns, has already marched far down the road.

And there is yet one more cognitive bias within the type 2 undemocratic election. This is the bias of time. Within each election cycle, there used to be a time for the campaign and a time for those seedbed pre-political movements that allowed individuals and groups to accumulate their thoughts and aggregate their allies. Whether it was the woman's movement, the civil rights movement, the gay pride movement, the environmental movement, or whatever, there was a time between the elections in which publicly spirited citizens could speak, write, assemble, and petition on a variety of topics that may not have received fair hearing in the context of the traditional political campaign.

When elections were not practically all that the American political system did, as they are now, such issues got their fair time at bat. In short, there was a time when public-spirited citizens could, first, learn more about what they needed to know and then craft an issue that they would bring to the government, not solely to a campaigning politician. They also searched for allies and alliances along the way.

But what has happened to all of that when the election campaign started to dominate the entire political timetable? Consider the cognitive form of an immediately past campaign issue, whether it be school vouchers, tax cuts, social security, or whatever. Today, the immediate campaign issue is almost invariably an over-refined issue. It has been reduced like a sauce in the most exaggerated nouvelle cuisine, and then reduced again. It has been purified of all nuances and interstices, numbras and penumbras. It has been honed, and honed.

Some will argue that campaigns should be dealing only with the well-refined issue. But if we concede the right of campaigns to deal with only that well-refined issue, then we should only more vigorously insist that when the election is over, that refined issue, and the singular interests and candidates who proffer it, get off the stage.

Overdue is the time for the American public to tell candidates, and their ever growing and enriched handlers, to get out of our faces for a goodly time and permit the richly embryonic political aggregations of regular citizens to have their day outside of the electoral context. Let the citizens who would grapple anew with an as yet less well-defined issue, or who would redefine and reinvigorate the well-honed issue, have their time to do what they must do. Let mini-dialectics do what they should around the country, finding contradictions here and there and embracing a synthetic cognition that will bring the orange to the apple, the synthetic form to the analytic, and maintain the subatomic balance that electoral campaigns alone can never maintain. Maybe the recent growth of blogs on the net will initiate that process.

The democratic political sequence begins with dialogue, the citizenry newly learning about and speaking to what troubles them. It proceeds to political, but pre-electoral, interaction. It then moves to a citizenry that asks of itself "Do you hear it too?" and "What do you think it is?" Then, and only then, the sequence proceeds to a movement—for example the civil rights movement—as cohorts within a citizenry that are similarly troubled and demanding of redress gather and protest. Finally, only after the mini-dialectic, the process at least ostensibly brings resolution, whether through administrative, judicial, or, yes, even elective processes. It may well end with the electoral process and there is nothing wrong with that. But it cannot begin with the electoral process because the electoral process is only cognitively analytic and cannot get to the contradiction alone.

If there is one rule of historical progress that is clear, it is that there are no shortcuts in the dialectical sequence. The analytic and the synthetic must share, in alternation, the stages of political life. The dialectic of the alternated cognition requires it. Aristotle's constitutional democracy requires it. But with each election cycle, unfortunately, America moves farther and farther away from it. The analytic encroachment, at the aristocratic, or oligarchic, pole of Aristotle's subjectivized continuum, continues within the very campaigns that pretend to so much democracy. In fact, America is the less democratic for them.

In sum, as we would identify the over-short campaign mandated by the tyrannical potentate as undemocratic at one end of Aristotle's continuum, let us now clearly identify the over-long campaign with Aristotle's aristocracy, indeed with aristocracy corrupted, or oligarchy. The latter is no more a representative democracy, or a polity, than is the former. The variable, again, is trichotomous, not dichotomous, and the cognitive range, as with Aristotle's range, was a trichotomy all along. Both poles of the trichotomy are, as they always have been, equally undemocratic. As we would easily identify the impoverished campaign with Aristotle's corrupted monarchy, or tyranny, let us then use a subatomic, psychological perspective to clearly identify the flush orgy of over-moneyed campaigns, run by only a restricted few from our population—with the undemocratic oligarchy it represents and sustains.

As for the new armies of campaign workers, the new swarm of mechanics who currently populate what was once our nation's democratic exercise, let us clearly identify them for what they are. They carry the water for Aristotle's oligarchy. Some are sincere. Some are valuable. But, as with Aristotle's trichotomy in all its other contexts, too many of them, like too much time and too much money, are not the symptoms of more democracy. They are the symptoms of democracy betrayed. Let us now quickly look at what I call the "compressed distribution."

The eighth worst nautical disaster in all of history occurred just three years after the sinking of the *Titanic.* No, the *Lusitania* was 1917. It was the *Eastland*, in 1915, whose sinking cost 815 lives. What is curious about the loss of the *Eastland* is that it did not occur on the high seas, or on any sea at all. Indeed, it did not even occur in a lake, although Lake Michigan was the ship's eventual destination, just a half-mile away. The *Eastland* Disaster, as it is known, happened while the craft was still docked in the Chicago River.

In the late nineteenth and early twentieth centuries, it was fashionable for those who lived on or near the Great Lakes to take summer cruises. Such cruises wound through at least four of the five lakes, the Welland Locks making Lake Ontario a bit of a stretch. Cruise ships typically docked at various towns or historic sites and offloaded the members of a social or service club, employees of a business or law firm. The *Eastland* Disaster involved a goodly number of employees from the Western Electric plant, located in Chicago's suburbs. Western Electric was affiliated with "Ma Bell" or A.T. & T., the company that assembled switchboards, phones, routing boxes, and the like.

What was even more remarkable about the *Eastland* Disaster was not just that it did not occur in any large body of water, but that it did not hit anything, or have anything hit it, or even submerge because of some mechanical failure. The boat simply rolled over, the result of Western Electric employees having climbed up the many decks and leaned over to one side in order to say "goodbye" to loved ones and hear the band play. It was all over in a minute.

Why did it happen? There are two kinds of indicators in virtually all statistical information. The first includes things like the mean, the median, or the mode of the variables, each designed to render some sense of a significant point where some core happening within the larger group occurs. The second indicator is the variance, or the degree of deviance or "spread" off of the significant, usually more or less center place, of the first indicator. The builders and subsequent owners of the *Eastland*, it seems, pretty much forgot about the second statistic. The boat, which had had a long history of trouble and a long history of being retrofitted but never quite fixed, was simply too tall or, if you prefer, not sufficiently wide, to be stable.

The structural problem with the *Eastland* was not a matter of accident or miscalculation. The story goes that the builder of the *Eastland* had naively assumed that since there were no great waves in the Great Lakes (not true—recall the *Edmund Fitzgerald*—1975), he could get away with building a very narrow and not very deep boat, topped by several layers of deck for those who wished to see the shoreline from a few miles out. This was the kind of feature that attracted groups such as the Western Electric employees.

When you think of it, it is hard to make a mistake with the mean, or balance point, of a boat. I've never seen a keel that was not pretty much at the center of the craft, and in this introduction to a metaphor, I am going to assume the centrality of the mean position. It is much easier to make a mistake with the variance, or the width, of a boat. Of course, if the ship is too wide, the cost is solely to speed and agility. I would not want to cross the Atlantic in a broadly girthed tugboat. But the other error, as with the *Eastland*, is invariably more serious. This boat, again, rolled over at the dock.

So what does all of this mean for politics? It is not much of a stretch to say that the fair representation of all the elements of a political society, aligned roughly along a normal bell curve, is necessary for the maintenance of democracy. Interests, we should not forget, are individual, and ideology is far more than just an ideological left and right. But, on balance, most interests do fall along the left-right continuum at some point, and they tend to coordinate with similarly flavored groups far more frequently than they do with groups on the other ideological side.

There are three well recognized perversions of a normal, or bell curve within politics. Clearly, if one ideological side is in full control, the curve is distorted to that side, and democracy loses in either of those two cases. Thus with Communism or Fascism. Almost as clearly, a bimodal distribution, two positions too near the poles of continuum, such as that which existed in Germany in 1932 or in so many Latin American countries in the 1950s and 60s, is at least a portent of democratic loss. If democracy has not already suffered to some degree from the strains of containing, or not containing, political extremism, a bimodal distribution will ensure continued strain on democracy.

But I suggest that there is a fourth perversion of democracy, one represented by an altogether different alteration of the bell curve, and one not yet described. What, after all, is the opposite of the bimodal ideological distribution? My view is that the opposite of a bimodal distribution, and every bit as much a signal of declining democracy as is a bimodal distribution, is not the normal bell curve. It is the other extreme, or what I call a "compressed" distribution curve, or a curve in which the generous width of a normal bell curve is lost and the high point on the curve becomes a narrow spike. Again assuming the more or less central location of this spike for the moment, I suggest that a compressed distribution can be every bit as undemocratic as a bimodal distribution that pulls the polity to its extremes, or a unimodal distribution that leans too far to the left or the right.

What I offer in relating this fourth perversion of the bell curve to politics is really quite simple. As money—inordinately large sums of money—has increasingly dominated America's late twentieth-century elections, and as those elections have become more representative of type 2 undemocratic elections at the citizen-to-institution layer of the American political arrangement, such now-routine and necessary political activities as polling, focus groups, huge, well paid professional staffs, and expensive TV ads have produced a level of similarity of political forms that I do not think American politics has ever seen.

Also, within the halls of Congress, with its increasingly insular committees, its increasingly hostile partisanship over narrower and narrower issues, its wholesale undermining of traditional leadership prerogatives, and the continued reduction of truly competitive electoral districts that bring solons to Congress (agreed to by both parties), the compressed distribution diminishes democracy as well.

What I suggest is that even if the substantive inputs of both the right and the left were still roughly equal in their ability to bring their respective views before the public, which I do not believe they are as I will speak to shortly, just the narrowness, the near singularity of the *forms* of political access, or the shrinking of the variance in the ways that citizens are able to have their voices heard, harms the political system. With due respect for new, largely internet-based citizens groupings such as ACT, MoveOn.org and other new "527" loophole organizations, I believe that what has happened with the dominance of increasingly large sums of money in political campaigns means that the increasingly expensive methodologies of politics, including particularly the growth of the highly paid election industry, makes the way that our nation's politics work more similar as between the two major parties than at any time in our history. Notice that the Republicans are now creating groups similar to ACT and MoveOn, exploiting the same loopholes in code section 527 to their advantage. The necessity of campaign finance reform, including public funding, is greater than ever and the specific prescription for it, I believe, begins in the next chapter.

Now, let us talk about whether or not the narrow "spike" that I suggest is a fourth instance of undemocratic politics, is generally near the ideological mean of American politics. Let us begin by looking at the "spike" in two very separate ways. The first is substantive, that is the proximity of the two major parties on a variety of economic and distributional issues. I suggest that that proximity has increased the chance that both parties, more recently the Democratic Party, get along all too well with the corporations that have kept real wages frozen for over thirty years while executive salaries and shareholder value have surged. Of course, this compression is detrimental to democracy, as someone like Ralph Nader has pointed out, the real policy choices of the electorate being limited as a result.

But, regarding the more central point, that regarding the very *form* of electoral process that has become nearly identical as between the major parties, what I suggest is that the "above the water" similarity of policy choices within American elections reflects, and indeed is reinforced by, a similarity of "below the water" form of how the policy choosers are selected. That similarity is in the usage of such extraordinary sums of money that it is the political right that has won out below the water. The keel of American politics, our very form of electoral selection, is not at the center. Once more, I praise groups like MoveOn, ACT and the liberal "527" groups that at least partially reduced the money advantage of the Republicans over the Democrats in the election of 2004. But, let us not forget, what the liberals were doing was monetary, using and if anything ratifying, the currency of money, if you will, within

American politics. The cruel fact is that ratifying huge sums of money as the coin of the political realm is, in the long run, a losing game for the left. The crueler fact is that such ratification is a losing game for government itself, which of course invariably harms the left. There must always be enough of the left, far enough away from the center of the spectrum, to fight for a government that is sufficiently strong to complete the humanitarian agenda. There must be an adequate governmental form to accommodate the synthetic form, and so arguing for parties themselves, cohesive governmental institution themselves, and the restriction of campaign expenditure itself, is part of what the left must do.

I put it bluntly. Beginning with the time when Sir Edward Coke helped finish off English feudalism, greatly mature the common law, and enhance the position of rising commercial interests, and then continuing with the time of the Glorious Revolution of 1688 that dismissed the largely anti-commerce Stuarts from the government and installed a supportive, mercantilist government in its place, the private sector, and its increasingly unencumbered analytic cognition, has been in the ascent. In America, with its even more individualistic and commercial culture, the sectoral, and cognitive, balance was tilted further still. The electoral result that grows out of the fact that the corporate right will always have more money than the left, and that the increasing quantities of money are still central to American politics, is that the right will continue to dominate our politics.

Oh, to be sure, there will be times when such awful corporate excesses, and such fawning before the corporations by the Republicans, occurs that the other side might temporarily win. But, in the long run, the growing Aristotelian imbalance toward oligarchy, in the context of the largely privatizing Anglo-American history of the last 400-plus years, does not favor the political left. Reforms like public sector funding of political campaigns, aided I hope by a political perspective that includes the Natural Left, will become even more necessary if our system is not to roll over and drown its passengers.

What I have been concerned with throughout this work, of course, is a deeper, more psychological and particularly cognitive, understanding of what are called the forms. The Natural Left that I offer focuses on the forms of knowledge themselves and, secondarily, on such things as these forms' respective choices for governmental structure and process. The pre-democratic balances that I am speaking to are balances between and among the different ways that our citizenry can influence its government. When a political system is healthy, there is a balance not only between particular public policy views. There is, at a higher level, a balance between those who wish the contractual, cognitively analytic form to dominate governmental interaction on the one hand and those who wish for more aggregative interaction on the other. Maintaining that balance of form requires some variance, or range, among the ways that citizens prefer to access their government. Even were the keel to be at the center, the occluded access range for the public diminishes democracy—the bell curve, again, does not have its necessary width at the top—and the left half of the ideological spectrum will pay far more of the cost for that compression. The occluded distribution, although nominally non-ideological in the sense that both sides are entitled to raise all the money they want, prevents the kind of collective action that strong parties, uncompromised office holders, and publicly interested regulators provide. The structural preferences of the Natural Left, founded on a firm understanding of the need for subatomic equity within all public institutions, are the key to such equity.

Briefly, there are two more costs that will inevitably be paid for a compressed distribution of politically relevant forms in government. The dialectic, recall, depends upon the alternative movement, or oscillation, of cognitive forms between the analytic and the synthetic. Clearly, such oscillation is only possible when there is already a fair degree of width to the continuum of cognitions within a given polity. Should the forms become compressed, there will not only be little range of policy alternatives at any static time, there will also be little chance of movement along the range over any extended period of time. From the perspective of the Natural Left, this condition ensures the inability of achieving the synthetic, contradictory form that is the essence of the dialectic's second stage. A political system cannot reform itself. It cannot change.

Finally, there is one more cost that grows out a compressed distribution of political forms. Many political observers assume that the closer that the two sides of an argument are, the less vigorous the argument will be. The notion makes a certain, superficial sense. Indeed, at the level of substantive, or policy, argument alone, it may well be that closeness breeds moderation. But, at the level of the forms of government, I suggest the opposite is true. I suggest that the acceptance by both the Republican and the Democratic parties of the narrow rules of a non-innovative political game means that they, these competitors, are essentially fighting over the same thing. Neither side, put simply, is trying to innovate; neither side is trying to step outside of the current form of argument and present new forms of thinking about the country's great and growing problems. The dogs fight, and continue to fight, over the same bone, over and over again, whereas if one side were to innovate, a circumlocution of the other side would take place; a flanking maneuver would occur on the battlefield, with the energy directed originally toward the citizenry rather than toward the old rival. The Natural Left, in my view, must begin to address the inequities that result from the "below the water" forms of our government. Restructuring our government in ways that return our system to the constitutional democracy that lies at the center of Aristotle's continuum should be the principal goal of the Natural Left within American politics. Only then will the oligarchic nature of our government, and its accompanying contractual, cognitively analytic, form be brought back into balance.

Citizen-To-Citizen Bias— The Constitution's Private Layer

As I mentioned earlier, I believe the Constitution to have three layers, the institutional, electoral, and, finally, the private layer. Immodestly, I do not believe that anyone has explained the private layer in the way that I think it should be. I believe that the private, or citizen-to-citizen layer, not only exists; I believe it is the most important layer in the Constitution. Indeed, I believe that, with a very small exception, it is what the entire Constitution revolves around. Virtually all the writings on the Constitution, scholarly though they may be, accentuate the structures of the American government and the pulling and hauling between and among those structures. My suggestion is that, as important as those writings are, and as important as the provisions they discuss undeniably are, the structures are fundamentally only instrumental. They are, in other words, only the means by which various political interests engage in their competition over governmental favor. But, I would ask, what is the argument over? I suggest that what the argument is over is knowable, and that we find it within this third layer of the Constitution, the layer that deals with citizen-to-citizen interaction.

As I will elaborate in greater detail in the next chapter, I believe the original seven articles of the Constitution, and the Bill of Rights, make up the balanced document that the Federalists, and the Anti-Federalists in opposition, designed. But I further believe that the core position of the Federalists was manifested in but two provisions of the Constitution. These were terribly important provisions and they, again, were substantive, private sector related provisions, not procedural or existing in the public sector.

The first is the Full Faith and Credit Clause of Article Four. That provision was in the Articles of Confederation as well but, as with all confederations, the enforcement of private contracts across a sub-jurisdictional boundary was iffy at best. The Federalists wanted to up the chances of effective debt collection, and so they reiterated full faith and credit in the new federal context.

Still on the Federalist side, the other provision that assisted the enforcement of contracts was the prohibition against the "impairing of the Obligation of Contracts" in Section Ten of Article One. The Federalists had seen enough of paper money, moratoriums and, probably most importantly, the appointment of judges (often for very short terms) who could be expected to accept jury fact findings on the existence of "onerous conditions" that would negate enforcement of the contract. Section Ten is talking directly to state legislatures, telling them that these kinds of encumbrances on the contract would no longer be permitted.

What, then of the Anti-Federalists side? Where do they come into the private sector portion of the American constitutional arrangement? To answer that, we need to go back a little in time, for I suggest that two very important events occurred that both presaged, and accentuated, the position of the Anti-Federalists in the Constitution's private layer.

The first event is well studied. It is Shays's Rebellion, that Western Massachusetts uprising of debt ridden farmers who claimed that the terms of their mortgage contracts were onerous, the result of hard times when the farmer's bargaining position was at a nadir. One of the catalysts to the writing of the Constitution was this private sector argument that ended in a brief military response to the farmers.

The second event that led to the Anti-Federalists' Bill of Rights response to the Federalists is seldom written of. Although James Madison's # 10 *Federalist* is almost universally declared to be the heart of the *Federalist Papers,* I differ. I believe that the most important segment of the *Federalist* is found within only three sentences, they appearing in *Federalist* # 80. Right in the midst of Alexander Hamilton's trenchant plea for an independent federal judiciary, a judiciary that would ensure lifetime appointments for judges, a judiciary free from congressional reduction of a judge's salary, and, most significantly, a judiciary capable of judicial review of the legislative acts of the Congress, three sentences put a caveat, hopefully a reassuring caveat, to those who might oppose the Constitution. The first of the three sentences simply describes the differentiation between the legal and the equitable jurisdiction. That first sentence was written to assure those who were expected to be opposed to the Constitution that Article Three's inclusion of the jurisdiction which frequently looks beyond the pure letter of the law, toward what might be a fairer resolution of a legal conflict, would be respected. The second and third sentences, elaborating on that distinction between law and equity, spell out the nature of the guarantee. Those sentences say:

> *It is the peculiar province, for instance, of a court of equity to relieve against what are called hard bargains. These are contracts, in which, though there may be no direct fraud or deceit, sufficient to invalidate them in a court of law, yet there may have been some undue and un-*

conscionable advantage taken of the necessities or misfortunes of one of the parties which a court of equity would not tolerate.

Is Hamilton writing in the abstract, or is he, more likely, writing in response to someone in particular, or at least a particular event? I don't think there's much question that he is. Hamilton is clearly attempting to reassure Daniel Shays and the other potential opponents of the Constitution that the powerful, independent federal judiciary that he was so strongly supporting would fully incorporate the most lenient standard of adjudication when it came to cases concerning private sector debts and debtors. I argue that this position, taken in #80 *Federalist*, does something that no other place in *The Federalist* does. It bounds the private sector on not just one side, as # 10 does, but simultaneously bounds the private sector on both the governmentally, specifically legislative, side and the legal, specifically equitable, side. For all of its undoubted eloquence and power, the # 10 *Federalist* is a single strutted argument. *Federalist #80* is double strutted.

And what then of the Bill of Rights provision? Where is it in the Bill that completes the trilogy of responses to onerous terms, or hard bargains, regarding those who felt so beleaguered by their creditors as well as by their political allies who wrote the original seven articles of the Constitution? The answer to that question is easy once you see it, but the Bill is not readily apparent for a simple reason, that being that few who think of the Bill of Rights think of it as having anything to do with contracts. Well, the Bill of Rights does have something to do with contracts, and although the specific provision in the Bill of Rights that relates to contracts is of little contemporaneous importance (and gets very small mention in today's Con Law textbooks), it is historically and theoretically very important. It is the Seventh Amendment.

I suggest that the Seventh Amendment is nothing less than the follow on of Shays's Rebellion and Hamilton's # 80 in the third, private, layer of the Constitution. In its ensuring that "the right of trial by jury shall be preserved" in federal civil cases, and that "no fact tried by jury, shall be otherwise re-examined in any Court of the United States," what the Anti-Federalists were doing was preserving what in almost all cases was a debtor favorable ruling, on the facts, in debtor-creditor cases. Put another way, if the Federalists were going to ensure that contracts could not be impaired by state legislative action in Section 10 of Article One, the Anti-Federalists would correspondingly ensure that individual debtors who could show that they were the victim of what even the father of American conservativism Hamilton had called a "hard bargain," would benefit from the fact findings that came from local juries.

The combination of Shays's Rebellion, #80 *Federalist,* and the Seventh Amendment, is what I call the "little trilogy" of the Constitutional order. It links the three private sector events, the last being within the Bill of Rights itself, that balanced the private sector layer of the constitutional order against what the Federalists had included with their full faith and credit and Obligation of Contract provisions in the original seven articles. Only one question remains, I think, and I also think that the answer to it is obvious. What kind of mind, wholly apart from any objective identification with a debtor or a creditor, is inclined to acknowledge the importance of extraneous, extra-legal considerations, such as having a favorable bargaining position or, conversely, being caught in the kind of economic trap that necessitated agreeing to onerous, hard bargain, terms?

The Seventh Amendment, if nothing else, incorporates the cognitive position that extraneous variables should be given full consideration in the issue of contractual equity. It all comes down to whether something outside the contract should be under consideration, whether the orange should be next to the apple, and that, of course, necessitates asking about what kind of mind naturally deals with that kind of issue. Is it the Kantian, linear kind of mind that, all things equal, would read only the terms within the contract, or is it the Hegelian kind of mind that would search outside the contract and include external variables as a part of the consideration? And so, I submit that not only is there a third layer to the Constitution, again a private sector, substantive layer, but that that layer is what the Constitution and the Bill of Rights, more than anything else, was arguing over. The balance was only achieved by the writing of these two ideologically differentiated documents.

And so, what is the impact on democracy when the balance between the above perspectives on the private contract is lost? We think of the loss of democracy as falling to a Hitler, a Stalin, a Mao or a Pol Pot. But that is only one side of the spectrum. When an oligarchy reigns, it is the existence of powerful private actors that undermines democracy; it is the natural product of the oligarchs. And what is the natural product of the oligarchs? It is nothing more, nor less, than the hard bargain contract. Think beyond Hitler and Stalin. Think of democracy's death that is the result of a thousand contracts, all onerous contracts, all relatively unencumbered contracts, and recall that what I suggested earlier that, with one small exception, the entire Constitution is centered on the single issue of to what degree contracts will be encumbered. Virtually all the rest, virtually all the structures and processes of the Constitution, are merely instrumental in the determination of that single issue: to what extent should the private contract be encumbered. Obviously, I think this is all best understood from the perspective of a subjectivized, moderately relativist, updating of the classical Idealist philosophical position.

Please permit me now to conclude this chapter with a few reflections on why I believe that America is at that point in its political and legal history in which the psychologically based perspectives on that I have been spelling out above are taking center stage.

The Subatomic Moment

In the first chapter I identified specific events of the year 2000 that I think were of considerable significance. The first was the challenge to the age-old political voting predictor of economic condition by the variable of whether or not a citizen is a regular attendee of religious services. That change, along with the rise in political importance of a variety of social issues, as I wrote earlier, signifies continued movement from an objective to a subjective basis for political identification.

The second was the naming of a Jew, Senator Joseph Lieberman of Connecticut, to the Democratic national ticket. The Senator was the first member of his religion to be on a major party ticket in American history. The courage of then Vice President Al Gore in doing such a thing has properly been commended. The objective barrier of religion, and particularly one often-oppressed minority religion, has fallen. But, again, the removal of that objective variable, along with others, only accelerates movement to the subjective from the objective.

The third significant thing that happened in the year 2000, I submit, was not at all subjective but ironically is one more example of why objectively based political ideologies will no longer promote victory for the left. This event was the culmination of many years of movement that, by 2000, found nearly 50 percent of all Americans to be owners of stock equities or bonds, whether through private accounts, retirement 401(k) s, or some other asset-owning vehicle. As we've mentioned, Lawrence Kudlow loves to say in his Friedmanesque micro economic classes on the business channel CNBC, that by the year 2000, 50 percent of Americans became members (Kudlow's voice usually drops in solemnity here) of "the investor class." That class may or may not always do as well as it might like financially, 2000, 2001, and 2002, bringing nearly universal loss on the major exchanges. But the coming together of this group is, without question, of considerable political significance. Its objectively rooted identity leaves little room for contradiction, at the level of objectively based political discourse.

Over the years, even a larger percentage of Americans will participate in the equity markets and will, over the long haul of their participation, enjoy rewards such as those of the 1990s and the recent year 2003. In spite of my politics, I would be no part of any restriction on public participation in those markets, although the cleansing of Wall Street surely has a long way to go. The way to respond to the objectively based influence of the investor class, in other words, is not to argue about the objective validity of enterprises such as personal investing. The way to respond is to move the entire political discussion to a higher, subjective level of discourse that trumps rather than confronts the investor-in-politics issue at its own level.

Why, after all, is the investor class politically significant? As I said earlier, the isolated fact of the growth of an investor class is part of a much larger context. This context, quite simply, is that America's distributional pattern, like Aristotle's trichotomy, is no longer well described as a pyramid. It is now better described as a very tall diamond. Franklin D. Roosevelt in the 1930s frequently and correctly referred to the distributional pyramid. With the caveat of a slight bulge in the bottom line of the pyramid, he was correct. But were he here today, I do not think that Franklin Roosevelt would use the pyramid symbol anymore.

With CEOs making twenty times more than they did twenty years ago, and with the average CEO today making over one thousand times what the average worker makes, the height of the American income distribution has clearly and dramatically increased. With 1 percent of the nation's population now owning over 60 percent of the nation's wealth, and with the net worth of that 1 percent equaling the net worth of the bottom 95 percent's net worth, the wealth distribution is even taller than the income allocation.[9]

And what about the bottom of the distributional configuration? Has not this become distended too? No question. Robert Kuttner reports that in recent years, corporate profits have increased by over 50% while wages have gone up only marginally.[10] It is now accepted that one-fifth of America's children go to bed hungry and forty-four million Americans have no health insurance. Recent figures show that, in real dollars, the minimum wage is $2.15 lower than it was in 1968.[12] Over two million Americans, seven-tenths of a percent of the population, are in jail.[13] In fact, a quarter of the world's imprisoned population is in The United States. The lowest quintile, or 20% of Americans' share of the income pie, has fallen from 6.4 percent twenty years ago to 4.9 percent today, and in the meantime, the top one-fifth of Americans has seen its share of the national income grow from 38.4 percent to 45.4 percent. After a decade of the greatest increase in wealth in our history, more than thirty million Americans still live in poverty.[14]

Though I am a great admirer of Franklin Roosevelt, let us remember something about his New Deal coalition that, I think, clearly distinguishes it from how a redistributional administration, and Congress, would need to act today. The Roosevelt coalition was a melding of disparate groupings, including the Old South, which was still smarting economically from the Civil War and thus financially needy even though it was socially conservative. Ethnic groups, unions, urban populations, and discomfited small-town and rural American voters who were suffering from the Depression made up the rest. But look at the form of the Roosevelt coalition.

The form of the old Roosevelt coalition is important to consider in the context of democracy, because if the distribution that Roosevelt was dealing with what was in fact a pyramid, then FDR's strategy for victory, brilliant in some ways as it is frequently characterized, was made up of little more than an additive collection of select objective groups. It was an amalgam, largely put together four years earlier by the 1928 Democratic nominee Al Smith, of different objective groupings that, because they were on or near the bottom of the pyramid, outnumbered those on top. Smith failed only because of the South's inability to accept his Catholicism, and the not-so-irrelevant fact that the Depression had not yet happened.

To be sure, there was an element of synthesis within the 1932 Roosevelt coalition. There had to be mortar between the bricks, and Roosevelt, along with the members of his "brain trust" and a few, usually university-housed, intellectuals, supplied that mortar quite well. But overwhelmingly, the Roosevelt victories were an objective achievement, greatly assisted, as is traditionally reported, by the Depression and the Second World War, with their accompanying hard times and need for sacrifice. Would Roosevelt have been able to do what he did with a differently shaped pyramid, say a diamond? Would he even have been able to win, or at least win as easily, if the distributional pyramid had been in the new, diamond shape?

I don't believe that Franklin Roosevelt could have won in the same way today that he did in the 1930s and early 1940s. No politician can advance what the left needs to do today with the support of only objective groupings and a few intellectuals. With a diamond rather than a pyramid form of distribution, something like what happened in William McKinley's landmark 1896 presidential election continues to happen, with enough of the scared middle class fearing the loss of their position and thus voting conservatively. Also, the rise of "culture war" issues has thrown most of the middle class into a more conservative mood. Something else will have to attract large numbers of citizens from other places on the distributional ladder than the bottom. The numbers do not add up.

And so today, I put it simply. I don't think, barring an economic downturn even more significant than the one America experienced from 2000 to 2003, that any left-of-center American politician can ever again win the presidency solely by mortaring together a combination of objective groupings. Again, the numbers just are not there. If we have reached a point where more citizens' votes correlate with regular religious attendance than with economic standing, and if we have reached a point where the last objective barriers to full citizenship are falling, and if we also have reached a point where the workings of a cognitively imbalanced economic system have created an increasingly disproportionate distributional diamond rather than a pyramid, then we are near the time wherein a wholly different calculus of electoral victory will be needed for the left. If the left comes to understand and utilize that new calculus, we are on the verge of a significant moment in American political history.

In a word, I believe we have arrived at that time when only a conscious courting of the subjectively synthetic voter, up and down the *entire* vertical, or objective, dimension of the distributional diamond, will bring about a left-of-center majority. Yes, some members of the Natural Left already participate on the left side of American politics. The contributions of movie stars, significant athletes and artists, etc., often top Democratic Party fund-raising lists. Some Natural Left voters do participate, although we have no measurement that can test how many of us do. But large numbers of Natural Left citizens who are not public figures, I suggest, are now so repelled by the increasingly Whole Group, interest group orientations of what today passes for the left in American politics that they, in my opinion, do not participate in American politics in anywhere near their full numbers. Only the conscious move from an objectively based to a subjectively based politics will bring these voters to the polls.

In the final analysis, what I am increasingly convinced of is that the unholy trio of undemocratic decentralization, type 2 undemocratic elections, and the compressed distribution are but three manifestations of the current ideological and structural imbalances that exist and grow within the American government. I think those imbalances and the distributional inequities that they have clearly fostered now reveal the United States to be at or near the oligarchy that is the corrupted form of Aristotle's aristocracy at one pole of the institutional spectrum.

Only by understanding undemocratic decentralization, type 2 undemocratic elections, and the compressed distribution within the context of an essentialist, theoretically Idealist and subjectively relativist political philosophy, are U. S. citizens going to comprehend why our country, before any other, has reached what I earlier called the subatomic moment. I believe that, before any other political system in the world, we have reached that point in history from which only a conscious recalibration of subjective, subatomic balances, beyond the mere correcting of objectively based injustices that are still often exacted upon objective groups, will restore true equity in the American political system. Subatomic equity must now accompany, if not precede, Whole Group Equity, and that is what a psychologically based political theory must both describe and prescribe.

The novel form of political recalibration I recommend will not be easy. And I think it will come only when the Natural Left supplants the objective left as the principal thread of American political left-of-center thought. It will come only when what I have called the Natural Left fully integrates the objective left, in much the same way that the Natural Right has enjoyed a fair degree of success in merging with, and to a great degree assimilating, the objective, largely corporate, right.

Again, the twenty-first century, objective residue of the New Deal coalition, though it may win particular elections, will not ever again make up a winning coalition. But the liberal-to-left political position can create a new configuration of numbers that has at least a fighting chance of winning if it understands and embraces the notion and the reality of the Natural Left.

Three More Campaigns

In 1984, I entered the New Hampshire Democratic primary, and over the period of two months I presented twenty-two forums at various universities and colleges across New England. These forums were designed to assist public understanding concerning what I believed to be the structural decline of the American government.

In 1992, I took leave without pay from the university once more. Headquartering outside Washington, D.C., I appeared at venues ranging from the Thomas Jefferson Society at the University of Virginia, to Haverford College in Philadelphia. Again, I spoke to students and faculty about the structural problems of the government. I formally entered the South Carolina Democratic presidential primary. As in New Hampshire, a presidential candidacy in South Carolina was available for a fee, rather than for a large number of petition signatures.

Most states, as the reader may know, have what they call "national recognition" laws. These laws mandate a secretary of state, or the head of the election commission, or whoever, to come to a decision over whether you are a desirable candidate for a ballot, without thousands of signatures. A Dick Strout article on this 1984 campaign, published in the Boston-based Monitor, *along with earlier Strout and other articles, cut no wood with the Massachusetts Secretary of State, to whom I twice made appeals to be on the ballot. In 1992 the District of Columbia, my original ballot target, was not interested in having someone who so generally criticized the government campaigning so close to the home of the outrage.*

And then in the spring of 2000 I entered the South Carolina Democratic presidential primary. This time I openly sought a large number of votes, putting together a small but capable organization, including a paid campaign manager and an inventive, generous media advisor. I went around the state speaking to colleges and universities, unions, League of Women Voters groups, county Democratic Parties, churches, Sierra Club chapters, and whoever else would listen to me.

The election was held March 9th, three previous dates having been changed. What was to have been a primary was also altered, at the last minute, to a caucus. Only Bill Bradley, Al Gore, and I were on the ballot, although voters had the choice of voting Uncommitted if they wished. Then Senator Bradley dropped out the day before the caucus. The final date of the caucus fell during Spring Break week for the state's colleges, something that may or may not have been intentional, and many of my early supporters wound up voting for John McCain in an attempt to defeat George Bush in the nasty and all too consuming Republican primary.

Nonetheless, I received a sprinkling of votes statewide and fully 7 percent of the vote in the Second Congressional District, running from Columbia south through most of Aiken and Orangeburg Counties and on to Beaufort County on the coast. In that district, Al Gore received only 85 percent of the vote, not winning the fifth of the five assigned delegates at the ward levels. I actually was leading Gore for that fifth delegate. The Washington Post *called to ask if I would continue to contest the delegate, but I told them I would throw in. Had I been able to garner nearly all of the Bradley and Uncommitted votes at the county and state levels, I might have made it past the 15 percent threshold that the national Democratic Party requires for a convention delegate. The enormity of that task in any case, along with the fact that the ward and county voting lists were not made available to me in so many areas, along with a genuine wish I carried all along, and had expressed to many, not to help George Bush by publicly fighting with the presumptive candidate Gore, persuaded me to concede the last delegate to the vice president.*

I want to say that I found the great majority of South Carolina Democratic county chairs to be both generous in their inviting me to speak to something like a county party meeting and honorable in their reporting of voting results. Nonetheless, there were irregularities in a few counties, the Gore totals simply being made up or increased. In some cases, my supporters were not named on ward lists when they and I knew they had attended the meeting. Statewide, Al Gore did not receive the 90 percent plus vote that the South Carolina Democratic Party reported to the press.

Why did I run? In the 2000 South Carolina campaign, I challenged the existing set of campaign laws, their lack of enforcement by the feckless Federal Election Commission, and the entire body of Buckley v. Valeo *follow on rulings. I did so by purposely violating selected campaign laws and hoping for a test case of those laws based upon the legal position that I have described. I did not violate the law merely to "raise consciousness." In violating the law, I specifically did three things.*

First, I declined to name four $200-plus contributors, the law stating that any contributor of $201 or more must be listed, with occupation, address, etc. Second, I deliberately withheld the filing of a Personal Financial Statement beyond the statutory thirty days after declaration of candidacy. I was punished by receiving the requisite $200 fine, then turned in the Financial Statement but refused to pay *the fine in the cover letter. I have never paid the fine. Third, I declined to file the fourth-quarter, 1999, FEC report altogether. This report, including contributors' names, expenditures, money on hand, loans if any, etc., is the core of the FEC reporting system. I did not file the fourth-quarter report, and I responded to a dunning letter regarding that non filing by declaring I had no intention of filing.*

And so, I am a lawbreaker. I had hoped to be a law tester. What I was trying to do was develop a case that would attack the Buckley *ruling on the theory that I have begun to describe here. Unless* Buckley *and its progeny are overturned and America's electoral processes returned to the public sector, no mere legislation—on soft money, false issue advertising, free television time, joint party and candidate committees—will make any difference. Even the passage of McCain-Feingold, as I said earlier, only erected barriers that can easily be circumvented.*

I am sorry to say that the FEC did not bite regarding my deliberate legal transgressions. But all was not lost. We learned something. We learned that the system is even more corrupt than many, including myself, had thought. We learned that the finance system's regulators, those charged with enforcing the law, look the other way, and the American oligarchy grows. Below, I share some of the documents from my attempt to be brought before the bar of justice and make a federal case out of my efforts

Itemized Receipts

Schedule A-P
Federal Election Commission
999 E Street, N.W.
Washington, D.C. 20463

ITEMIZED RECEIPTS

Use separate schedule(s) for each category of the detailed summary page | PAGE 1 | OF (total pages) 1 | LINE NUMBER -0-

NAME OF COMMITTEE (in full): The Kreml Campaign

Any information copied from such Reports and Statements may not be sold or used by any person for the purpose of soliciting contributions or for commercial purposes, other than using the name and address of any political committee to solicit contributions from such committee.

NAME, ADDRESS, CITY, STATE, ZIP CODE	NAME OF EMPLOYER / OCCUPATION / AGGREGATE YEAR-TO-DATE	RECEIPT FOR (specify other)	DATE (MONTH, DAY, YEAR)	AMOUNT OF EACH RECEIPT THIS PERIOD
Will Not Disclose		☐ Primary ☐ General ☐	Short to 9-30-99	# 201
Will Not Disclose		☐ Primary ☐ General ☐	Short to 9-30-99	# 287
Will Not Disclose		☐ Primary ☐ General ☐	Short to 9-30-99	# 500
Will Not Disclose		☐ Primary ☐ General ☐	Short to 9-30-99	# 600
		☐ Primary ☐ General ☐		
		☐ Primary ☐ General ☐		
		☐ Primary ☐ General ☐		
		☐ Primary ☐ General ☐		

SUBTOTAL OF RECEIPTS THIS PAGE ....

TOTAL THIS PERIOD (last page this line number only) ....

FE5AN047

First page of letter from Federal Election Commission on Failure to File Personal Financial Statement

FEDERAL ELECTION COMMISSION
WASHINGTON, D.C. 20463

December 2, 1999

CERTIFIED MAIL
RETURN RECEIPT REQUESTED

William P. Kreml
111 Southwood Drive
Columbia, SC 29205

Dear Mr. Kreml:

On October 19, 1999, you were sent a letter requesting the completion and transmittal of the financial disclosure report required by the Ethics in Government Act of 1978, as amended. A copy of that letter is attached.

As of the date of this letter, the Commission has not received your completed report. If it is not already in the mail, please forward the completed form to the following address within ten days:

Federal Election Commission
Office of the General Counsel
999 E Street, N.W.
Washington, DC 20463
Note: Ethics Act Report

Reasonable extensions of time for filing of up to forty-five days may be granted by the Commission's Office of General Counsel. Request for extensions of time in excess of forty-five days must be made to the Office of Government Ethics.

Under section 104(d) of the Ethics in Government Act of 1978, as amended, "[a]ny individual who files a report required to be filed under this title more than 30 days after [the due date] shall...pay a filing fee of $200." The statute allows the Director of the Office of Government Ethics (an independent agency separate from the Federal Election Commission) the authority to waive the late filing fee in extraordinary circumstances. An example of an extraordinary circumstance would include the failure to file a timely report as a result of personal/family illness. Therefore, you should either submit a written waiver request with your completed report, or include a $200 late filing fee for deposit with the United States Treasury.

Second page of Letter from Federal Election Commission on Failure to File Personal Financial Statement

William P. Kreml
Page 2

You may be referred to the Department of Justice for civil action under 5 U.S.C. app. § 104(a) if you do not provide your public financial disclosure report. That statutory provision states that the United States Attorney General may bring a civil action against any individual who knowingly and willfully fails to report required information.

If you have any questions regarding the Ethics in Government Act of 1978, as amended, or the filing requirements, please contact the Office of Government Ethics, 1201 New York Avenue, N.W., Suite 500, Washington, DC 20005-3919; Telephone: (2020) 208-8000. For additional forms, contact the Office of the General Counsel, Federal Election Commission at the above address; Telephone: (202) 694-1650 or toll-free (800) 424-9530.

Sincerely,

Scott E. Thomas
Chairman

Attachment as stated

My Letter of Reply to the Federal Election Commission on Failure to File Personal Financial Statement

William Kreml

For President

MIDLANDS COMMITTEE

Robert Angel
Eileen Barry
John Bryan
James MacGregor Burns
Timothy Driggers
Sheila Elliott
Benjamin Franklin V
Toni Goodwin
Sandra Hall
John Ray Harper
Jeff Hubbell
Rickey Hill
Rhett Jackson
Janice Love
Carolyn Matalene
Rebecca Mbuh
Peter Sederberg
Cleveland Sellers
Molli Steele
Karen Sundstrom
Robert Watkins

Federal Election Commission
Office of the General Counsel
999 E Street, N. W.
Washington, DC 20463

December 9, 1999

Dear Sir or Madam:

Enclosed is my personal financial disclosure report.

I am a presidential candidate, FEC # C0034773.

The $200 fine for late reporting is not included.

Thank you.

Sincerely,

William P. Kreml

Letter from Federal Election Commission on Failure to File Fourth Quarter, 1999

999 E Street, N.W.
Washington, DC 20463

WESTERN UNION MAILGRAM
UNITED STATES POSTAL SERVICE

Ø85910ØØØ383 02/24/ØØ CLB2 - CLBB
EN16105

WILLIAM P KREML
KREML CAMPAIGN; THE
111 SOUTHWOOD DR
COLUMBIA SC 29205-3219

February 23, 2ØØØ

IDENTIFICATION NUMBER: CØØ347773

REFERENCE: YEAR-END REPORT (1Ø/Ø1/1999 -12/31/1999)

DEAR TREASURER:

IT HAS COME TO THE ATTENTION OF THE FEDERAL ELECTION COMMISSION THAT YOU MAY HAVE FAILED TO FILE THE ABOVE REFERENCED REPORT OF RECEIPTS AND EXPENDITURES AS REQUIRED BY THE FEDERAL ELECTION CAMPAIGN ACT, AS AMENDED. YOU WERE PREVIOUSLY NOTIFIED OF THE DUE DATE FOR THIS REPORT.

IT IS IMPORTANT THAT YOU FILE THIS REPORT IMMEDIATELY WITH THE FEDERAL ELECTION COMMISSION, 999 E STREET, N.W., WASHINGTON, D.C., 2Ø463 FOR HOUSE CANDIDATES, OR THE SECRETARY OF THE SENATE, 232 HART SENATE OFFICE BUILDING, WASHINGTON, D.C. 2Ø51Ø FOR SENATE CANDIDATES. A COPY OF THIS REPORT SHOULD ALSO BE FILED WITH THE SECRETARY OF STATE OR EQUIVALENT STATE OFFICER, UNLESS THE STATE IS EXEMPT FROM A FEDERAL REQUIREMENT TO RECEIVE AND MAINTAIN PAPER COPIES.

THE FAILURE TO FILE THIS REPORT MAY RESULT IN AN AUDIT OR LEGAL ENFORCEMENT ACTION.

IF YOU HAVE ANY QUESTIONS REGARDING THIS MATTER, PLEASE CONTACT Robin Kelly IN THE REPORTS ANALYSIS DIVISION ON OUR TOLL FREE NUMBER (8ØØ)424-953Ø. OUR LOCAL NUMBER IS (202)694-113Ø.

SINCERELY,

JOHN D. GIBSON
ASSISTANT STAFF DIRECTOR
REPORTS ANALYSIS DIVISION

MGMCOMP 16:46 EST

My Letter of Reply to Federal Election Commission on Failure to File Fourth Quarter, 1999

William Kreml

For President

March 13, 2000

MIDLANDS COMMITTEE

Robert Angel
Eileen Barry
John Bryan
James MacGregor Burns
Timothy Driggers
Sheila Elliott
Benjamin Franklin V
Toni Goodwin
Sandra Hall
John Roy Harper
Jeff Hubbell
Rickey Hill
Rhett Jackson
Janice Love
Carolyn Matalene
Rebecca Mbuh
Peter Sederberg
Cleveland Sellers
Molli Steele
Karen Sundstrom
Robert Watkins

Mr. John D. Gibson
Assistant Staff Director
Reports Analysis Division
The Federal Election Commission
999 E Street, NW
Washington, DC 20463

Dear Mr. Gibson:

In receipt of your message to me dated February 23, 2000, please know that there will be no audit of the fourth quarter reports of The Kreml Campaign.

As my letter to the FEC of January 12, 2000 indicated, my failure to file a fourth quarter report was deliberate. It was part, perhaps only a small part, of a process of revealing the deep corruptness of the American electoral system, and the FEC, before the American people.

I delayed responding to you in February because of my hope that our campaign would make a showing in the March 9th South Carolina caucuses. I am happy to say that we did do well in certain districts, our 7.4% in Lexington County, our 9.8% in Allendale County, and our present 13% in Richland County (a figure that will decline) indicate that we were a viable campaign.

Although I am no longer campaigning, the FEC should know that our candidacy remains active, at least for the immediate future.

Again, save yourself, and me, the time of requesting an audit. No data from the fourth quarter will be available to you.

Sincerely,

William P. Kreml
FEC # C00347773

111 Southwood Drive, Columbia, SC 29205 • 803-799-7203 • kreml@mindspring.com • http://kreml.home.mindspring.co

Paid for by The Kreml Campaign

CHAPTER SIX

The Supreme Court and Cognition

The Constitutional Challenge

What can America do regarding its increasingly oligarchic political system? If we have indeed arrived at the point where America's constitutional democracy has been sold out from under us, and if that sellout has been facilitated by things like undemocratic decentralization, type 2 undemocratic elections, and the compressed distribution, what can we do to restore our polity? Similarly, what can we do to restore a measure of public-sector strength through a degree of structural recentralization, a term no American politician has ever used, or more than likely ever would?

First, we can begin that restructuring and restoration of public-sector strength by doing the kinds of things that were recommended by the Committee on the Constitutional System (CCS) in January of 1987. We should extend the congressional term to four years. We should exorcise Section 6 of Article I from the Constitution, thus permitting members of the Congress to serve in the administration. We should also adopt James MacGregor Burns' notion of the "team ticket," a device that permits one lever to approve all the federal office seekers of one party.[1]

But apart from the CCS recommendations, we should encourage state governments, particularly in small states, to adopt unicameral legislatures. We should encourage annexation and merger within metropolitan areas, along with smart growth land use policies and meaningful zoning. And, we must continue to reduce the influence of race-based reapportionment designs in legislative districts. Overuse of an objective, in this case race, variable has substantially harmed the left side of the political spectrum, along with the African-American community. The Natural Left would have dealt with the deserved claims of the African-American community in a different way.

If all else fails, we should consider movement to a parliamentary system, a step that I have vigorously opposed in the past but which must never be abandoned as an ultimate fallback. Separation of powers and federalism, which is what the American political system is based on, are both centrifugal arrangements. They were intended to be. I do not think it possible, ever, for Americans to give up their states. In spite of the "state's wrongs" that many state governments engage in, some not even maintaining minimal educational and health care opportunities for their citizens, states are probably forever with us. The move away from the American Constitution to a European style parliamentary system would be within an inch of being as hard. But an inch of support may be all we have to build on.

Let us be sure that we know why a government that is overly decentralized limits political equity. Excessive decentralization is undemocratic because of the public policy biases that come from a contract-dominated political system. Excessive decentralization is also undemocratic because it is the cause of what those in the Washington Beltway sheepishly call gridlock. The utter nonperformance of government in a variety of policy areas, like dealing with the health care crisis in any meaningful way, combined with the biased performance of a decentralized government in other areas, is the result of an overabundance of the analytic cognition, manifesting itself in the occasional outright scandal but, unfortunately, barely masking itself in the everyday misappropriation of the public good by barely legal political activity. Remember that the weakest government possible is best, from the perspective of the analytic private sector. Just as the Federalists crafted a moderately decentralized system to curtail democracy, our generation, not unlike those who argued for the Bill of Rights, must restore the structural equilibrium that the Bill of Rights attempted to ensure in its counterbalancing of the original seven articles. As counterintuitive as it may sound for many Americans, the recentralization of the government, to at least some degree, will make the government more democratic.

But there is another requirement for a U. S. return to the equilibrium of Aristotle's trichotomy. I believe there will be no recovery of the cognitive balances needed for constitutional democracy until a fundamental reform of the American electoral system takes place. In 1976, the Supreme Court case of *Buckley v. Valeo* overturned significant portions of Congress's 1971 and 1974 restrictions on excessive campaign spending.[2] Principally, the *Buckley* decision held that Congress could not restrict the amount of money that candidates spent on their own campaigns. It further held that Congress could not restrict the amount of money spent on someone else's campaign by an independent citizen working as long as there was no coordination with the candidate or her campaign. In other words, *Buckley* held that campaign expenditures could not be regulated, although campaign contributions could.

Although *Buckley* did permit Congress to legislate in the area of campaign contributions, specifically upholding the limits that Congress had placed on what a citizen could give to someone else's effort, it used some of the most tortuous reasoning of any twentieth-century Supreme Court case in doing so. Its differentiation between campaign contributions on the one hand and campaign expenditures on the other was specious at best. The Court argued for this differentiation as if the two were not intrinsically linked, or as if someone would raise campaign money and then not spend it. More significantly, the Court blanketed its favored campaign expenditures under a wholly incorrect interpretation of the First Amendment's free speech guarantee. Though recent legislation has been approved by the Court that permits some limitations on so-called "soft money" (money funneled through the national parties) and on negative "issue" ads that immediately precede elections, both small triumphs are already being subverted. Excessive contributions are already being given through interest-group-based "527" organizations, and pre-election money is simply being diverted to non-television expenditures. Only through a correct understanding of the Bill of Rights can *Buckley* and its successor cases be wholly overturned and real campaign finance reform achieved.

Let us recall that, in effect, what *Buckley* ruled was that money equaled speech, and that therefore any money expended by the candidate, or by independently acting individuals or interests on behalf of a candidate, is only the equivalent of that individual's or interest's holding up a sign on a street corner. More importantly, *Buckley* and subsequent rulings did not prevent money from being given beyond the statutory limit if it were routed through the national political parties. Even after the passing of the so-called McCain-Feingold legislation, money continued to be funneled through state parties, again because the Court has consistently misunderstood the First Amendment and held that expenditures constituted free speech and that money equaled speech. In short, the Supreme Court ruling in the *Buckley* case, along with that host of confirming rulings that the Supreme Court has issued in the ensuing years, has contributed more than any single event to our country's becoming an oligarchy.

I do not doubt that all who called for legislation to curb "soft" money, false issue advertising, or for the continuing need to close the ever more creative Georgetown lawyer loopholes on such things as joint party and candidate committees, honestly believed that this legislation would substantially cure the abuses of campaign funding. I urge them to keep pushing for expenditure legislation, but I urge them as well to come to a better comprehension of the problem. I do not believe that even expenditure-directed legislation alone will solve the problem. I believe that only public funding, which has been successful in some small states, will cure the problem of unbalanced political influence. In order to do that, I say once more, *Buckley* will need to be revisited, and overturned. As I write, two cases are before the Supreme Court on this issue and I urge the court to consider the deepest equities of the American political system in its deliberations.

After all, the campaign finance reform issue is a constitutional issue. It will only be dealt with by constitutional change, either through Supreme Court interpretation or by the kind of constitutional amendment that was introduced by my old friend and onetime political opponent Senator Ernest F. Hollings (D-SC), now retired. This amendment, which would enable Congress to pass meaningful campaign reform law, has not gathered sufficient support in the Congress to give out country immediate hope for success.

In Chapter Seven, I will explain how I think a new Supreme Court case must be argued in order to overturn *Buckley*. The argument touches on the most fundamental division in the American constitutional order, the division between the private and the public sectors. But it will also include the role of the analytic and synthetic cognition within those sectors, a consistent identification of sector and cognition being apparent when a full analysis of American constitutional history is involved. To come to an understanding of that identification, I think it is necessary, first of all, to look at the five dichotomies that have formed the core of constitutional interpretation since the beginning of the Republic. It will also be necessary to apply what I believe to be the correct understanding of *Shelley* v. *Kraemer* that I described in Chapter Two.

Five Constitutional Dichotomies

In my judgment, to say that *Buckley v. Valeo* is fundamentally wrong is understatement. *Buckley* not only is the most improperly decided Supreme Court case of the twentieth century but, perhaps not surprisingly, it almost precisely mirrors, in its cognitive form, the most improperly decided case of the nineteenth century: the slavery-protecting case of *Dred Scott*.[3] As an introduction to the specific problems of *Buckley*, I ask you to consider a brief analysis of the five dichotomies that make up the American constitutional order. This analysis, I believe, will reflect the importance of the cognitively subatomic, psychologically based philosophical outlook that I have been describing in a specific constitutional context. I frankly do not think that we get to the bottom of the *Buckley* case, or to the strategy for the correction of *Buckley*, without using a subatomic perspective.

To focus on *Buckley*, we should begin with the facts that a) there are five central dichotomies in the American constitutional order; b) these dichotomies have arranged themselves in certain patterns for very long periods of our constitutional history; and c) there is only one "line up" of the five dichotomies that has remained almost wholly consistent throughout the entirety of American constitutional rulings. I do not suggest that every Supreme Court ruling, in every constitutional period, followed the exact configuration of alliances that I use here. I do suggest that the biases of various Supreme Courts have generated patterns among the Court's major decisions that are visibly consistent when these decisions are laid next to one another. With knowledge of these consistencies, we can get to the core of *Buckley*'s difficulty.

The five dichotomies that I believe lie at the core of the American constitutional system are as follows:

1) Ideology. The first dichotomy is the division between liberalism and conservatism, in an every day understanding of those terms. During most of American history, the liberal to conservative continuum has been concerned with economic haves and have nots. In more recent times, liberals and conservatives have also differed over a variety of social, even moral, issues, such as school prayer, abortion, protection of the flag, etc. A tolerance for a more diverse resolution of these issues makes up the liberal position on these issues. A preference for a more singular orthodoxy almost invariably represents the conservative position.

2) Legislative vs. Judicial Prerogative. One of the great tensions in American constitutional law is that between the rule of the statute and its enactor and the rule of the Court. In democracies, the rule of the statute grows out of the legislated law of a representative body, that law, of course, usually reflecting the input of the executive as well. The rule of the Court, naturally, comes from judges and, to a lesser extent, juries acting in concert with judges.

On the one hand, a representative democracy like that of the United States must ensure its citizens that the elected government will make necessary statutory law. At the same time, the English common law is still the foundation of our private law and even a good bit of our public law. The unchallenged arbiter of private and public disputes is the body of laws governing property, contract, bailments, and the like, along with the judicially decided case law interpreting statutes on the above topics, other private-sector topics, and various public concerns. The private law is represented in modern codifications such as the Uniform Commercial Code, while the public law is represented in statutory codifications such as those protecting civil liberties.

True, the argument will always continue over the extent to which judicial review, wherein a court overrules a statute, should be used. However, the principles that have grown from centuries of common law development, along with the Federalists'clear allocation of a rule-making jurisdiction for the courts, provide for a healthy degree of judicial decision-making within the overall system. The balance of legislative versus judicial rule-making has shifted back and forth during our country's two hundred plus years. Legislative versus judicial rule-making prerogative makes up our second dichotomy.

3) National vs. State Prerogative. In creating the American federal system, the Federalists allocated power between the central government and the state governments. Though the Supremacy Clause and other provisions of the Constitution made it clear that the federal government was to be superior, the state governments were just as clearly meant to maintain reserve powers. Over time, there have surely been shifts of relative power between the federal and state governments. The Supreme Court has frequently ruled on the correct allocation of that power. Judicial favor for one or the other of these two levels of government makes up our third dichotomy.

4) Private vs. Public Sectors. Although no structural provision in the Constitution specifically addresses the allocation of power between the private and public sectors, provisions exist regarding property and contract, as, of course, do provisions ensuring public governance. These guideposts import a balance between the two grand sectors, the one encouraging a broad entrepreneurial activity and the other affording the citizenry the opportunity to check that activity's excesses. That balance too has surely shifted back and forth over the life of this Republic, while the Supreme Court has ruled on where it believed the correct demarcation line should be. The private and public sectors make up our fourth dichotomy.

5) Analytic vs. Synthetic Cognition. Finally, I suggest that the cognitive dichotomy, that is the analytic versus the synthetic cognition dichotomy that under-girds a subatomic theory of politics, is evident throughout the history of American constitutional development. This is so even though there is no evidence that Supreme Court justices have ever consciously been aware of it. But we can, I argue, now locate the analytic and the synthetic variables that make up the subatomic variable within America's constitutional history. The analytic versus synthetic cognition, therefore, makes up our fifth dichotomy. Understanding this dichotomy, I suggest, will go a long way toward explaining why *Buckley v. Valeo* is wrong. It should also help us see how to change it.

Having listed the five constitutional dichotomies, let us move to a description of the configurations of those balances that various Supreme Courts generally adopted. We should see unmistakable evidence of the most fundamental dichotomies within the American political/judicial system. I will now refer to the most obvious leanings within these dichotomies, or the shifting of ideological balances within each dichotomy.

First, the ebbs and flows between state and federal jurisdiction are readily identified. Surely, the highly nationalistic orientation of the John Marshall, Joseph Story, post-Constitutional Court contrasts with the states' prerogatives in rulings of, say, the Roger Taney Court during the mid-nineteenth century. The nationalist underpinnings of Earl Warren Court rulings surely contrast with the state-oriented rulings of the late Chief Justice William Rehnquist Court.

Second, the oscillations between strong or "activist"Courts and Courts that more readily defer to legislatures are also clearly drawn in American constitutional history. On the one hand, the Marshall Court introduced the notion of judicial review to the American legal system, and courts such as the Stephen Field dominated body of the late nineteenth century also frequently denied legislatures the power to interfere with America's then almost purely capitalistic ethic.

On the other hand, a greater tolerance of legislative initiative came from the early Roger Taney Court and the twentieth-century Charles Evans Hughes Court, after what court watchers call "the switch in time that saved nine." The "switch" referred to the movement from a less legislatively friendly Court to a more amenable Court after President Franklin Roosevelt threatened to "pack" the Court with a new member for every then current member over seventy years of age. There were six septuagenarians at the time.

And so it is for the first two dichotomies, both structural. Now let us move to the remaining three: the ideological dichotomy, the sector dichotomy, and the cognitive dichotomy. The balances within these three dichotomies are very important to our analysis of *Buckley*. I believe we cannot understand the mischief of *Buckley* without a clear understanding of these three dichotomies, particularly the internal oscillations along their continuums over extended periods of time.

Even casual students of the Supreme Court are familiar with the ideologically conservative nature of the John Marshall Court, the first Supreme Court to serve any length of time in the early days of this Republic. Most Americans are equally familiar with the generally liberal nature of the Earl Warren Court of the 1950s and 1960s. The ebbs and flows of conservatism and liberalism in American judicial history are relatively easy to track. We will trace them in more detail shortly.

The pattern of oscillation between America's private and public sectors is visible just below the surface of many Supreme Courts periods. The Marshall

Court, although it spoke a good deal about the institutions of government, consistently ruled in favor of the private sector in its principal cases like *Marbury v. Madison*[4] and *McCulloch v. Maryland*, for example.[5] The same is true of the late nineteenth-century Stephen Field, "robber baron," Court and the early Charles Evans Hughes Court, before the "switch." The later Hughes Court, again, was far less protective of the contractual and property rights that it had vigorously embraced in earlier going.

The same was true for the Earl Warren Court, as I think friend and foe of that Court agree. I would also argue that for most of the Roger Taney Court, particularly in the early going, there was a favorable responsiveness to the Jacksonian democratic environment, and there was also, all things equal, a responsiveness to the public sector's legislation, at least more so than that Court's predecessor, the Marshall court. The latter-day Taney Court, the Court of the *Dred Scott* decision, was an altogether different matter, of course. The private-public sector favor in various Courts' patterns of decision is more hidden than the favor for one end of the first three dichotomies or the other, but it is still there.

One complication must now be included in the description. The fact is that, at the beginning of the Republic, the United States was very much in need of the kinds of public-private cooperation that were still a long way from what we would today call free enterprise. The crucial writings of Alexander Hamilton on matters such as paying off the Revolutionary War debt, or the development of "Manufactures," as he called it, or even the creation of a national bank, which was deliberately left out of the Constitution because it was a political hot potato, mirror the Federalists' favor for what was typically called mercantilism. Mercantilism signified the cooperation of the private and public sectors in order to encourage infrastructural and other productivity-oriented economic activities.

Please do not misunderstand. The Federalists surely had a deep preference for the private sector. James Madison's # 10 *Federalist* still stands as America's greatest paean to private property and contract.[6] But the Federalists were realists if nothing else. They understood that their new government would need to construct a sub-flooring under the fledgling enterprises of the day, as well as encourage a few new ones in the bargain. Was there sufficient private capital, and willing private capital, available at that time for the building of ships, post roads, harbors, and canals? The answer at that point in our history was "no,"and the government, accordingly, needed to assist in their construction.

In the overall, it is important to remind ourselves that the private and the public sectors were nowhere nearly as separated in this country's early years as they are now. What can be misconstrued as pro-public sector rulings by

John Marshall, for example, were merely supportive of that mercantilist combination of private and public economic enterprise, and were still ideologically conservative, and overwhelmingly pro-private sector, in their direction.

Moving on, I only suggest that by the time of the Jacksonian revolution, when mercantilism was increasingly disparaged as granting economic favor to a few well-connected interests by those of a new, increasingly risk-taking entrepreneurial generation, the sectors began to separate from each other. As a general statement, I think it fair to say that by the close of the Jacksonian period, the private and public sectors were more distinct than they were directly after the founding.

Let us now examine the final dichotomy: cognitions. Cognitions, as I have said before, are the key subatomic variable. An application of the analytic and synthetic cognitions to America's constitutional development is somewhat less obvious than the patterns of the other four dichotomies. But I assure you that the patterns are there, and they are helpful to understanding constitutional error. In the simplest example, it was the cleanest form of contract, the contract without encumbrances, that marked much of the Stephen Field, or "robber baron," late nineteenth-century cases. Whether it was in the so-called railroad cases or in the striking down of a variety of other legislative attempts to encumber private contracts in the name of the public good, the Field Court kept the private contract analytically pure.

In the twentieth century, with state regulatory cases such as *Nebbia v. New York (1934)*[7] even before the Hughes Court switch, and federal regulatory cases such as *N. L. R. B. v. Jones and Laughlin Steel (1937)*[8] which at least partially marked the switch, contracts were increasingly encumbered by public legislation. A cognitively synthetic, encumbering variable was being added to the judicial formula, usually ratifying an encumbering variable that a legislature had passed into law.

In short, the cognitive patterns of the American constitutional experience are as discoverable as are the patterns of the other four dichotomies. And, as I shall point out shortly, the cognitions are easy to find because they frequently parallel the path of both a) the sectors and b) ideology. Cognitively, as the public sector increasingly shed its partnership, or mercantilist, role in favor of newer forms of entrepreneurial endeavor, the public sector became a source of regulatory, that is synthetic, encumbrance on the private contract. To restrict child labor, women's labor, excessive hours, dangerous labor, harmful products, and eventually products that destroy the environment, the public learned to use its sector, and the synthetic cognition that it is usually a part of, to ameliorate what the private sector had inflicted on them. This is not complicated stuff.

What the public wanted cognitively, although they did not think of it in these terms, of course, was almost invariably a synthetic addition to a contract. The public wanted an encumbrance on the otherwise pure contract of money for a good, money for a service, money for land, etc. I do not think there is any question that these encumbrances, like those that were overcome in *Shelley's Case* as far back as the sixteenth century and *Shelley v. Kraemer* in 1948, were cognitively synthetic.

The rise and fall of this latter-day synthetic cognition, once isolated within a separate, fifth dichotomy of judicial considerations, is quite easy to trace. The progressive period, the New Deal period, and the Lyndon Johnson eras, for example, all represented legislative periods of synthetic, contractual encumbrance in such areas as labor, women's and children's rights, and civil rights. The 1920s, the 1950s, and the 1980s Ronald Reagan period, on the other hand, successfully pared a good deal of public encumbrance from the private contract. These periods, all things equal, were analytic from a cognitive perspective, in concert with their being ideologically conservative.

And so, these are what I believe to be the core judicial dichotomies. I have briefly tried to define what they are, and even more briefly I have tried to prepare for an analysis of the alignments of these dichotomies by referencing how some of them have progressed during different periods of American constitutional history. I suggested earlier that there are patterns to how the preferences for different positions within these various dichotomies have aligned themselves with one another. It is now time to look at these alignments among the dichotomies, using the cognitive distinctions of the psychologically based political philosophy in the context of a contemporary political and legal dispute.

The Patterns of Alignment

The first significant alteration of the classical alignment of a) conservative-to-liberal ideology, b) legislative-to-judicial prerogative, c) national versus state jurisdiction, d) private-versus-public sector ascendance, and, most central to our purpose, e) analytic versus synthetic cognitive preference, occurs in the horrific case of *Dred Scott*. Yes, *Dred Scott* is the second case of judicial review, a fact that is not unimportant but, in my view, not as important as something else. I suggest that that case's greater lesson is that it is the first significant case that reconfigured the original alignment of the dichotomies, whether cases were decided on the Marshall side in favor of the federal position over the state position, and so on with the five dichotomies, or on the other side as in the earlier Taney, Jacksonian rulings. The alignments of the Marshallian dichotomies, once more, were not changed until *Dred Scott*.

But in *Dred Scott,* the alignments surely were changed, with the salience of the federal-to-state dichotomy being so grand at that time in American history that Chief Justice Taney had no qualms about shifting the position of that one dichotomy so that "state's rights" now teamed with court ascendancy, a conservative ideology, the private sector, and the analytic cognition in the general protection of slavery and the destruction of the Missouri Compromise. I submit that an understanding of this realignment, and the other realignments within the five dichotomies, is at least as structurally important in the understanding of the Supreme Court's history as are traditional things like judicial activism and judicial review. I will say more about *Dred Scott* when our brief chronology of the Court gets to the Warren era.

So when, then, comes the second realignment within the dichotomies? The second realignment does not come until the beginning of the twentieth century, resulting from the grandest switch in ideology-to-structure relationships in America's history. As we know, the Hamilton-to-Jefferson contrast throughout the first hundred years plus of our nation's history pitted a strong federal government, generally on the side of business, against the notion of stronger state governments that were still generally on the ideological side that is descended from the Anti-Federalists, and protected the little guy, often a debtor. Liberal Illinois Governor John Peter Altgeld could still make an impassioned plea for state's rights at New York's Cooper Union after the Cleveland/Olney intervention into the Pullman strike of 1894.

But the classical alliance was reconfigured shortly after that, specifically in the early twentieth century, in response to populist and, later, progressive state governments. It could respond to the increasingly national scope of robber baron industries like the railroads, the oil companies, and the tobacco companies. The famous quotation of Herbert Croly concerning "Jeffersonian goals by Hamiltonian means" marks this departure from the standard Marshallian perspective and judicial alliance.[9] From the turn of the century, liberals would ask for federal government assistance in fighting off what were by then interstate private enterprises of considerable power.

Within the Supreme Court, the acceptance of federal governmental activity found in legislation like the Sherman Anti-Trust Act of 1890 is illustrated in the *Standard Oil* (1911) and *American Tobacco* (1911) cases.[10] The federal-to-state dichotomy was changed at least a fair percentage of the time with, again, the federal government, and the Supreme Court, moving into an alignment that more often placed the federal courts in league with liberal legislative initiative, even state initiatives in areas like worker protection. See *Muller v. Oregon* (1908).[11] The court approved a synthetic encumbrance on a contract.

Moving to the next significant period of American judicial history, I would point out that traditional analyses place much emphasis on the Depression-era "switch in time that saved nine" that differentiated between what I will simply call the Hughes I and the Hughes II courts. The first came before the *N.L.R.B. v. Jones and Laughlin Steel* (1937) that approved labor protecting federal legislation and the second came after.[12] As we've said, this was the "switch" that, under the threat of Franklin D. Roosevelt to pack the court in order to "help" those over seventy years of age, would have added a new member for each of the septuagenarians. Obviously, those appointments would have been liberal and the new, fifteen justice court could have been expected to approve New Deal innovations.

But I suggest that there is something that is more important than the ideologically liberal and legislature affirming "switch" of 1937: although there was a reversal of the winning side from Hughes I to Hughes II, there was no variation *within* the alignments whatsoever. What happened from 1936 to 1937 in the Supreme Court did not bring change to the alliances themselves, among the dichotomies we have reviewed.

Thus the pre- *J & L* position imported a favor for courts over legislatures, a restriction of the role of the federal government in ameliorating the impact of the Depression, a conservative ideological perspective, kept within the private sector, and, yes, the analytic, unencumbered contract cognition on one side of the alliance. The *J & L* position, and subsequent Depression mediating opinions, embraced legislative solutions, many of which now came from the federal government, endorsing ideologically liberal public policies, the public sector's ameliorative role in fighting the Depression, and the synthetic cognition's contribution of permitting something other than purely bilateral unencumbered contracts from ruling, and ruining, the day.

A case like *Schecter Poultry vs. United States* (1936)[13], which would have permitted market sharing and artificial price maintenance, is perhaps the best pre-switch example of that configuration of dichotomies. Coming before the switch, the public sector and the synthetic cognition clearly lost in *Schecter.* But, after the switch, arrangements like those in *Schecter* were generously tolerated. But, again, there was no variation within the alignments. There was only a switch in the ascendancy of one alignment over another, something nowhere as significant as a change within the alignments to the theoretical understanding of the Court's history. To Warren.

It is accurate to say, I think, that the most controversial of all periods in the history of the United States Supreme Court was the Earl Warren period. Conservatives are not wrong in claiming that something quite extraordinary happened during that period, whether one agreed with what it was or not.

As a rough statement, there were four court periods of what traditional constitutional analysis calls "activism" within the Supreme Court before Warren. The Marshall judicial review Court in the early nineteenth century, the Stephen Field "substantive due process" and robber baron protecting Court of the late nineteenth-century, the Taft anti-progressive legislation Court of the 1920's, and the Hughes I anti-New Deal Court of 1933-36, were all Courts that placed judicial authority above the prerogatives of legislatures. At the same time, the first two of these Courts generally favored the federal institution over the state jurisdiction, Marshall's suspicion of renegade state legislation being mirrored in Field's rejection of initiatives like railroad safety regulation, while the Taft Court and the Hughes I Court suspicion of federal regulatory legislation placed them on the other federal-to-state side.

So, after the "Croly switch" of Jeffersonian and Hamiltonian institutional-to-ideological positions, we not unexpectedly find that Taft's opposition to what he thought to be errant legislation also included national laws that had responded to the populist and progressive initiative, and Hughes' first response to national legislation during the early nineteen-thirties at least partially altered the federal-to-state variable within the grand coalitions. But regardless of jurisdictional preferences, these four "activist" periods all demonstrated a clear ideological bias, a conservative bias, in favor of the analytic cognition.

Then, with Earl Warren's Court, something altogether different happened. Whereas the first four traditionally understood to be activist periods were all protective of a private sector, conservative, unencumbered contract position, achieved through a judiciary that stood up to what these Courts saw as out of control legislatures, the activist Warren Court, for the first time in Court history, had a liberal ideological orientation. And, whereas "non-activist" courts like Hughes II and other legislatively compliant courts only went along with more liberal, public sector and contract encumbering legislation, what happened with the Warren Court went far beyond a simple change in the ascendancy of one dichotomous condition over the other. What happened, in a way that is different from any switch *between* coalitions as found in the movement from Hughes I to Hughes II, was the *significance* of one of the five dichotomies was accentuated more dramatically than in any previous time.

What, after all, so riled the conservatives about Warren's court? Some claimed that it was the activism, pure and simple. But that wasn't it. Conservatives still heartily applaud the first four activist periods. They were riled, unquestionably, because of the ideological content of the activism. Even more intensely, they were riled because of the *form* of the activism in the sense that Warren and his supportive judicial colleagues were in fact "making law" while activist forays that used common law, private law, principles were not. There is no argument. Indeed, the Warren court did make law. But it did so in a way that on the one hand confirmed the configuration of dichotomies that traditionally existed, after the Croly alteration, and on the other hand initiated the novel use of a synthetic cognition within the court's own deliberations.

Again, looking at the configurations of the dichotomies, what Warren and his Court did was far different from what Hughes II did in merely accepting the legitimacy of the federal jurisdiction in making broad, anti-Depression laws, placing the courts into a receptive position vis-à-vis those laws, and thus approving ideologically liberal, public sector, and cognitively synthetic initiatives.

Put another way, for the first time in the court's history, rulings on key issues like civil rights, reapportionment, women's rights, and the like were self inspired. They came from a deep sense of a need to face the great contradictions between promise and reality in American society. And they came, I believe justifiably, from the Court as one component of the traditional post-Croly alignment. The cognitive component was emphasized in a way that was very different from any previous Supreme Court.

As soon as they could, quite naturally, the conservatives had their way with their desire to end the above, "wrong" kind of judicial activism in the Supreme Court. But, I suggest what they did went well beyond a returning of the Court to a measure of conservatism after Richard Nixon made a liberal activist court a centerpiece of his 1968 presidential campaign, and three of his four court appointments soon did what Nixon expected of them. The Burger, and later Rehnquist Courts, surely returned the entire set of dichotomies to a conservative ideological, and allied position. But they did more. Before we examine what they did in detail, and particularly how what they did is reflected in *Buckley v. Valeo,* let us ask the question of whether the constitution's institutional variables, the state-to-federal and legislative-to-courts variables in our dichotomies, are inherently of one ideological flavor or the other. If they are not, we might further our understanding that something other than institutional variables may lie at the heart of America's constitutional balances.

Think on it for a moment. Is there any *inherently* liberal or conservative tilt to a court or to a legislature? I know of no reason why there would be. Courts can be and have been both liberal and conservative, and legislatures can be and have been both liberal or conservative. Similarly, is there any *inherently* liberal or conservative tilt to a state or to the federal government? I don't know why there would be. States can and have been liberal and conservative, as has the federal government.

There is, in short, no constitutionally aberrant reason why the kinds of coalition alterations that we have just examined should not have, and should not continue to have, perfect legitimacy within the American political system. The only difference with Warren's Court, again, was that what liberalism there was in the courts, before Warren, had been expressed almost solely by courts accepting, or ratifying if you will, liberal legislation. Warren, again with its use of the synthetic cognition (much like Edward Coke), placed that cognition within the Court itself and created law from it.

Buckley and Dred Scott

But what, secondly, of the other coalitional alteration? Specifically, what about the case that I believe to be the key theoretical case of the twentieth century? What is the specific configuration of dichotomous variables within *Shelley v. Kraemer*? In this case, I suggest agaom, something very unusual happened. Rather than have one of the institutional, or constitutional, dichotomies change sides, and thus alter the coalitional lineup, it is one of the other variables, one of the non-institutional variables, that underwent reversal. In *Shelley v. Kraemer*, it was the ideological variable that kept itself out of the original configurations.

Ms. Fitzgerald, who wished only to alienate, or sell, her house, which as we've noted became one of the sacred rights of property coming out of the feudal period, was pleading for judicial acceptance of what by our cognitive analysis is clearly an analytic contract. She was pleading, in other words, for judicial sanction of a contract without encumbrance. She won her approval within a coalition of variables that otherwise embraced the federal over the state jurisdiction, and embraced the legislative over the court jurisdiction (that had previously enforced restrictive covenants such as those in *Shelley*.)

But, far more importantly, she won her case, once more, in the context of a reversal of that one dichotomy within the other three, non-institutional variables. That is, her ideologically liberal claim to be able to sell her home to a black family was assisted not by the public sector or by the synthetic cognition that usually runs with the public sector. Beyond the purely substantive understandings of the case, that is those that deal with the fourteenth amendment and "state action," it was the private sector, and the analytic cognition, that really won the case.

Now, why is this important, both for itself but also with regard to the way this all reflects on *Buckley v. Valeo* and the legitimacy of expenditure related, and public funding, in campaign finance reform?

Besides the lack of ideological inherency of institutional variables that we have already examined, we must recall that *Shelley v. Kraemer* marked the beginning of the sole American legal dialectic. That is why, unlike almost any other American case, it produces a liberal result (the home is sold to the black family), with a usually conservative, private sector, and cognitively analytic form. *Shelley* demonstrates that the analytic form may advance history a bit. At the same time, however, it shows that the analytic cognition, lodged within a contract, can only take history so far. The analytic form, at the beginning of the three stage, alternating cognition dialectic that even Hegel's "single, ordered whole" dialectic did not cognitively understand, does not get to the historical contradiction. It cannot get to the historical contradiction because the analytic cognition, the minimal designation of the 5 + 7 = 12 as synthetic that Hegel said could never advance the dialectic, cannot deal with the apples and oranges cases such as those concerning desegregated education, fair apportionment, and the right of women to choose. The mere enforcement of a contract is not going to alter those areas of law. Dialectically, the analytic cognition may start the ball rolling, but that's all. Let us now look at *Buckley v. Valeo* and the post-1969 Nixon court within the context of the above understanding of *Shelley v. Kraemer.*

Without question, the *Buckley* case is an institutional victory of a court over a legislature. The Supreme Court struck down a congressional law regarding expenditure, whether from a candidate or from independent supporters. And, while the Court permitted campaign contribution limits to continue, it left the loophole of what was called "soft money" through state parties, and which, even now after McCain-Feingold, permits the "527" group and other money channeling artifices to flourish. That loophole predictably demonstrated that the court did not fully proscribe outrageous contributions that, directly or indirectly, wound up assisting one candidate or another. I think the court-to-legislature balance, or should I say imbalance, is clear.

Secondly, let us look at the state-to-federal variable in *Buckley v. Valeo.* Admittedly, this is more difficult because the case does not directly address the federalism issue in campaigns and elections. But let us look at where we are, particularly at this writing after the 2004 election. Restrictions on the federal government in the arena of contributions and expenditures surely have some link with restrictions on the government in the area of campaign and election spending. Without revisiting all of the horribilia of the 2000 presidential campaign and election, I suggest we merely focus on the single question of where the authority lies in matters like registration, ballot access, and vote counting.

What we can see is quite clear when we look at it. Examine, please, the location of jurisdiction in Florida, down to the differences in how counties, not even the state, registered voters, threw voters off the roll, counted or did not count ballots, or even allocated different machines with far different performance standards within the different voting districts. That location of jurisdiction begins the analysis of how best to deter voter harassment, voting roll "cleansing," and the problems of various voting instruments. Is it too bold to suggest that if we are voting for a president, there should be some minimal federal standards, beyond the Voting Rights Act of 1965, that protect voters' rights? After all, we federalized laws governing the assassination of a president, and even the threatening of a president. Are there no federal standards regarding the selection of a president?

Let's make no mistake here. Nothing in *Buckley* specifically prohibits the passage of such federalizing legislation in the arena of federal elections. But even when passing the Help America Vote Act, that afforded federal money to improve voting instruments after the 2000 election, the Congress shied away from significant alteration of the level of responsibility for holding elections. In matters like provisional voting, there are lawsuits, at the state and federal levels, and lawsuits concerning voting rolls, ballot access, and the validity of various machines and how they count (or don't count) votes. Legal "teams" now stand at the ready in federal elections, for what the parties and candidates believe to be the inevitable post-election voting debacle. I believe *Buckley,* within its alignment with other dichotomous variables in our analysis, implicitly restricts effective federal control of federal elections.

In order to understand fully why the country that likes to think of itself as the beacon of democracy for the world can only hold an election that, even before it happens, seems certain to produce highly contested results, I suggest that we now look beyond the court-to-legislature and state-to-federal dichotomies, and examine the other variables, specifically the non-institutional variables that I believe have rested more consistently within the Supreme Court and its cases than have the institutional, atomic, variables. Maybe they can tell us something that the institutional variables cannot.

I believe that the first thing that the subatomic variables tell us about America's elections lies at the heart of the analysis of *Buckley v. Valeo* and, ultimately, its relationship to *Dred Scott.* We need merely to review the cognitive nature of the huge campaign contribution. Unmistakably, the large contribution is cognitively analytic. In one way, it is not really a contribution at all. It is a contract. The narrowness of the purpose imports a bilateral relationship with the receiver of the contribution, and only a bilateral relationship.

Second, the imbalance of the contractual form of contribution is, over the long haul, conservative. Yes I am aware of what ACT, MoveOn, and George Soros did for the Kerry campaign and some other Democrats in 2004, but I am sorry. The Bush campaign still raised more money than Kerry and the fact that the right will always outraise and outspend the Democrats is something that the euphoria over the new fund raising sources for the liberals will not undo.

Third, and most importantly, the issue of sector, or more specifically preferences for sector, is a key subatomic linkage within the American constitutional order. When all the argument over *Buckley v. Valeo* is completed, and when one has the perspective of time to look back on this case, there is one thing that stands out above all else. It is that the Supreme Court, in its *Buckley* ruling, essentially privatized the American electoral system. While political systems around the world have electoral structures that are essentially run by the general government, as representatives of the citizenry entire, the United States does not have that. The American political system is not just looking for, but has already found, a few good (usually) men who have bought the political system and assured a conservative bias under the protection of *Buckley.*

The loopholes of *Buckley*, whether they still indirectly permit inordinate campaign contributions like those of Mr. Clement Stone who gave two million dollars to Richard Nixon in both 1968 and 1972, or in a way that George Soros with his twenty million dollars circumvented our democracy in 2004 with his twenty million dollars, make the American electoral system subject to the excesses of a few very wealthy people. If that is not oligarchy, I do not know what oligarchy is. But beyond all of this, even beyond the variable of sector which is surely important, the fact is that the key dichotomy in *Buckley v. Valeo* is the analytic-to-synthetic cognition, with the analytic cognition, as in *Dred Scott,* in full ascendance.

Let's look at the cognitive dichotomy more closely. Putting the subatomic considerations of cognition, ideology, and sector together, what do you come up with in *Buckley?* To answer that, let us remind ourselves of the simplest fact of the case. The public did attempt to forestall the privatization of their electoral system. They did it through their elected federal representatives who passed legislation that changed something for the better, they thought, and they did it at the federal, not the state level.

So here is the link. From early in the twentieth century, though certain progressive states were often the "laboratory" of democracy as some political scientists like to think of it, it was the federal government that ultimately dealt comprehensively with whatever the issue was: women's suffrage, worker protection, civil rights, and the like. But the very election of federal candidates, the president, the senator, or the congressperson as the principal players in the democratic "laboratory," was largely kept from federal oversight.

The result was predictable. And so, whereas in *Dred Scott* Chief Justice Taney ruled that there was no federal jurisdiction over slavery in the territories, in *Buckley v. Valeo* the Burger court assured that the federal political jurisdiction could not limit expenditures in political campaigns, and, perhaps inadvertently, that there could really be no federal control over contributions as well.

In other words, whereas *Dred Scott* weakened the federal jurisdiction in physical areas that were not yet a state, forbidding federal action on the slavery question in the territories, *Buckley v. Valeo* weakened the federal jurisdiction throughout the country in the primary political area of electing representatives for an ostensibly democratic government.

Further, whereas *Dred Scott* disenfranchised "negroes" from federal citizenship, *Buckley v. Valeo* disenfranchised all non-millionaire citizens who did not wish to prostitute themselves to a variety of interest groups in order to offer for a national public office. By the early twenty-first century, the American electoral system became the primary example of oligarchy within the overall political system. It also became the primary example of oligarchic excess in the developed, democratic world.

Finally, although *Dred Scott*, along with other events, surely accelerated the momentum towards the secessionist initiated Civil War, *Buckley v. Valeo* did nothing less than assure the continued disassembling of the American political system with apparently no redress for those who sought to restore the structural integrity of the system. And, don't forget, all of the above aberrations of *Buckley* were achieved through an inordinate attachment to the cognitively analytic form of the large contribution contract which we have well discussed.

And so, to the central point: whereas Earl Warren's Supreme Court led to the cognitively synthetic extension of basic liberties to African-Americans, women, voters, and the like, *Buckley*, just seven years after Warren's retirement from the court incidentally, swung to an extreme position that ignored the most obvious and system damaging analytic variable of the fat contribution that had been addressed by the Congress and the Presidency. *Buckley*, just as *Dred Scott* ignored the dreadful human cost of the cognitively analytic, unencumbered slave contract, similarly ignored the dreadful political cost of the cognitively analytic, unencumbered excessive contribution. I think that's the essence of *Buckley v. Valeo.*

To review, in this segment we have used a cognitive understanding of a small handful of key Supreme Court decisions to show how the patterns of alignment within court rulings have worked over time. We have, in other words, looked at patterns of core constitutional cases in what I hope is an original and revealing way, a way that assays the deep cost to our nation of the *Buckley* ruling.

But we are not through. We need now to take what understandings we have gained from this section and place them within the context of the American political and legal system entire. Specifically, we need to see how the subatomic balance between the analytic and synthetic cognitions underpins even the intricate institutional balances of the original seven articles of the Constitution and the Bill of Rights. We also need to see how these intricate balances have been altered in the recent past. Whereas in this chapter we have analyzed *Buckley v. Valeo* in its historic setting, and introduced a kind of cognitive impact analysis of *Buckley* and *Dred Scott* taken together, in the next chapter, we will look at the philosophical roots of the differences between the original seven articles and the Bill of Rights, and then apply that differentiation to the case of *Buckley v. Valeo.*

Moscow

A faculty member at the Naval War College in Newport, Rhode Island, read some of my writings and saw to it that I was invited to a small conference in Moscow in late August 1992. The conference was officially hosted by the Newport Institute, the Committee for Science and Culture of the Russian Parliament, and the Center for the Study of Psychology in the Nuclear Age. I prepared a paper and flew to Moscow, not long after the Russians had abandoned Communism and begun their long and I'm afraid very uneven journey toward democracy.

The three soldiers still changed the guard at Lenin's tomb in Red Square, and Gum's, at the corner of the square, still provided the best shopping in the city. I was taken by the height of the wall around the Kremlin and very much taken by St. Basil's at night, with lights shining on it, almost always through a misty fog. I was also taken by the long parade of neo-classical architecture on the other side of Red Square, buildings that were rarely photographed but that house the legislature and are really quite impressive in their own right. I was always amused by the Russians who were amused by my name. I was treated well.

The conference lasted three days. Among the speakers were the Russian deputy minister of education Alexander Asmolov and high (and usually quite angry) officials of the Russian Orthodox Church. Wolfgang Giegerich, Director of the Jung Institute in Zurich, gave a paper, as did the renowned Dutch rabbi Awraham Soetendorp, and other religious and political leaders. Our topic was ethnic hatred and its increase in the early post-Cold War era.

During the conference I sat across from a Buddhist who had the most expressive face I have ever seen. He listened intently to every speaker, often tilting his head one way or the other but rarely lifting his eyes from the speaker's. At times he was deeply pensive and at other times clearly pained. Often he radiated a joyousness that came from deep inside. He was capable of great laughter, giving in to that full hearty body laugh that signified surrender to a moment, and its insight.

And yet, beyond all of the above, there were other moments for him, moments that occurred when perhaps he thought no one was watching. I don't know how many others saw him in those moments, but I did. In those briefest of times I saw something very different from his reactive expressions, his usual gaiety. It was al-

most an internal expression, an inside peeking out and then climbing back in again among all the mirrors of what someone else had said.

And it was sad. It was unmistakably sad.

In the morning of the third day, the Buddhist had his turn to speak. He did not approach the podium but sat in front of a burly monk whose silver briefcase had brushed the back of the Buddhist's chair from the conference's beginning. The Buddhist asked for a translator, although it turned out that he knew nearly all of the English words he used.

He spoke of the loss of his country. He spoke of where he used to live and of where he had gently ruled. He told us how the Chinese had driven him from his country. And he told us how he longed to return before he died.

Here, the sadness was no longer elusive. It was transparent. He gave into it but never gave in to what would have been understandable interruptions. He continued apace, telling the full story in one sitting, then thanking his audience and leaning back against his chair, only inches from the briefcase. The man who lost his country had told his tale.

After lunch on the third day, I sat again where I always sat. One of the last presenters was giving her paper when the door opened. A burly man entered, alone. It was someone who had not been to any of the previous sessions. And he was Russian.

I was sitting in the first bank of the two rows of chairs. The second row, back from the table, was never full and was usually disorderly. It was a small conference. Out of a corner of my eye, I saw the Russian pause for a moment and then proceed down the little space between the rows, through the little aisle behind me.

This new man walked slowly, speaking to no one, and shuffled sideways when the chairs were too close together. He carried no notes, nor much of anything else.

Within a moment he was behind me. There he found a chair, just obliquely behind mine, and sat down. He still had said nothing to anyone, and the speaker continued until she had completed her presentation.

After her paper, there was the usual applause, and then an awkward silence. No one seemed to know what to do. To my surprise, no one moved to greet the new visitor. Some glanced at him, only to glance away.

I soon realized I was the closest to him. So I stood up, turned to my left, and held out my hand. "Welcome, Mr. President," I said, with the enthusiasm I genuinely felt. And, though he speaks little English, he clearly understood. He bolted to his feet with a huge smile and said something back to me, in Russian. Immediately the translators were there and, for an all too brief period, I conversed with this man, alone.

Unlike the Buddhist, there was little variety in his expression. It was almost universally boisterous, with an encompassing Slavic smile. And yet, even in that short period, the dominant expression could not hold. Briefly, ever so briefly, there was a contradiction. And the contradiction signaled a different emotion. And that emotion was fear.

Fear? With me? In a conference room, in Moscow, with all those others around? Yes, it was as unmistakable as was the Buddhist's sadness. The expression, undeniably, was fear.

Unlike the Buddhist, he did not speak later to his contradictory expression. But then I did not need to hear it. After a moment with him, I remembered. I remembered that this was the anniversary. This was the first anniversary of the day he, and his family, were taken prisoners in their vacation home. They had feared for their lives, as they were taken prisoner by the revanchist Communists. This was the anniversary of the day when he had almost lost his life.

After speaking with the Russian, and when others came, I thanked him and then turned to pick up a copy of my recent book. I walked across the front of the long presentation table and then turned toward the Buddhist. This was the last day of the conference, and I wanted him to have the copy that I had autographed for him. After giving him the book, I spoke momentarily with him about it.

But after that moment, I heard a rustle in the room. I looked behind me and saw that the Russian was now walking behind the presentation table, just as I had. Others were following him, and then he turned, as I had done, and came back toward the Buddhist and me.

I realized, of course, that he was coming to see the Buddhist. I realized, but only then, that he and the Buddhist had never met.

As the Russian neared, I stepped aside from the Buddhist, and as our photographer edged beside them, the translators wedged between. But the translators were not needed, and the photographers, after taking a picture or two, looked over their lenses and then lowered their cameras, in respect.

The man who lost his country and the man who almost lost his life did not speak to each other immediately. They did not need to speak. The Russian and the Buddhist merely embraced. There was one more picture taken, and then, after a long silence, they talked to each other through the translators. The two men both wore new expressions, expressions of deep affection and even deeper understanding. And while they talked and continued to look into each other's eyes, their expressions never changed.

CHAPTER SEVEN

Buckley v. Valeo

The Federalists and Their Constitution

The American political system is, or at least was, extraordinary. If I sound patriotic about the American constitutional order, it is because I still believe that the two sets of Founders (do not think of the Founders as a singular group), were an exceptional lot. What they gave to our young nation was an extraordinary founding document. I recall, however, what Benjamin Franklin said to the lady who asked him what the Constitutional Convention had given to the country. Throughout the Constitution's living history, it has always been a matter of whether we, as the inheritors of the document's government, could "keep it" a republic. The Anti-Federalists made a great contribution toward keeping it a republic with their Bill of Rights.

Why, then, are so many critical of the American political system now, and specifically of America's electoral system? The answer, quite simply, is that I believe that our entire sub-constitutional order has been significantly altered, and I believe that what was once a well-balanced order, one that properly mixed all three elements of Aristotle's trilogy and that made our nation a republic, has been wrenchingly misaligned in recent years. As I said in Chapter Five, I think that the American political system now increasingly reflects Aristotle's oligarchy, the corrupted form of aristocracy.

How did this occur? There are many reasons for the gradual misalignment of the U. S. government. Within the subjective context of a subatomic political philosophy, the organizational dynamics that Anthony Downs and Howard Aldrich wrote of and the long-cycle, historical dynamics that those like Arnold Toynbee and Oswald Spengler portrayed, have clearly revealed the corrosion of our political institutions.[1] The natural ascendance of the analytic over the synthetic cognition in the interactions of America's institutions over time has now fully manifested itself in America's political system.

Put simply, the Congress's overly centrifugal 1970s reforms, more than anything else, have made it easier for the oligarchs to make the system their own. The Congress's interface with interest groups of whatever objective stripe has, if anything, accelerated what would be naturally-caused imbalances. Objectively based interest groups have endured the same internal sorting out of psychologies as the public institutions they interact with. When a subatomically imbalanced interest group interacts with a subatomically imbalanced public institution, the result is predictable. As Plato, Zeno and the classical dialecticians would have us do, we need to first look to the form of how institutions are interacting, and the subjective biases there should become both inevitable and clear.

But there is even more to it than that. The recent imbalancing of the American political system grew in great part from a lack of understanding of what lies at the core of any governmental system. It grew out of the failure to understand that the American political design was based on balances that, without intent, went far deeper than the checks and balances between and among institutions that make up America's usual governmental understanding.

These deeper balances, I argue, are capable of easy understanding. They are, and I think the Federalists and the Anti-Federalists knew of them intuitively if not consciously, cognitive balances. As outlandish as it sounds at first, I believe these cognitive balances, again as part of the sector/ideology/cognition trichotomy, are the core of the American Constitution, just as much as I believe that they are at the core of any governmental arrangement that purports to be organizationally functional and politically equitable. I therefore believe that describing the American political and legal systems within the context of these cognitive, subatomic balances, and not the traditional institutional balances between states and the federal government, and Congress and the Courts, will guide us to what has recently gone wrong.

At least to some degree, Americans know the history of their political and legal systems. For a time immediately after the Revolution freed the colonies from the British, the Articles of Confederation provided the nation with a loose, state-dominated order. We know that that order began unraveling within a very short time and that something needed to replace it.

During the time of the Articles, the states were charged with such national obligations as paying off the Revolutionary War debt. Some states, to be sure, contributed their share, but some gave less and some nothing. The states' lassitude about the new nation's credit surely contributed to the Articles' unraveling.

Something else wounded the early order, where many states were as selfish regarding the development of a common market as they were regarding the debt repayment. Tariffs sprang up between and among the states, designed of course to protect home enterprises. Licensing was restricted to home industries in many states, and a neighboring entrepreneur found it difficult if not impossible to set up shop across a state line. Full faith and credit, as we've discussed, was not granted to the debts of those who had slipped across a state line. Once a debtor made it across the state line, there was no way to collect the debt. All of these state practices, and others, contributed to the national unraveling.

But the problem of keeping the country together under the Articles was not simply a matter of how states were not repaying Revolutionary War debts or were irresponsibly dealing with sister states in matters relating to private debt. The problem also had a good deal to do with how several state governments treated their businesses and their large private-property holders. Some states, to the horror of the propertied and creditor classes, intruded into the private sector in ways that were highly unfavorable to those whom many considered to be the wealth-creating classes. Whether it was the printing of paper money, Rhode Island being the chief culprit, or the overtaxing of wealthy estates which more than one state engaged in, or even the judicial unwillingness to engage in loan foreclosures, because judges were usually elected for a short time and juries overwhelmingly favored debtors, some states were thought by some of their better-off citizens to be moving toward the mob rule of Aristotle's pure democracy.

The Constitution, in replacing the Articles, greatly shifted authority to the federal level. The states had had their chance. But on the continuum of centralized-to-uncentralized government, the new federal governmental design was substantially more *de*centralized than the state governments. The legislature, as it was in so many state governments, would no longer be king. Under the Articles, state legislatures had dominated most state governments, with weak governors and weaker courts typifying their tripartite arrangements. Such legislative overbearing meant that a state such as Rhode Island was already every bit as participatory in its late eighteenth-century legislative responsiveness to the average citizen as were most Jacksonian states more than fifty years later.

But this often-irresponsible state government activity led the Federalists to do more than simply place state governments under a federal union. They simultaneously felt it necessary to create a variety of institutional separations that their new federal constitution eventually reflected. Beyond that, they also felt a need to protect the private institutions of property and contract within the new constitutional order. So they did this as well.

With the new federal design, would there be opposition to what the Philadelphia convention had birthed? Of course there would be. But though it is well known that there was opposition to the constitution, the Anti-Federalists were not studied substantially by more than a few scholars until recently. Smarting from the loss of their state-level authority, and from what they perceived as the right to counterbalance overbearing creditor interests in their states' governments, the Anti-Federalists argued, first against the ratification of the Constitution altogether, and then in favor of a Bill of Rights that would at least balance the original seven articles.

Let us not forget that capable Anti-Federalists, such as George Mason of Virginia, saw so little of representative democracy in the new government that they thought favored an autocratic executive, a creditor-favoring federal court system, and an aristocratic Senate. They thought little authority was left for the sole "people's" institution, the House of Representatives. The institutional arguments of the Anti-Federalists are still nowhere near as well known to the general public as is the nature of the eventual bargain between the Federalists and the Anti-Federalists. It is accurate for constitutional commentators to focus on the Bill of Rights as the Anti-Federalists' last, and only, successful bargaining chip. The granting of this Anti-Federalist demand is what support for constitutional ratification in the wavering states eventually came down to.

But settle they had to, and the later ratifiers of the Constitution, including New York, Virginia, North Carolina, and (finally) the ever truculent Rhode Island, were far more willing constitutional partners after the Bill of Rights handshake. Let us now, within the context of a subatomic, psychologically based political philosophy, briefly reflect on the cognitive flavor of the two grand halves of what most American citizens think of as one Constitution.

In that context, I merely suggest that the institutionally disparate seven original articles of the Constitution are structurally aristocratic, in an Aristotelian setting, and overwhelmingly analytic within a subatomic, cognitive setting. The three branches, and the state governments, are not only dispersed but, as we discussed with undemocratic decentralization, are also most available to those who best make their own, cognitively analytic contract with the government. In reprise, I believe the first seven articles of the Constitution to be clearly of the cognitively analytic form. By themselves, as the Anti-Federalists argued though on other than cognitive grounds of course, they would not have produced an equitable government. In contrast, I also believe that the Bill of Rights is very much of the synthetic cognitive form.

The Anti-Federalists and Their Bill of Rights

Most politically informed Americans have read *The Federalist*, or at least some of the more important of what were really just op-ed pieces, as they made up the beginnings of America's political science. They know of James Madison's fear of "factions," a kind of pre-party aggregation of like-minded people. They know of Madison's advocacy of the separation of powers just mentioned. Finally, they know of Alexander Hamilton's argument for what was not politically wise to place into the Constitution: judicial review. But, as I just mentioned, what many informed Americans still do not understand very well is the nature of the Anti-Federalist position.

Perhaps the very first opposition to the Constitution came from Patrick Henry, the radical democratic constitutional delegate from Virginia who scorned the Convention shouting, "I smell a rat." From there, opposition to the Constitution was not only slow to rise but, even when called to arms, did a far poorer job of coordinating a nationwide campaign against the Constitution than the concentrated pro-constitutional efforts of James Madison, Alexander Hamilton, and to a lesser extent, John Jay.

As a result, even today there are not many informed Americans who have read *The Anti-Federalist Papers.*[2] But these papers contain the writings of many talented citizens, people beyond George Mason of Virginia. Melancton Smith, (who in great part reflected and expounded on the thinking of Virginia's Richard Henry Lee), John Lansing, Elbridge Gerry, and others all argued against the Constitution's ratification and then for the Bill of Rights. As we have noted, their core complaint against the Constitution was that the new document enthroned a political aristocracy.

There has always been another reason why *The Anti-Federalist Papers* have not been widely read. Unlike *The Federalist Papers,* which were available as a volume a year after their newspaper publication, the much larger collection of Anti-Federalists writings, scattered all over the East Coast, was never assimilated and published as a body until the year 1981. The other side of the constitutional argument, those who did not favor the ratification of a government very different from what they had in their states and that would take precedence over their states, was not fully in intellectual play for nearly two hundred years after the Constitution's ratification.

What specifically did *The Anti-Federalist Papers* argue for? To be sure, *The Anti-Federalist Papers* have a greater variance within them than did the opposition liturgy. The former, as I've said, were written by far more people than wrote *The Federalist Papers,* and those people were in nowhere near as close communication as were Messrs. Madison, Hamilton, and Jay. But there are still central themes in *The Anti-Federalist Papers.* Most maintain that only the better-off would benefit from the dispersion of powers within the federal jurisdiction, as well as the triumph of the federal jurisdiction over the state jurisdictions and the Constitution's specific protections of property and contract. The better-off, and the creditors who were frequently a part of their numbers, would surely benefit from a Constitution without a Bill of Rights and with a strong executive, a strong judiciary, and an aristocratic half of the legislature. Also, the new arrangement would restrict the general populace's ability to participate in their government in a way that could counterbalance the wealthy. The Anti-Federalists were unhappy, in other words, not only with what they thought the Constitution did to help the better off, but also with what the Constitution specifically prevented the middle class from doing, politically, to respond.

What the Anti-Federalists dearly wanted, in short, was something that would be both ideologically and institutionally complementary to the Constitution's first seven articles. They wanted something that would balance the original seven articles with something more procedurally democratic, and something more ideologically liberal, as we would understand it today. Most importantly, they wanted something that was what I have argued was more clearly of the cognitively synthetic form because they wished, collectively, to respond to the public's needs by placing publicly generated encumbrances upon the often-government-sponsored contracts of the emerging mercantilist class. I will review the cognitive nature of the individual provisions of the Bill near the close of this chapter.

Reluctantly, the Federalists went along, although "high" Federalist figures like Hamilton and Pennsylvania's James Wilson never truly believed that anything like a Bill of Rights was necessary. As above, the Federalists only agreed to go along with the Bill of Rights because of the foot dragging of some states on ratification. But they also agreed because even some Federalists, Madison most importantly, felt on reflection that the original seven constitutional articles had, perhaps, tilted too far toward the aristocratic side of things. Some rebalancing was probably in order, and Madison, along with some "low," or moderate Federalists, was ready to make the bargain.

In spite of opposition among his old allies, for Madison a bargain was a bargain regarding the Bill of Rights. And, even beyond the deal, the influence on Madison of Thomas Jefferson, the influence of James Monroe (whom Madison traveled with in his first congressional "campaign"), and the growing acceptance in Madison's thinking of what the high Federalists would never countenance, open political competition and even political parties, sealed his affirmation.

By 1791, Madison was ready to bring to the Congress the Anti-Federalists' price for constitutional reconciliation. It was not an easy task since the Federalists who overwhelmingly populated the first House of Representatives showed little interest in bargains made by others three years earlier. The rudeness shown Madison by Federalist legislators as he tried to interpose the Bill of Rights on an agenda filled with protections for American commerce is one of the more appalling, if retrospectively somewhat humorous, moments in American legislative history.[3]

Indeed, we are now at a key point in American history. In great part because the entirety of *The Anti-Federalist* has been available for only a quarter-century, and in part as well because of the ideological interest of such groups as The American Bar Association; and conservative think tanks such as The Cato Institute and the Heritage Foundation which have insisted on seeing the Bill of Rights solely as a protector of individual rights, the Bill continues to be misunderstood. Let us try to undo that misunderstanding and thus begin to deal with *Buckley* and the campaign finance reform issue from the perspective of what the Bill of Rights really means, and not what the conservative think tanks and the drafters of *Buckley* mistakenly believed it means.

To begin, we should look briefly at the most pointed commentary of the Anti-Federalists regarding the Constitution. George Mason, fully the intellectual equal of his fellow Virginian James Madison, exclaimed after reading the Constitution that "there is not the substance, but the shadow only of representation" in the new constitutional document. According to Mason, even the House of Representatives, ostensibly the voice of the people, would "never produce proper information in the legislature, or inspire confidence in the people."

Mason continued his attack by arguing that the House of Representatives would always be overwhelmed by the Senate, which had the "power of altering all money bills, and of originating appropriations of money, and the salaries of the officers of their own appointment, in conjunction with the President." As for the remainder of the government, Mason saw a richly empowered president as an accomplice of the Senate. Most forbiddingly, he saw the federal courts as destined "to absorb and destroy the judiciaries of the several states."

For Mason, the new arrangement's policy output, as we would label it today, would be "tedious, intricate, and expensive." Further, justice would be "unattainable, by a great part of the community." In sum, Virginia's Mason saw the newly empowered federal government as a "moderate aristocracy," but something that could easily degenerate into a full "monarchy or a corrupt oppressive aristocracy."[4] Before we can restore our limited democracy today, I suggest, we need to understand how the Anti-Federalists meant to balance the new government they were forced to accept at the outset of the constitutional period. Look first at the simplest meanings of the Bill of Rights language. I think that language, taken at face value, tells us what it was all about, both for the Anti-Federalists and for us today. When the first amendment prevents the "abridging of free speech," I would ask if this is merely a solitary right, a right of a lone individual that is being protected. I do not think so. We speak, after all, to others. We speak to those whom we wish to convince of something. As a result, the speech right is inherently aggregative, implying the limited democracy of Aristotle's polity, or the necessary interaction of a free people's communicating with each other, about what concerns them politically.

And what does "or of the press" mean? Would you publish a paper for yourself? No, the press's product is to be read. It is part of a dialogue between and among citizens. It is surely part of the constitutional democracy, and it is, at a minimum, another part of the democratic exercise. And would not "the right of the people peaceably to assemble" be aggregative too? The answer should be obvious, for an assembly is an aggregation. It is limited democracy cohered. Without assembly, there would be no coming together of the people. Without assembly, there would be no constitutional democracy. The citizenry must meet.

The same is true with the fourth political right of the first amendment, "the right of the people to petition the Government for a redress of grievances." This freedom goes back at least to Edward Coke and the Petition of Right. We get to complain in a limited democracy, and if that is not democracy, there is no democracy. To the second amendment.

The second amendment, preserving the right to bear arms, was unquestionably an aggregational amendment. Though some liberals do not wish to concede this, and I support the kind of gun legislation that was passed during the Clinton administration, the second amendment was nonetheless the creation of those who feared an overweening government, controlled by the Federalists. An organized opposition had to meet collective force with collective force.

The third amendment, concerning the housing of troops in one's home when it is not a time of war, is also an oppositional amendment. A citizenry can not organize an opposition when the boots of the government are resting on its hearth.

Naturally, democracy also means that the government can not pry into your "persons, houses, papers, and effects." Just as naturally, citizens should be protected from "unreasonable searches and seizures," as the fourth amendment requires. How else does aggregated political opposition grow than with dissenters keeping records and corresponding?

And should anyone "be twice put in jeopardy," or be compelled "to be a witness against himself,"or be deprived of "life, liberty, or property, without due process of law," as the fifth amendment forbids? The sixth amendment's guarantee of counsel, expanded as have been so many of the amendments by significant cases, also protects the protester, while the eighth amendment's prohibition of "cruel and unusual punishment" speaks to the protection of those not only convicted of crime, but to those who might consider breaking the law, or to those subjected to it after conviction for the purpose of eliciting information. We have discussed the Seventh Amendment, where the referent is clear. This response to the prohibition against impairing "the Obligation of Contracts" ensured balance in the private, resultant section of the Constitution and, in my view, overshadowed all of the procedural provisions of the entire document.

This, again, lies at the crux of the Constitution, the essence of what was being most argued over. But beyond the substance of their argument, these two provisions of the Constitution best demonstrate how the cognitive preferences for or against encumbrances on the debt contract boil down to preferences for the analytic (unencumbered contract) and the synthetic (encumbered contract) position. Even better than the undemocratic decentralization of the Constitution's institutional level, and beyond the Type 2 undemocratic elections and compressed distribution of the citizen-to-institution level, this third, citizen-to-citizen level of the Constitution, reflects the cognitive contrast. In fact, it reflects that contrast every bit as well as *Shelley's Case* and *Shelley v. Kraemer.*

But I have left out something, haven't I? Yes, I have, deliberately, left out two important provisions of the Bill of Rights, the "establishment" and the "free exercise" clauses of the first amendment. Are they different, qualitatively different, from the other provisions of the Bill of Rights? Remember when I said that beyond the core provisions of Section Ten in Article One and the Seventh Amendment, and beyond the vast majority of constitutional provisions that are procedural in nature, there was one more exception, beyond the Article One/Seventh Amendment section, that also demonstrated the cognitive contrast? Well, this is the exception. This is the other private sector part of the Constitution and it deals with faith, or religion, and it is, looking back on a long and winding road, the forerunner of the "culture wars" that currently rage in our country. This is the last piece of the Constitution that we need to examine to discern the position of the Natural Left regarding America's principal document. Please remember while we do so that the Federalists had taken the threat of monarchy out of the Anti-Federalists' bag of criticism by including the four year term and the election by states in Article II. They had also taken the threat of titled nobility away by guaranteeing against the Society of the Cincinnati, George Washington's officers and their male descendants, from becoming such a nobility in Article One, Section Nine as well. But the Federalists themselves left something out, didn't they? They left out any reference to an established church. On that point the Anti-Federalists were still insecure.

And so how do the "establishment" and "free exercise" clauses of the Constitution salve that insecurity? Although many argue, at a purely substantive level, that the religious clauses import a reference to the Judeo-Christian tradition, my position is that a sectoral analysis and a look at the *form* of the provisions provide a very different answer. The sector side of it is easy. Clearly, the Anti-Federalists wanted the religious portion of a citizen's life to be in the private sector. They did not want for there to be either a preferred, state-sponsored religion, like what the English had and still have, and they did not want for there to be conflict over which religion would be favored.

The drafters of the Constitution's original seven articles, and the Bill of Rights, were extraordinarily well read. They knew of the English Civil War, the Thirty Years War, the Edict of Nantes and the Revocation of the Edict of Nantes. They wanted Henri Quatre, not Louis Quatorze, and to keep religion in the private sector was the best way to ensure the absence of bias and conflict. Here, like the case of *Shelley v. Kraemer* (1948), the private sector rests in the liberal sector ideologically. The absence of government in this instance assures the best result but, again, this is the citizen-to-citizen portion of the Constitution which, apart from the citizen-to-citizen layer of full faith and credit, the protection of contract, and the complementary protection of favorable jury rulings in the Seventh Amendment, mirrors the cognitive relativity with such clarity.

With regard to the *form* of the "establishment" clause, I would suggest it is synthetic, and I say that only because the clause maintains a plurality of permissible religions, or the existence of very different kinds of worship. In that sense, the case mirrors *Roe v. Wade* (1973), insisting on a plurality of alternatives in the public sector. The drive for orthodoxy, seen at the fringe of far too many religions today, is really a drive for singularity. Maintaining the rainbow is inherently synthetic.

As for the "free exercise" clause, much the same is true at both the sectoral and cognitive level. In order to protect against bias, and to protect against conflict, although this time it was more likely conflict including a small, minority religion rather than the conflict of major religions who wanted to be the "official" religion, the Anti-Federalists also put this clause in the private sector. Your religion is a private matter and it is protected.

With respect to cognition, the maintenance of the full rainbow is even more evident than it is in the establishment clause. Even if you are member of a small religion like, say, Taoism, you will be protected from religious persecution so long as you are not breaking the law with human sacrifice or something of that nature. The range is expanded here, just as with the establishment clause. Those who wish to tie our constitutional origins to a particular religion are, at best, speaking only at the lowest level of abstraction. At worst, they are missing the point of the Bill of Rights entirely.

So what, in sum, does the Bill of Rights protect? What is clear is that the Bill of Rights does *not* protect individual rights, at least in the sense of the Greek word *telos* or in the sense of the *purpose* of the right. It protects individual rights only in the sense of the *locus* of the right, or in its original placement within an individual citizen. Yes, a citizen has an individual right either to be a part of a group or to act on her own, and in those senses only the right is singular, or individual. Such is not the case in any other sense.

What, after all, was the Bill of Rights designed for? It was designed, as we've said, to enable democratic opposition. It was designed to provide citizens of the still-new nation with a guarantee of meaningful involvement in a general government that was far more powerful than the Articles of Confederation government. Much of the white male American citizenry had become accustomed to public involvement in the state governments. There were political parties within many of those governments before the Revolutionary War. From our subatomic, cognitive perspective, the Bill was clearly designed to provide the kind of synthetically formed aggregation of protest and participation that could only be assured by what we understand as the second stage, the contradiction stage, of the cognitively alternating dialectical progression.

In short, there simply should be no argument over the Bill of Rights being a collective document, a largely democratic document, and, again, a document that is synthetic from a cognitive perspective. When properly understood, it should, and I believe will, provide the legal antidote to the disastrous ruling in *Buckley v. Valeo.*

Before closing, I wish briefly to refer to one example of recent, far more legally centered research on the Bill of Rights that I think seems to confirm what I have suggested so far. The distinguished constitutional scholar Prof. Akhil Reed Amar of the Yale Law School has put it simply regarding the Bill of Rights. His research has led him to the conclusion that the Bill of Rights was never drafted to "impede popular majorities, but [instead] to empower them."While the conventional understanding of the Bill, according to Amar, focused on the protection of minorities from the majority, the essence of the Bill of Rights, in his judgment, is in fact far "more majoritarian than counter."[5]

Of course, Prof. Amar comes to his conclusion from an altogether different theoretical foundation than mine. But he comes, without a doubt, to the same conclusion. The Bill of Rights is a democratic, majority-empowering document. We can only restore the limited democracy that the Federalists *and* the Anti-Federalists jointly created with their ideologically, and cognitively, *complementary* documents: the Constitution's first seven articles, and the Constitution's Bill of Rights. Let us now begin to detail how the above complementary understanding of our Constitution and the Bill of Rights specifically enables the overturning of *Buckley v. Valeo.*

The Bill of Rights, *Dred Scott*, and *Buckley*

So what more, then, of *Buckley v. Valeo*? If *Buckley* is a cognitively analytic ruling, protecting the increasingly unencumbered contract that makes up the current large political contribution, and if the Bill of Rights is in fact a cognitively synthetic, publicly aggregative document, then I believe *Buckley* can be overturned for reasons related to the contradiction between the cognitive form of the Bill of Rights and the misinterpretation of that form in *Buckley.* Recognizing that the campaign finance reform cases that have occurred since *Buckley* have not changed the essence of the *Buckley* holding one iota, I think that only a wholly new way of arguing the campaign finance reform issue will lead to meaningful change. I think that strategy should also, unabashedly, add to the parallels I have already drawn between the *Buckley* case and the case of *Dred Scott,* as well as contrast the misunderstandings of *Buckley* with the misunderstandings of *Shelley v. Kraemer* and, ultimately, link the travesty of *Buckley* with the right's misrepresentation of the Bill of Rights.

The sins of *Dred Scott* were great indeed. An objective, pre-cognitive analysis finds *Dred Scott* at the aristocracy end of the Aristotelian trichotomy of aristocracy, polity, and monarchy—the trichotomy, again, no longer being structured as a vertical pyramid.

Dred Scott, recall, was not only the first case to alter the classical conservative, federal jurisdiction, court prerogative, private sector, and cognitively analytic alignment that had existed since the time of Chief Justice John Marshall. It was the case in which the state government, rather than the federal government, became the ally of an ideologically conservative court over legislature, private sector over public sector, and analytic cognitive position. As I argued earlier, this change in the classical, Marshallian alignment of the five dichotomies I have outlined helps show how extreme the subjective biases of the case really were.

Beyond that, I have argued that *Dred Scott* extended the positions on the cognitive dichotomy to mark an extreme position for an unencumbered, or analytic, contract. The subject of the contract, after all, was slavery, and the slavocracy was determined not to let any human consideration, no matter how dire, get in the way of slave property, or the contract for the purchase and sale of such property. Just as *Buckley* equates free speech with money, the slave contract equated a human being with money, except that in *Dred Scott* the nonmonetary element enjoyed less protection than free speech did.

In short, the burden of *Dred Scott* is a burden of application. It is an extreme application of the unencumbered contractual legal obligation, with the crying need for an encumbrance of a contract making the cognitive polarity of the decision so obvious. How does this compare with *Buckley*? In my view, the sins of *Buckley*, if not as malevolent in human terms as the sins of *Dred Scott*, are at least as malevolent as *Dred Scott* in the sense of the suffering that the case has caused the American political system.

Remember from Chapter Six that the three judicial decision-making dichotomies that have proven themselves to be the most consistently aligned were a) ideology, b) sector and c) cognition, not state versus federal jurisdiction, or legislature versus court jurisdictions. With reference to the sectoral dichotomy, *Buckley* privatized the political processes by which our onetime limited democracy chooses its public officials. The United States, though it surely suffered the indignities of too much money in the political process before now, made a radical turn toward the private sector with *Buckley*, opening the floodgates to the ever increasing sums of money that now habitually drown our elections. As a result, few without their own private wealth, or direct access to someone else's private wealth, can seriously offer for major public office.

But if sector, ideology, and cognition are in fact the core variables of America's constitutional history, I suggest that *Buckley*, more than anything else, ratified the recent significant shift in the subatomic, cognitive makeup of America's campaign contributions. As I wrote earlier, the large contribution is not just more powerful than the small contribution because of its size. The large contribution is more powerful also because it is cognitively different from the small contribution. The large contribution is almost invariably more cognitively analytic. Though still an eyelash away from a bribe, there is rarely any question about what kinds of legislation a large political donor wants or what kinds of administrative rulings a regulated interest wants, that ruling, in turn of course, frequently being influenced by a legislator.

Small donors across the ideological spectrum rarely want anything more than better protection of the environment, better enforcement of automobile safety standards, a fairer tax code for middle-and-lower income earners and the like on the left, and a more "moral" society, more tax relief, and a stronger national defense and the like on the right. I have already suggested that this is the kind of public input that is not of the contractual form and is clearly more synthetic in its cognitive nature than the large contribution. You are contributing to an ideology, maybe with the double pleasure of contributing to a candidate you genuinely like.

What precisely, then, is the error of *Buckley*? As I've said, the core error, from a sectoral, noncognitive perspective, is that *Buckley* privatized the American electoral system. From a subjective, cognitive perspective, it radically altered the electoral system from one in which the small, largely ideologically based contributions mentioned above became overwhelmed by large, analytically formed contributions. From that perspective, I also suggest, *Buckley* repeats the cognitively analytic extremity of *Dred Scott.* Denying the recognition of encumbrances on the contribution "contract" mimics the denial of recognition of encumbrances on the slave contract. This is not what the Bill of Rights intended.

Why did *Buckley* do what it did? Was the Warren Burger Court as insensitive, or as wedded to the analytic form, as the Taney Court? Well, in some ways it was, but I would note that it came to its insensitivity by a very different route than did the Taney Court in *Dred Scott.* I would argue that whereas Taney's decision protected an extreme form of private property, just as it evidenced an extreme form of the analytic cognition, it at least did so with knowledge of what it was doing. Taney, for all of his misjudgment, knew where the sectors were in his ruling. He at least, if intuitively, got the cognitive form to line up correctly with its appropriate sector, even if he had to alter the classical state-to-federal balance among the original Marshallian dichotomies to do it.

Buckley, in a very important constitutional way, did something even worse than *Dred Scott.* In *Buckley,* the Burger Court entirely misunderstood what sector, and intuitively what cognition, underpinned the Bill of Rights. *Buckley*, recall, claimed that its ruling assisted the public sector in its decisions regarding elected public officials. The Burger Court in *Buckley* claimed to be enhancing the quality of limited democracy and, inferentially, the moderately synthetic mix that makes up a limited democracy. It had no idea that in fact it had done the exact opposite, in cognitive form as well as in objective substance.

In both its form and its substantive errors, therefore, the Warren Burger Court did no less than mimic the errors of understanding of *Shelley v. Kraemer* that the almost Supreme Court justice Robert Bork and the late Supreme Court justice William Rehnquist made. These ostensibly notable jurisprudents wholly misunderstood both the sectors, and the cognitive forms, of what I have argued to be the century's most important theoretical case.

To be sure, it will be difficult to overturn *Buckley*. But I think the introduction of the subatomic, cognitive perspective on the original seven articles of the Constitution and the Bill of Rights provides the best theoretical base from which *Buckley* can be overturned. Even if the new chief justice of the Supreme Court, Justice Roberts, does not understand the essence of *Buckley*, he and his Court can be taught to comprehend both the sectoral and the cognitive biases of *Shelley v. Kraemer, Dred Scott,* and, most importantly, the Bill of Rights. From there, the biases, and the damage, of *Buckley* might become obvious to him and to the rest of the Supreme Court.

As I said earlier, even a sectoral analysis alone finds the Bork/Rehnquist rendering of *Shelley v. Kraemer* to be wholly inaccurate. The neighborhood group was far more public, far more politically aggregative, than the private individual, Ms. Fitzgerald, who wished merely to sell her house by using a simple bilateral contract. But from a subjective, subatomic perspective, the case is clearer still, with the race-based, cognitively synthetic encumbrance on the sales contract being championed by the neighborhood association, and the cognitively unencumbered, analytically formed sale coming from the interaction of Ms. Fitzgerald and her buyer alone.

Yes, as I conceded earlier, *Shelley v. Kraemer* is that rare exception to the tight bonding of ideology, sector, and cognition that I find to be the central alliance of American constitutional law. But then *Shelley* marked the beginning of what I believe to be the only significant dialectic within all of American constitutional history. It parallels *Shelley's Case* in Coke's dialectic, and it leads to the synthetically formed, dialectically second-stage contradictions that are addressed in the *Brown, Baker,* and *Roe* cases, along with many others, in the Earl Warren Supreme Court.

Please do not misunderstand. I write with some certainty about the catastrophe of *Buckley v. Valeo* only because, as appalled as I am by the *Buckley* Court's misunderstanding of the Bill of Rights (as well as by the horrific impact of that misunderstanding on America's politics), I concede that given the theoretical tools that were available, it was difficult for the Supreme Court to see the error of its ways. Immodestly, what I suggest imports an entirely new jurisprudential framework. I submit again that unless one uses a subatomic, cognitive analysis like the one I have created, no one can readily see the relative private-to-public nature and, more importantly, the analytic-to-synthetic nature of the *Shelley, Dred Scott,* and *Buckley* cases.

Put simply, one must simultaneously consider which party represents the more cognitively analytic, and the more unencumbered, contract, and which party argues for the cognitively synthetic, or the more encumbered, contract in each case. This is the key to understanding these cases, in the context of the great ideological, sectoral, and now cognitive balances of the Constitution, which I believe I have demonstrated to be the core trichotomy of constitutional interpretation.

In sum, even beyond discovering the correct cognitive placements within *Shelley, Dred Scott* and *Buckley*, only a cognitively based analysis clarifies the further question regarding which side of the ideological fence the Bill of Rights was on, from the beginning and, when interpreted correctly, still is on. When we see the subatomic cognition clearly, and when we see the objective, sectoral spectrum clearly, we have a good chance of coming to the correct conclusion regarding what both sets of the Founders would have wanted regarding campaign finance spending. In that context, is there any question but that the latter-day, Anti-Federalist-influenced James Madison of the Bill of Rights, would have been appalled by *Buckley v. Valeo*?

Most telling of all, I believe, is the simple fact that the current United States Supreme Court, as its follow-on rulings after *Buckley* make clear, still fundamentally misunderstands The Bill of Rights. I cannot say it more bluntly: the Bill of Rights is an ideologically liberal document. It balances the conservatism of the Constitution's seven original articles, more confidently believing in the ability of an educated polity to govern itself than the Philadelphia conventioneers did.

Sectorally, the rights that the Bill protects are overwhelmingly in the public sector, not the private sector. They are, above all, the rights of political opposition and the rights of political aggregation that makes that opposition worthwhile. What I add is what I believe no one has until now thought of, that being that the Bill of Rights is cognitively synthetic. It labels the $5 + 7 = 12$ equation as analytic because it requires a full-blown orange, not just another apple, to move history past its second stage of the dialectic. By doing so, it facilitates the aggregation of the populace through its dialectical contradictions within the constitutional order of a limited, or constitutional, democracy.

At its most fundamental level, the Bill of Rights embraces that vast array of opinions and perspectives that exist among a free people. At its best, it brings those people into inspired but non-violent, democratic conflict with each other, gradually synthesizing their views into new, adaptive, and hopefully more equitable, public policies. Beyond that, the Bill of Rights ensures that all citizens have an opportunity to compete in the political arena, and not just as a member of an already existing objective grouping that may or may not have a just grievance against the government.

Curiously, the Bill of Rights assures that citizens, apart from being members of an objectively based coalition that advocates a particular public policy, may even choose a subjective over an objective political identification. A citizen may request that her or his subjective perspective benefit from the same standard of equity that objectively deprived groups have asked for, and generally received, throughout America's history.

More importantly, the very discovery of a subjectively based, constitutional interpretation of campaign finance legislation, and a correct interpretation of the Bill of Rights that underpins such an interpretation, is just as legitimate as asking for racial, gender, and economic justice in any specific way. Once we understand what the subatomic moment in politics has brought us to, I think equilibrium can be restored. Ultimately, the Bill of Rights does not ensure only that all ideas are included within the political debate: the crux of it is that all *forms* of ideas are included in the debate. Anyone sitting on the United States Supreme Court in the twenty-first century should know this, and know it well.

In my judgment, only the above argument, made within either a constitutional case or in furtherance of a constitutional amendment such as my friend Fritz Hollings proposed, will overturn *Buckley*. Only this will rebalance America's oligarchy and peacefully return our country's politics to the Aristotelian center point of limited democracy.

The easy linkage between the *Buckley* line of cases with the *Dred Scott* case of nearly 150 years ago is a tragic commentary on the recent Supreme Court. And yet, just as *Dred Scott* presented the most compelling case for the recognition of a cognitively synthetic encumbrance on a contract in all of nineteenth-century American history, the current Supreme Court will continue to ignore the reasons for permitting appropriate encumbrances on the contributory campaign contract until the issue is couched in cognitive terms. Only then will the mistakes of *Buckley* and its progeny, like the mistake of *Dred Scott*, be so glaring that the United States Supreme Court, a less distinguished jurisprudential body than it would like to think it is, cannot ignore it.

The Flag

In South Carolina it is not necessary to specify which flag. Merely referring to "the flag" is all it takes because the Confederate flag has been an issue for a long time, and more than a few would have it continue to be an issue for a good while longer.

The year 2000 was one of great intensity regarding the flag. Having been placed informally on top of the capitol in 1961, after President Dwight D. Eisenhower had decreed that the years 1961 to 1965 be dedicated to a remembrance of the Civil War—and then officially sanctioned as the third flag on the flagpole by a legislative resolution in 1962, the flag attracted all ideological sides in the ensuing years.

The intensity only grew, and by the year 2000 the NAACP had voted economic sanctions against South Carolina. In the early part of that year, forty-four thousand citizens marched to the statehouse steps demanding that the flag be taken from the dome. The proflag group could muster but six thousand in a later rally, but by then the issue was drawn. As the boycott was beginning to have an effect, the South Carolina state legislature, if reluctantly, agreed to take up the matter of the flag.

To the credit of many who labored in good faith, and under the burden of no small derision from those who opposed any change at all, a reasonably broad consensus developed by late spring that the flag should be removed from the flagpole. Even most ardent flag supporters agreed that its current placement implied sovereignty, and thus a disloyalty to the national government. Something, therefore, should be done.

But the devil was in the details. Where should the soon-to-be-lowered flag be placed? One side argued that any placement on the statehouse grounds still implied sovereignty. For them, only museums, cemeteries, and other private venues would suffice. On the other side, there was a push for a prominent re-placement, somewhere that could be seen by all. The flag might need to be lowered, but it should not be hidden.

After various plans surfaced and submerged, plans that included ancillary issues such as the future of a Confederate Memorial Day or the maintenance of Confederate memorials throughout the state, a startling development occurred. One day the local TV stations carried an extraordinary news conference, covering no less than seventy-eight state leaders who had decided on a new place for the flag.

This assemblage of former governors, bank presidents, law firm senior partners, presidents of the University of South Carolina and Clemson, and a healthy smattering of black leaders had come to a compromise. The flag would be placed at the Wade Hampton III monument (Hampton being the first governor after Reconstruction), behind and slightly to the east of the capitol building. It was quite a gathering, a visible coming together of what any political scientist would readily call the South Carolina "establishment." In somber tones, the group announced its solution to the press and the citizenry, and I recall mumbling "that's it" to myself as I hit the off button on the clicker. The issue had finally been resolved.

Well, not so fast. Yes, the Hampton monument gathering was an extraordinary assemblage. And yes, their compromise surely seemed to have the voice of reason behind it. But soon there was something more unusual about it, and that is that this compromise, and the group that created it, were soundly beaten. In fact, they were not just soundly beaten; they were virtually ignored. Incredibly, in South Carolina what seemed to be the "establishment" overwhelmingly lost its battle to place the flag in an out-of-the-way place. After continued bitter wrangling in the legislature, the flag was eventually placed at a principal intersection of the City of Columbia, Main and Gervais Streets, still on the capitol grounds.

Also, the Confederate monuments around the state were guaranteed perpetuity, and the once optional Confederate Memorial Day was converted into a universal holiday, as was the King holiday. For the record, Confederate day is observed in but a few rural counties.

I thought for a long time about what I had seen, and obviously not seen, along with what the civic leaders had not seen. In rough terms, I finally came to the conclusion that what happened is that just as the nineteenth-century Whig version of the world had triumphed over an eighteenth-century Tory version of the world in the Civil War—the Tory vision having earlier beaten the Whigs in the declaring of the Secession within South Carolina—in the year 2000 a coalition of old-family Tories and their yeoman allies among rural, small-town, and suburban whites had beaten the so-called New South Whigs, and beaten them badly.

In thinking about all of this, I recalled something that had occurred approximately one year before the flag debate, something that lent a belated but powerful insight into what eventually happened with the flag. I had been in Charleston for a day, traveling there with my friend R. B. Haynes, who had bought, with me, a few shares in a small local company. We had gone to the annual shareholders' meeting, held at the Embassy Suites Hotel on Meeting Street, just off Calhoun Park.

Haynes and I entered the long lobby of the building a few moments before the meeting and began chatting with some of the people who had preceded us there. It was all random talk, mostly about the company, but after a few moments of meeting with those to whom R. B. introduced me, I noticed someone standing alone at the rear of the hall. He was a young man, with very black hair and he stood out in both the way he fashioned his hair, and the way he dressed. His suit was European in cut, almost foppish yet certainly of a style. And his hair was so different from anything I had seen before, flattened down at the top but bushing out at the sides. A natural curl gave the rigor of the cut a certain abandon in practice, waves of locks traveling all the way from the temple close to the back of his head. But it was set there, not waving when the gentleman moved his head. His part was square in the center. A certain order seemed to emerge from the chaos after all.

Looking more closely, I noticed this young man's incredibly deep-set eyes, eyes that hauntingly mocked a genuine smile and an otherwise generous countenance. He leaned, more for affect than comfort, against the large door frame, but, as I saw over time, he repeatedly stood away from the frame to shake hands with the almost constant flow of people who crossed the hall, just to shake his hand. Young people, middle-aged people, and even those of some years redirected their angled walk to the right-hand corner stairs to greet this young man, often with a slight bow and a far-extended hand. I kept looking at his eyes.

Finally, R. B. finished talking with some people and motioned me toward the stairs. It was time for the meeting. We began our little walk to the back of the hall, angling over to the stairs as everyone else had. Then, shortly before we reached the stairs, R. B. stopped abruptly, looked up at me, and placed his forearm over mine. "Have you met John Calhoun," he asked, and we turned and walked over to this young man. I extended my hand, shook hands with him, said "hello," and then weakly walked to the other side of the hall. I slowly climbed the stairs, realizing that someone who was a direct descendent of one of the most pivotal figures in all of American history was, 150 years after the death of his famous ancestor, the recipient of an inordinate deference among those who knew him well and not so well, and who obviously felt an affinity for him and his ancestor.

CHAPTER EIGHT

A STRATEGY

How Not to Do It

A panel at the American Historical Association meetings in 2000 judged President Bill Clinton to be an average president.[1] I agree. By standard definition a highly intelligent individual, and by all accounts someone who lent his enormous energy to the difficult office of the presidency, Bill Clinton was still but an average president. A great deal has been written about Mr. Clinton. His own book has appeared, and largely gone. I will not add substantively to the body of work on Mr. Clinton. In this brief subsection, I will merely outline what I think is the best way to think of him, with brief reference to some of what he did as president. I believe the best way to consider Clinton and his presidency is to look at them at ever-rising levels of abstraction.

To be an average president, Bill Clinton must have accomplished good things, and indeed he did. The period from early 1993 through early 2001 marked the most robust economic boom in human history. A great deal of the credit belongs to the private sector, which produced, and utilized, the computer-based technological breakthroughs that truly changed business. But some of the credit belongs to the public sector too, including the then president. Of course, some of the boom was hype, and a stretch, of the law and of expectations. America continued to go into debt and foreign trade balances continued as well.

But beyond the 1994 budget, which did bring a measure of fiscal discipline to the federal government by building on the Graham-Rudman-Hollings Act of 1986 and the George H. W. Bush tax increase during that president's single term, there were two gun control acts, both hard fought and justly won. There was family leave, Americorps, at least a minimal hike in the minimum wage, an increase in the Nixon presidency's earned income tax credit, portability and accountability of insurance, legislation on violence against women, and an agreement with the tobacco companies regarding the advertising of cigarettes to minors, as well as some reparations for the lives tobacco had already taken.

In foreign policy, there were successes in the old Yugoslavia, particularly Bosnia, with progress in Northern Ireland and even a bit with the intractable North Koreans. The Praxis of Good, The Old City and the Israeli-Palestinian conflict generally, only gets older, but at least Clinton tried. If his term had not run out, he might have succeeded, and his aggressive containment was surely preferable to the vote-and campaign-contribution-driven war that George W. Bush has since inflicted on our nation.

Also, Bill Clinton bonded with the nation's principal minority better than any previous president had, at the same time that his court and cabinet appointments more accurately reflected the nation's objective group diversity and protected a woman's right to choose. There was progress on gender pay equity and the protection of gays and lesbians. His embracing of the African-American community in particular perhaps correctly identified Clinton as the first African-American president that the poet Toni Morrison claimed.

On the negative, purely substantive side lies Clinton's continuation of support for the recently renamed School of the Americas, an institution that trains people to do very bad things. There was an inability, not all Clinton's failing to be sure, to have countries such as Haiti sustain a semblance of democracy and areas such as Sub-Saharan Africa pull back from ethnic violence, disease, political instability, and the ravages of long and brutal war.

Domestically, there were failures that balanced the successes as well. The ratio of executive to worker pay exploded to 475, far higher than anywhere in the industrialized world.[2] Since then, the ratio has grown to over 1,000. The use of "permatemps" more than doubled under Clinton, the worker without health care, retirement, or a pension accompanying the more than half of all laid-off workers who got back on the bus making less than what they made when they were told to get off. [3] Of course, not all temps were perma, although the thoroughly dishonest Department of Labor unemployment statistic, still the best example of interparty collusion in Washington, unashamedly counts them as employed. It also counts part-timers, and those who have given up hope altogether are not counted at all, thus artificially reducing the unemployed percentage. I wonder if Clear Channel Radio will ever play Berthold Brecht's original libretto from the *Three Penny Opera,* with its keeping the poor "out of sight," instead of the sanitized 1950s Bobby Darin pretender.

And so the average American, even the fully employed American from the trucker to the single parent that Clinton loved to talk about, found she had to work longer hours, frequently in two or more jobs, than she has worked since before protection for unions, the minimum wage, and the maximum hours laws of over a half century ago were passed. More than half the time now, she worked within a year of her baby's birth.[4]

The ultimate Clinton curse, of course, was health care. Bill and Hillary Clinton, and an army of all-too-closeted wonks, ensured that forty-four million Americans still have no health insurance, a figure that grew considerably in the Clinton years. In fact, the handling of the Clinton health proposal was so bad that the Republicans won the Congress back in 1994, and blocked much of what a friendly legislature might have done in other areas. Campaign finance reform, which should have been job one, was ignored, purposefully ignored in my view, even when the other branch was in friendly hands. Powerful corporate interests, as well as other interests within the Democratic Party, persuaded an all too flexible president that their help would remove the necessity of campaign finance change. And, incredibly, the Clinton administration acceded to pressures to reduce the number of I.R.S. agents, loose auditing of the wealthy and corporations at the close of the Clinton years being routinely acknowledged in Washington and chuckled about at the Versailles, excuse me, Georgetown dinner parties.[5]

The above, again, are merely substantive, objective accomplishments and failures. They are of considerable importance, without question, but they lie at the lowest level of abstraction. We learn more about Bill Clinton at higher levels of abstraction. At these levels, Clinton fares less well. Higher levels of abstraction, of course, are more revelatory of the subjective, subatomic cognitions that remain our principal concern. A ladder of abstraction exists in government just as it does anything else. So what happened under Bill Clinton, at the next level of abstraction, specifically at the level of the social contract? One would think that the social contract could afford to become more generous in flush economic times. One would think that the bonds of a community would strengthen, at least a bit, even if the bonds were purely financial. But, in fact, that did not happen.

The Republicans had complained about welfare (personal not corporate) for a long time, Ronald Reagan making much of the ersatz Chicago "welfare queen," her four Social Security cards, and her four checks. So Bill Clinton accommodated the Republicans, this New Democrat, under the tutelage of former Republican senator Jesse Helms aide Richard Morris, leading the charge for "welfare reform." The open collusion between the parties set their time limits for recipients and, in good economic times, may even have benefited the upper half of those recipients. These were the trainable citizens, those in generally good health and capable of absorption into a booming economy. For the bottom half, in spite of all the continuing hype, the record is not nearly so clear. When the good times became less good for three years, as mothers left their children with caregivers for a dollar an hour more than their welfare would have been and still well below the poverty line, politicians of both major parties collude again, touting a success that is partial at best.

And what happened when this piece of the social contract was chipped away? The rest became negotiable, of course. The Republicans surely came on, with their friends in the investment industry plumping for privatizing Social Security through individual savings accounts. The push for privatizing Medicare through HMOs followed, and then the privatizing of more prisons, and the privatizing of the public schools with magical vouchers, and the miracle of free trade that has prompted the wholesale exporting of jobs overseas, and a lot of other things with which the contract, within the private sector, became the operative mode. The analytics carried the day.

Climb higher still on the abstraction ladder, to the subject no one wants to talk about in Washington, or in political science textbooks: the balance between the legitimate government and the illegitimate government. How did the Outfit, the Wise Guys, do under Bill Clinton? The Russians lost their battle to these people in 1991, and, after seeming to recover, are falling back again. The outfit stills does very well here, particularly the new, ever more dangerous international aggregations, which often are led by Russians. While there were but two gambling states not so long ago, there are now forty-seven. Over forty states are part of lotteries, with more to come. And the gambling operations are all serviced by interesting little companies, that do the marketing, the selling of the machines, and the servicing of the machines and that contribute more than a little to compliant politicians and their handlers wherever they do business.

At that same, structural level of abstraction, must we not coldly evaluate the balance between the public and private sectors? That, after all, is the greatest divide within the American constitutional order? I think so. What, after all, did the megacorporations do to that private/public sector balance? They did a lot, but like Arthur Conan Doyle's dog that didn't bark, the issue was never joined. And so, the banks raised their ATM fees, when it was supposed to be cheaper not to have a teller.[6] And they raised their "spreads" between the interest consumers paid on their loans and the interest they earned on checking, savings, CDs, and the money markets. And their spreads grew when the friendly feds kept the rates low for the banks, falling for the "too large to fail" argument and "the Japanese are larger than we are" argument (untrue because of highly inflated real estate values), and thus keeping away the Antitrust Division of the Justice Department. They also fixed prices on credit cards and merged and acquired in a way that made collusion among the remaining banks, even with what the banks argued were still small market shares, easier than at any time since the 1920s.[7]

Consider only the growth of the "bounced" check fee over the last years, years in which dealing with the check and the customer is easier, and cheaper, than it has ever been. At Bank of America, the bounced check fee in 2003 was already thirty dollars. It is now thirty-two dollars. If you are on the bottom, you do not know how to complain, do you, and you don't have the resources, or the time, to do it either, do you? You just did not get to the bank on time this month, or one of the children got sick and you had to write one more check. Or maybe someone doesn't work somewhere, or anywhere, anymore. The private sector overwhelmed the public's feint attempts at consumer protection. The banks did not just gouge, they gouged at the bottom, and they gouged deep.[8] The analytics won again, and Clinton was with them, those quiet New York dinner parties doing more harm to the citizenry than those in Georgetown did. Why did the Clintons move to New York anyway? They moved there for the same reason Willie Sutton robbed banks.

And the insurance companies? How about the "inflation" adjustments on home insurance and the required 20 percent down payment minimum on home mortgages? And did you try to stop the payments when you got to the 20 percent? The insurance companies notoriously kept charging long after the 20 percent was reached, until you called, and called, and called.

And how about title insurance? Five or six hundred dollars for what could be done for twenty-five dollars, all the title data being in the computer for years. And credit life insurance, and the fact that there is no federal regulation of the insurance industry at all because … well, because the insurance industry does not want it. And what about the slack enforcement of insurance regulations within so many states? [9] The analytics, with Clinton as their friend, triumphed again, in a walk.

Consider alone the impact of the loss of local insurance and banking companies on the states that have no large insurance companies, or the states that have lost their large banks, as South Carolina did, to huge "money center" banks that may be only a few miles across a state line, as they are in Charlotte, North Carolina? More than ever, the big states bled the little states, and Bill Clinton winked at all of this, just as he winked at the securities industry that made billions from the hidden fees, the front loads, the back loads and the quarterly fees on citizens' IRAs, and the inside information going to the wealthiest customers, and the outright lying over stock and bond valuations.

Add to that the credit card industry, owned by the banks, and their increasing penalties, shortening of payment periods, charging when you discontinue a card, and keeping their interest rates high when overall interest rates dropped after the millennium. Then it happened, shortly after Clinton left office: Enron, and Worldcom, and all the conflicts of interest with investment banks and brokerage houses, and even the auditors such as Arthur Anderson who mixed the investment counseling side of their business with the auditing. Clinton loved "self-regulation," and the private sector ran riot with it. Another victory for the analytics, and Bill Clinton.

Lastly at this level, what about telecommunications, the industry that more than ever cradles our speech and our press? Test your memory. Gold stars to those who remember the other newsworthy event on the very day that Bill Clinton gave his 2000 Democratic Convention speech? That was also the day that Rupert Murdoch bought up ten more American television stations, mostly in large markets like San Diego and Houston. He did it under Bill Clinton's Telecommunications Act of 1996, the act that shrunk the Bill of Rights a bit, and made a shrinking number of companies very wealthy indeed.

A week before Bill Clinton left office, AOL and Time Warner had their merger miraculously approved by the Justice Department, and the fees for intrastate phone service in particular just never quite came down, did they? And later, the FCC approved further consolidation, although the Congress later had second thoughts. The private sector, and the analytics, overwhelmed the public sector again.

And so, to the highest level of abstraction which, of course, is cognitions in the government. What happened within the public sector under Bill Clinton? What happened to the cognitively synthetic variable, the core cognitive variable in the public's government? Beyond undemocratic decentralization, type 2 undemocratic elections (recall the more than three billion dollars spent in the 2000 election and the half a million dollar dinner plate with the president and the "I slept with Lincoln" towels), as well as the compressed distribution, what happened under the president who said that "the era of big government is over," just when the global megacorporation was exporting more and more manufacturing jobs and depleting the American middle class?

Was the increasingly analytically biased, oligarchic nature of the government challenged by this Democrat? Or was it enhanced, by one who was just as comfortable with the *form* of it all as the Republicans? At this last level of abstraction, I return, naturally, to the forms. What is the *form* of the mind who smokes marijuana but does not inhale? Who has high school sex but says he did not have sex? To have it both ways, of course, and never, ever have to distinguish; that is what the analytic cognition is all about. Deny the distinction in the first instance, and then you don't have to deal with the contradiction. It is the form of the mind that not only would not differentiate but who often worked the other side, the antigovernmental side, in the always-fluid struggle between the private and the public sectors.

Clinton was the first Democratic president, at least since Grover Cleveland, to advance the oligarchic forms from what substantively looked like the liberal side of the spectrum. He betrayed the forms; he betrayed the shift of the liberal position to the Hamiltonian centripetal structure that the progressives had discovered at the beginning of the twentieth century and that would have fought the barons of the private sector in our own time.

How did Clinton do it? As I began to explain earlier, he did it by sloughing the issue that I believe to be the most important of all contemporary issues: campaign finance reform. He did it when he had majorities in both houses of the Congress, or when he reneged on the essential small "d" democratic promise of popular government, as well as the Bill of Rights' protection of engrossing the aggregated citizenry through the cognitively synthetic form.

Clinton elected not to improve the system but rather to beat his opposition at their own game, taking the money from the corporations he kept so comfortable, as well as the Hollywood set, a group so useful for candidates and causes but which has proved wholly incapable of addressing the more important structural difficulties of our government. At the highest level of abstraction, at the level of the forms, Clinton invariably opted for the analytic cognitive form that, as Chapter Five argues, favored the oligarchy that the Jeffersonian side of America's original ideological divide had always opposed. This less-than-first-rate abstract mind readily made the Faustian bargain concerning the balances between the government and the corporations regarding campaign finance reform, as well as regarding the failure to create an original jurisprudential position that would overturn *Buckley*.

To "walk a fine line" between not helping the questioner and telling the truth? This is the mind that begins his presidency with "don't ask, don't tell" (I can still hear my brother screaming on the phone); and though admittedly there are minds, highly synthetic minds, who would see a contradiction too easily, or who would see the world too readily as a zero sum game, so too there are minds who will never know the contradiction, or its dialectic, and Clinton's mind is one of those.

The forty-second president regaled those who would listen to him about how they could always balance the interests, without victory for either side, on matters of the environment, the economy, the economy's distributions, and on and on. And, incredibly, many people, including even those who wrote critically of him, believed that Clinton was very smart. In fact, Bill Clinton, as I said above, has but a second tier abstract mind. Hegel would have made fun of Clinton, for precisely the reason that he made fun of Kant.

And so, the linkages between the private sector and the public's government became ever more contractual under this Democratic president, as the number of lobbyists on the Beltway and K Street grew, and the number of campaign consultants grew, and the government became less and less a government and more and more a self-checkout private store. The nation's institutional balances, rather than remaining true to the cognitive balances of the subatomic understanding that I believe came unconsciously from the two sets of Founders, became ever more analytic and brought America ever closer to Aristotle's oligarchy.

This is the president who, when Rupert Murdoch was buying more of our television stations, walked down one corridor of white cinder block walls and then another, and another, and popped up on the podium to brag about how he had beaten the other guys with a look on his face that would scare a moose. But the form of competition is not the same as that of contradiction. Competition will never include the new variable—an original, disparate, synthetic variable. Competition merely ratifies the game. It is only the can of Coke fighting the can of Pepsi. It validates the contested, already rationalized variable, always in the form of the analytic cognition. And that is how he had governed. Not to have anticipated the political encumbrances that the Mexican government placed on the NAFTA contract was summa cum dumb.

What is so extraordinary about those who typically write about Bill Clinton is how easily he distracts them by having them think about his character. Even in recent memory there were far more troubled characters. Both Jack Kennedy and Richard Nixon were far more tormented men, and both paid higher prices. It is not easy to leave a political party that you have written a constitution for, but after the president's pre-departure interview in January, 2001, in which he did not use a single synthetic cognition and trumpeted the virtues of automaticity and self-equilibriation within and between the American private and public sectors, I left the Democratic Party.

I cannot put it more plainly. The middle stage of the dialectic, the contradictory stage, is and always will be synthetic. It is the contradiction, not of substance, but of the forms themselves. The contradiction is nothing more, nor less, than the historical apple confronted by the historical orange, the bottle of Coke confronted with the can of Coke. Without the synthetic form, the contradiction is never faced, much less resolved, and history, for Bill Clinton or anyone like him, does not move. The contradiction is never faced by the kind of mind who cannot differentiate between the forms, and who labels the $5 + 7 = 12$ equation as synthetic. Toynbee's "mimesis" or "kind of drill,"like the corporate carousels of the Philadelphia and Los Angeles 2000 political conventions, increasingly make America "deaf to the dull ears of Orpheus' lyre." This is not how to do it.

How to Do It

What happens once a political system becomes an oligarchy and the analytic cognition dominates the system? There are only two ways out. You either return to the center gently or you rush past the center without stopping, ignoring Aristotle's *meson,* or middle, in a dash to the other extreme. One never knows which will happen, but one thing is certain. An unequilibriated system will not stay that way for long.

Can America reequilibriate gently? I hope so, and I will suggest how I think it should be done. But first let me refer to what kinds of political coalitions might initiate reequilibriation. There are many coalitions in politics. But politics' most enduring coalition, I venture to say politics' classical coalition, is that between a strong leader and the populace, in opposition to a variety of more or less aristocratic groups that represent interests, and the continuation of the privileges that the aristocratic position had ensured. Shakespeare's *Julius Caesar* describes this alliance better than any political writing. It was Caesar's aggregation of the citizenry, circumventing the tribunes, that fired Cassius's lean and hungry look, and Brutus's et tu.

I am old enough to remember 1949, when Clement Atlee's Labour government clipped the wings of the Lords, limiting their jurisdiction, as well as the delay they could inflict on legislation from two to one years. But, incredibly, the British task is unfinished into the twenty-first century. The once decisively elected Labour prime minister Tony Blair has still never removed all the hereditary peers.

In response to America's untitled lords, or those who controlled the banks, the insurance companies, and the investment houses, among others, American political history has traditionally witnessed either the Populist position, the William Jennings Bryan perspective for example, or the more sophisticated Progressive perspectives of, for instance, Theodore Roosevelt, Woodrow Wilson, and the great Governor Robert LaFollette of Wisconsin. These perspectives signaled the rise of leaders who aligned themselves with those who could not fight the aristocracy alone. But these were also American leaders without the excesses of a Caesar, for they were, at one level, mere citizens who saw their role as assisting other citizens in the overturning of privilege. In such times, America was fortunate to have moderate but powerful left-of-center leaders, men, and sometimes women, who were committed to true, if limited, democracy. Those leaders confronted the robber barons' imbalances with creations such as the direct election of senators, the graduated income tax, suffrage for women, along with sub-constitutional antitrust enforcement, and protection of the worker, without a hint of the authoritarian left.

At one time in American history, of course, the risk of passing through Aristotle's constitutional democracy, and coming to what may have been a very real tyranny was possible. That time was during the Great Depression, when one figure, the only man Franklin Roosevelt ever politically feared, plotted to gain political power, even within the federal government, and rule in an almost Caesar-like way. The figure was Huey Long, the kingfish, the American demagogue, who promised to make "every man a king"and the one figure who, in all of our political history, probably most threatened our democracy.

Not surprisingly, Long's path to tyranny would have grown out of Aristotle's corrupted form of constitutional democracy: direct democracy. After all, the Louisiana governor, and senator, rose to power with a direct appeal to the little people, evidenced and made simpler in his home state of Louisiana by the combination of the Depression and the long-standing excesses of the state's Bourbons. The Aristotelian spectrum in the United States, at least through the Depression period, was still an objectively based, not subjectively based, spectrum.

Long, Father Coughlin, and others of the objective left who propagandized for their little tyrannies were almost wholly of the subjective, or psychological, right. But remember that Bryan, for all of his concern for the little man, wound up his career with fundamentalism and little else. In fact, the subjective left has been manifested but rarely in the real world of political leadership, such European figures as Ignace Paderewski in inter-war Poland, Vaclav Havel in the Czech Republic, Willy Brandt in Germany, and Olaf Palme in Sweden perhaps being the best twentieth-century examples. In the United States, the subjective left has had but meager political representation, recent figures such as Eugene McCarthy, George McGovern, and perhaps most notably, Dr. Martin Luther King Jr. heading a short list. In the Eastern world in the twentieth century, none was greater than the Mahatma, although long ago the Buddha and Taoism's Lao Tze taught political and moral lessons that were much more of the subjective left than the lessons of the Western faiths.

Yes, before the subatomic moment, tyranny has almost universally been imposed by those of the analytic mind. The conceptually horizontal, that is the subjective, representation of Aristotle's trilogy, has not been appropriate until recently. The psychologically analytic tyrant gave the polity its overaggregation, not from a desire to bond the citizenry in productive and equitable ways, but from a desire to rule alone. Nonetheless, it is fair for critics of the left to suggest that an extreme synthetic perspective can also create a tyranny at the other end of the psychological spectrum. It can be as oppressive as Plato's philosopher kings or Jean-Jacques Rousseau's forcing all men to be free.

Similarly, history's corrupted aristocracies have not always been the products of the analytic mind. But the subatomic moment signals the time when that mind's very favoring of the most structurally centrifugal and procedurally contractual side of the spectrum does support oligarchy. What I offer for the gentle turn away from America's oligarchy, back to a limited democracy, is a strategy for change that must include those constitutional and subconstitutional, cognitively synthetic, alterations that groups such as the Committee on the Constitutional System proposed. I proffer these ideas in the spirit of our twin Founders' limited democracy, ever cautious of the Huey Long variant of objectively left tyranny, as well as the excessively synthetic subjective tyranny of a Plato or a Rousseau.

What, after all, is the place of the objective left and the subjective left within the framework of a subatomic, subjectively based theory? What should become of the objective left, the left with its deep and justified commitment to so many issues and groups in twentieth-century politics? To all who have been deeply involved in objectively based political activities, the economic, gender, sexual orientation, racial, and similarly based kinds of activities, I have only urged the addition of the full-blown subjective variable to politics' theoretical map, not the wholesale rejection of what you have already been doing. My suggestion, I think, diminishes your claim on equity not one bit; in fact it enhances it.

All fabrics have a warp and woof. The political right has benefited from at least a fair degree of cooperation between those who want only to advance their objective positions in one way or another (i.e., making money) and those who are cognitively comfortable with entities such as the contractual, analytic form and are thus similarly comfortable with an oligarchic governmental order. On the other side, The Natural Left must do no less than bond all of us far better than the contractually based objective interfacing of income, gender, race, or sexual orientation ever did.

Though I am an unqualified supporter of unions, women's groups, gay and lesbian groups, and almost all other objectively left aggregations, I suggest that their lobbying and electoral activities alone have frequently failed to challenge, and in subtle if unintended ways have even ratified, the oligarchy. They may have inadvertently contributed to the cognitively analytic domination of our legislative, judicial, and executive branches. Although objectively the unions have fought the corporations, and women and their allies have fought the misogynists, and gays and lesbians have fought gender-preference intolerance, and so forth, none of these groups have ever sought to reform the system, as a system. I suggest that there will be no reform of the system, no change in America's systemically caused inequities, without the full participation of a subjectively based political orientation, specifically the orientation of the Natural Left.

Only the Natural Left will successfully bond the components of the objective left. Only the Natural Left is intellectually inclined to give its first attention to the very forms of the political system itself. It does so in ways that will help ensure the victory of the objective left positions, but it will do much more. I say this in the context of the new American distributional diamond rather than in the traditional pyramid-shaped distributions of income and wealth. The Natural Left will ensure the fairness of wages, a fairness that only comes from an unashamedly result-oriented sense of proportion. For those who seek proportionate distributions for proportionate contributions, and for those who do not see the world in purely economic terms and who wish to lead the kind of balanced life that includes both economic and noneconomic pursuits, I think an understanding of the Natural Left is crucial. It is the Natural Left, not the objective left, that addresses the forms themselves, within a subatomic notion of balances among different kinds of minds and the different personalities that house such minds. This, I suggest, is the necessary third level of theoretical equity that the twenty-first century must move toward.

It is now time for America's psychological left, in other words, to commit to a subjectively centered entity such as a national, and eventually an international, movement and/or political party that consciously includes the Natural Left. Of course, each citizen can easily continue their identifications with objectively based, Whole Group Equity groupings or political parties. But I believe that only a Natural Left-based political entity can incorporate all of the objectively based pleas for equity, that is, the equities of all specific groupings of citizens, into a global coalition. Only a global coalition will both maintain the integrity of each objective grouping, and bind these groups together as they have never been bonded before.

As you have gathered, I believe that the subjective political thread is richer than any strategic, contractually based threading of objective groups. This new hemp should bind together those who, by being naturally favorable to the synthetic cognition, transcend the single economic or social cause that so often relies on contractual forms of alliances in order to achieve what are all too often momentary coalitions. It alone moves to the permanent, subjectively bound, embracing of justice for all, within a subjectively as well as objectively varied human society.

Let us not forget our ideological history. We on the left, throughout political history, have been defeated by our own conflicts more than by anything else. Like the Popular Front in the Spanish Civil War that was greatly subverted by the subjectively analytic and right wing Stalinists, so many left-of-center American movements have fallen short because of their own bickering, and because of the eventual dominance of the objective left that turned out to be subjectively right wing within objectively left organizations. I can look back to the left of the 1950s, curiously, and find more of the subjectively left glue there than I find in any other American period, even the 1960s. I now urge that that kind of bonding, reflectively understood within a new, psychological, and particularly cognitive context, be a permanent part of the left.

The 1950s, remember, gave us Jack Kerouac, William Burroughs, and Allen Ginsberg. It gave us J. D. Salinger's Holden Caulfield, Robert White's *The Organization Man*, Sloan Wilson's *The Man in the Grey Flannel Suit*, and it gave us James Dean, whose greatest movie was *Rebel <u>Without</u> a Cause* (emphasis mine). Most importantly, of course, it gave us *Mad Magazine*, and Alfred E. Newman, a.k.a. Melvin Coznowsky. In the 1960s many of us marched for civil rights and attended anti-Vietnam War rallies, but the fifties, speaking out against McCarthy, was somehow deeper than the sixties. There was more solitude, and thus more of a bond.

And, regarding the subjective left's relationship to the objective left, I cannot fail to refer once more to the figure whom I have argued needs now to be supplanted. That figure, as you know, is Karl Marx. Though I have never been a Marxist, and though there is no question that some of the last century's worst tyrannies came from perverted forms of Marxism (Stalin, Mao, Pol Pot, etc.), this individual was still and all the most imposing left-of-center theorist for 150 years. We do not walk away from him as that principal left figure lightly. Neither shall we remember him through the vulgar interpretations that saw him only as a philosophical Materialist, without his genuinely human concerns and respect for the great Idealists like Hegel.

A brilliant, disciplined, passionate, and tireless advocate, sitting at his table in the British Museum or in his unheated London flat, Marx did no less than bring the entire second-tier political debate into full flower. As I suggested at the outset, it is Marx's thought, more than anyone else's, that still underpins so much of the Whole Group Equity arguments that will inevitably remain a part, if now a more junior part, of a subatomic, subjectively based political movement.

In one way, we stand on Marx's shoulders. Yet, in another and more sobering way, Marx impedes our progress as we must now learn to walk by ourselves. More than ever, I believe that knowing who we are is even more important than knowing what we are. The human mind's responsibility for the path of history cannot be subjugated any longer to the twin notions that our personality is no more than the sum of our social relations, and that the objective realities of the world are what lead us through history. Our personality, though marvelously adaptive, is still largely inherent, real and essential. Our common destiny is in the hands of our common, if very differentiated, human minds.

In short, Hegel was doing just fine on his feet, unlike what Feuerbach said about him, even if the greatest philosopher since the Greeks only intuited the psychological side of his extraordinary insights. Now that a subjectively based grounding is available to us, and now that that subjective grounding can be seen in all of its marvelous relativity, we can understand how Hegel's vision was always, at least potentially, more powerful than Marx's. My own contribution of what I believe to be a powerful, original political philosophy began with nothing more than a subjectivizing, or a reading through, of both Kant and Hegel, and then placing these philosophers along the principal subjective spectrum. From there, I hoped that something would take root that begins with an extension of knowledge beyond Hegel's synthetically a priori limits, or even Hegel's exclusively synthetic form for the dialectical improvement of knowledge.

We can now, more than ever before, have the subjectivized Kant and Hegel extend the limits to knowledge beyond Hegel's synthetic a priori to the simultaneous vision of both the analytic and the synthetic forms. At the same time, the newly subjectivized, and relativized, dialectic can incorporate the post-Hegelian vision that finds its historical stages, unlike Judith Shklar's accurate vision of Hegel's dialectic as a single, ordered whole, as something that occurs in cognitive alternation. The essentialist and the historically classical or Idealist visions are ready to reclaim their rightful place at the head of the philosophical train. A new political philosophy, and I fervently hope a new political movement, will thrive because of it.

That philosophy will answer, I think better than any other perspective, the pap from the right that argues that the world will adopt America's current form of democracy, our form of free markets, and our form of something that sounds a lot more like Christendom than Jesus to me. A new, cognitively relative political philosophy will not embrace a simplistic, linear progression of history. It is a truism to say that those who do not understand nonlinear history, like those who do not understand nonlinear mathematics, are invariably those who do not understand the dialectic. They do not understand the dialectic because, at the outset, they do not understand difference. They cannot envision 5 + Blue, and they will never understand why there will be no Pax-Analytica.

A Caution

With new understanding, of course, comes new responsibility, if only because there is indeed new danger at the level of the subatomic tier. I shall not overdramatize it, but I merely recall that at one time it might have been easy to comprehend the subatomic notions of Nils Bohr and Ernest Rutherford, or even comprehend Albert Einstein, with his specific and general theories of relativity that grew from the first subatomic vision, without thinking much of where it might all lead. Of course, it is no longer possible to think that way. Hiroshima and Nagasaki took care of that, and if you cannot travel to Japan then spend a moment just north of the corner of 57th and Ellis Streets in Chicago. This is where Enrico Fermi split the atom and sustained the nuclear reaction, under the stands at old Stagg Field on the University of Chicago campus. It is a humbling place indeed.

No, the potential problems of a subjectively oriented politics are not as dire as the bomb. But just as it was easy to pervert the benevolent intentions of Marx, so it would be easy to imagine something equivalent to what Arthur Koestler and George Orwell wrote of, even before we knew all that we now know about human psychology and, more recently, the human genome. I realize that a subjectively based political philosophy could be twisted in most undemocratic ways since one psychological side could well come to dominate the other as these positions become politics' front line.

There is nothing in my theory that assures that all psychologies will be treated fairly beyond our ever-deepening knowledge of the psychological differentiation itself. Its inherent plea for a psychological, subatomic standard of equity, and its assertion that all societies need all kinds of minds, must stand on its own feet. Anything less is bigotry, just as surely as was race-based, gender-based, sexual-orientation-based, and all the other objective kinds of bigotry. I can only guarantee that the conflict of the advanced democracies is now conceptually horizontal, or subjective, the United States perhaps more than any advanced nation shortchanging the synthetic mind in its political structures and processes.

In short, I believe that something that reflects a kind of cognitive bigotry within the American government has been going on for a long time. A form of psychological discrimination already exists within the Washington government, within the pack of lobbyists and most certainly within the exploding campaign industry with its pollsters, consultants, focus groups, and operatives that now control America's elections. It is the unanswered analytic cognition, the cognition that is both objectively and subjectively comfortable with selling itself to wealthy customers, in part for the money and in part to ratify the contractual, cognitively analytic form itself. This is what is clearly in charge. A new, second layer of oligarchy covers, and covers for, the old layer so easily because it reflects the exact same cognitive imbalances of the people over whom it fawns.

The Natural Left must not compromise about this. We must speak directly for the necessary political contributions of the Natural Left, to the necessity for a new bonding within the American society and the necessity for the inclusion of values that reflect more than the analytic form. The calculus of this psychological bigotry has already had more effect on the American political system than it has had on the more cognitively balanced political systems of Western and even Central Europe, Canada, Australia, New Zealand, and even India. For a long time I have not thought of the United States as one of the world's most democratic countries.

Interviewed on a PBS Nightly News show shortly after the 2000 election, former president Jimmy Carter noted that the United States would not be eligible for the election supervision so often offered all over the world by his Atlanta based Carter Center. The absence of a uniform set of election rules and the absence of a single overseeing election body, both damaging qualities of our undemocratic decentralization and oligarchy, now disqualify our country from Carter Center oversight.

Let us not forget that our system's inability to achieve political equity results from its objectively based politics' only offering incremental, nondialectical, forms of change. Whether it was the proletariat versus the bourgeoisie, men versus women, straights versus gays, or whites versus blacks, the objective groupings formed only a conceptually vertical duality. Even Marx's historical dialectic, by being of Materiality and not of mind, was largely if not wholly analytic. The Material position was not simply a reversal of historical leadership but a cognitive simplification of the dialectical form, as the economic proletariat confronted an economic, thus cognitively similar, bourgeoisie.

Taking full responsibility as the creator of the Natural Left, I concede that the subjective, psychological range will only gradually form a dialectical opposition. Remember that the subjective range is just that: a range. Though I have described it in shorthand as a duality (Kant's and Hegel's preferred analytic and synthetic cognitions, respectively), I said at the outset that we were always dealing with a spectrum. The analytic-to-synthetic cognitions make up a human continuum that exists within any objective group of people. I suspect that that psychological spectrum will, for a time, almost certainly spill over the sides of a still conceptually vertical, objectively based arrangement of public opinion aggregators such as America's political parties. In my view, the subjective range is already spilling out from the edges of America's objectively based political parties, Ralph Nader's 2 3/4 percent presidential vote after many left him because of the late-in-the-day realization that the election would be close, probably evidencing that subjective spillage better than anything we have yet seen.

Nader's votes were of a different cast, he speaking largely to the structural corruptions of the American government. Whether my reader is sympathetic or not to the Nader effort, it is curious that not one significant Democrat has had the courage since 2000 to stand up and say that Nader was right on the issues of corporate influence on the American government and the resultant centrifugal distortions of our political processes. I met Ralph Nader only after the 2000 election but his comments to me and a small South Carolina gathering demonstrated a considerable understanding of the American government's structural decay. Almost wholly ignored by the press, and with access to far fewer ballots than he possessed as a Green candidate in 2000, Nader still polled almost half a million votes in 2004, all third party candidates fighting the "compressed distribution" by gathering over 1% of the vote in an election that the two parties argued, with some justification in my view, was absolutely crucial to the country's future.

Objectively based orientations that existed at the poles of a conceptually "vertical" party spectrum have been dying out for some time, (like the American Communists on the left, or, much earlier in our history, the Federalists who affected and would have perfected aristocracy on the right). Subjectively based orientations like that of the Greens on the left, or even of those who follow Harry Browne on the libertarian right, now challenge the current, broadly centrist major parties and will not assimilate into the American mainstream without a truly relativisitic appreciation of the complementarity of different, subjectively derived, perspectives.

Again, the roots of these new psychological orientations are natural. They are essential, not existential. They are, therefore, deeper and potentially more intensely psychological than objectively based identifications. They grow out of who we are, not what we are. It is a fact of American politics that our country has avoided class conflict precisely because of the hopes for material improvement and the realization of those hopes by so much of its population. It has avoided deeper racial divisions than it has had because, eventually, African Americans and other minorities realized at least some of their just due. These groups' objectively based perspectives were always subject to change, but psychological orientations are less capable of either change or cooptation, particularly at their extremes, unless something is pointedly done to incorporate subjectively based politics into the American political system.

Put another way, although objectively based complaints about the American political system were historically either dismissed or co-opted, the system soon returning to its quiescent two party, procedurally democratic norm, such ameliorative processes will more than likely be more difficult to achieve with subjectively based criticisms. The subjective range makes ameliorative processes more difficult, and multiparty politics, in a political system that I obviously believe to be too decentralized already, may well occur. Believe it or not, I favor a more or less two-party political system, except when the polity is at the second or contradictory stage of the dialectical progression, or when the two parties, as I discussed earlier, have become compressed. The "di" in dialectic stands for something.

But third parties may, as they frequently have in the past, become necessary during the second, contradictory, or "for itself" dialectical stage of historical change, particularly if the two major parties choose not to confront a historical contradiction, and thus shun the cognitively synthetic variable. I do not believe in proportional representation. After mulling it over for a long time, I still favor first past the post. But I also believe that the current electoral barriers for third-party ballot access in many American states must be significantly lowered. Genuine opportunities must be available for third parties—to become second parties, or first—and public financing and at least long-term ballot status once a threshold has been achieved, must also be part of the bargain. I also believe in instant runoff voting, in which second choices are factored in when lesser candidates' votes are proven insufficient.

How do we deal, then, with an uncontrolled spillover of the subjectively oriented vote? We must first acknowledge the subjective range's ideological ascendance, and thus permit the analytic-to-synthetic cognitive distinction to peacefully become the bedrock of the American party, and eventually a global party, loyalty. I predict no less than that the analytic and synthetic cognition will soon become the central organizing principle of America's major political parties, with left-of-center candidates speaking openly of a bent of mind, or a psychological perspective, or of whatever else transcends the objective political identification. Some of this is already beginning to happen in Europe.

I believe that a disproportionate number of the citizens who do not vote in this country are of the subjective or Natural Left rather than the Natural

Right. On the whole, the Natural Right has done a better job of combining with the objective right, in great part because it can strongly identify with both religious and economic institutions, and also because its location within all institutions typically rests at the defining borders. This is why the warp and woof of subjective and objective variables on the left are now so necessary.

Having said all of that, however, I still remind the reader that the subatomic moment's coming means that the Natural Left's day has also arrived. It is time now for the Natural Left to do what it does best, that being to aggregate the political left, and oppose the Natural and objective right from an altogether new direction. Again, no temporary coalition of objectively based left-of-center groups can accomplish this. The new fight is subjective at its core. It is conceptually horizontal.

I said in my section on Bill Clinton and "How Not to Do It" that the key to the next level, the third tier of theoretical understanding, is never to stop seeing the system as a whole, and as it should be. My general sense of proportion in the distributions of income and wealth, for example, comes from nothing more complicated, or extreme, than the sense of proportion that Aristotle defined in *The Politics*, or that Pericles spoke of regarding Athen's politics and architecture, or that I learned growing up, looking up at Chicago's architecture.

With difficulty to be sure, we can bring America's party system together under the subjective tents of the analytic and the synthetic cognition. I think we do that best when we accept the deep balances and harmonies among the ideologically complementary founding institutions of our government: the first seven articles of the Constitution and the Bill of Rights. I think we are helped in doing that when we reclaim the natural balances among centripetal and centrifugal forces within core institutions such as the United States Congress.

The American political system will need to sustain a period of transition, a transition from a time when things such as social and economic identifications dominated political party arrangements. But that is the price for moving to a subjectively responsive politics. Certainly, the enhanced equity that will come from a subjectively responsive politics will greatly outweigh the short-term costs. Even disfavored objective groups will be better treated once the political system has rebalanced itself structurally, as well as addressed the entire panoply of equity issues from a broader perspective than what objective groupings alone can bring.

What is also very clear is that the psychological left, the Natural Left, is not going to support a wholly objectively based, that is interest-based, Democratic Party any longer. The Democratic Party will need to acknowledge the Natural Left and correspondingly remove a degree of influence from those objective groupings, like the banks and the insurance companies that have so recently increased their influence in that party. Little parties like South Carolina's and Illinois's United Citizens Party, as well as larger parties like the Greens who now exist in over one hundred countries, will increasingly haunt the Democratic Party. One little fact that has astounded me is that the American Democratic Party never attempted to become an international party at a time when such an activity would have united a moderate left across the world, and acted as a synthetic warp to the woof of global corporatism. Now, someone else has done it. One of the things that Mikhail Gorbachev assured me of was that global parties would come, in their appropriate dialectical way.

To be sure, I still have problems with America's Greens, many of whom mindlessly cling to a 1960s ideal of decentralization without any sense of what the imbalance of centrifugal and centripetal forces in the American government has caused. Many Greens also hang on to such dubious positions as statehood for Washington, D.C. Others now argue for giving a House vote to the District. But this does not help with Senatorial representation and, at the same time, it would lock in a House seat for a population that is already well below the House average and will be farther below after the 2010 census. Since the D. C. population has fallen to 550,000 (July 1, 2005) and Maryland's population has hit 5.6 million (July 1, 2005), isn't it time for the national government to vigorously persuade its junior federalist partner to permit the retrocession of Washington's residential neighborhoods, not unlike the South-of-Potomac retrocession to Virginia of 1846? Yes, it will take an amendment to do it.

Yes, the disenfranchising of the D. C. resident rivals the disenfranchising of two-thirds of America's presidential voters in something called the Electoral College in the State's Wrongs Competition of the American political system. If the Greens can debug themselves from its 1960s holdover positions and assimilate synthetically derived notions like undemocratic decentralization, type 2 undemocratic elections, and the compressed distribution, their party will grow here as it has around the world. The synthetic cognition is the Hamiltonian position, remember, the current lack of a strong federal government enabling the private sector to do what it has been doing, as we have been discussing.

Regarding all of America's institutions, a subjectively based political philosophy, one based on the Natural Left in my view, will gather strength because its roots are innate, growing out of the very essence of human nature within at least some portion of the population. It will not go away because the creative intellect, the intellect of the synthetic cognition, is every bit as powerful as the intellect of the analytic cognition. Indeed, in my judgment, it is only the Natural Left that can reverse the awful work product of those office holders, both Republican and Democrat, who have now greatly weakened this country's government by surrendering it in little pieces to the private sector institutions and their contractual forms.

Perhaps, as the global corporation and its national champions have brought the dominance of the analytic cognition to the level of global politics through the unbridled jurisdictions of the IMF, the World Bank, NAFTA, the WTO, and other overwhelmingly contractual organizations, the dominance of the analytics themselves will breed its own comeuppance, at the global level as well as the national level. It is the synthetic cognition that underpins the just considerations of human rights, the environment, wage parity and other burdens on globalization as proper encumbrances on the transnational contract. Only the synthetic cognition will build the alternative global institutions, such as a worldwide party, that challenge analytically based institutions and processes.

I suggest that a twenty-first-century use of outdated, twentieth-century terms like capitalism and socialism will only impair our political transcendence to the next level of theoretical and real-world understanding. I stopped using these labels years ago. The twenty-first-century ideological battle is wholly different from the twentieth-century battle, just as the twentieth-century battle was different from the nineteenth-century struggle. As advanced societies move to the third, or subatomic, tier of political opposition, the political contest will increasingly be between the analytics and the synthetics within those advanced countries, just as it will eventually be throughout the global order.

As I have said, the conceptually vertical ideological battles of the twentieth century's Whole Group Equity interests, like the ideological battles of the twentieth century at least in the developed world, are being supplanted by conceptually horizontal, subjective and subatomic confrontations. For every objectivity, there is a subjectivity. The Third World too will be differently impacted by how the developed world resolves those confrontations. But it will only survive when the subjective consideration is allowed to balance the objective, in their nations as well as in the West.

In the first instance, what will go on will be an intellectual battle, with the analytics already well financed in such intellectual whorehouses as the Heritage Foundation, the Cato Institute, the Hudson Institute, the American Enterprise Institute, and Stanford University's Hoover Institution. To label their work for what it is, to expose the cognitive biases behind their political biases, and to expose both those biases' impact on Washington, the IMF, the World Bank, etc. in terms that go beyond economics, will be the easy part. It is not difficult to show how these institutions' agendas invariably favor the analytic cognition, in every economic and political arena.

But to fairly balance the analytics, at the next level of theoretical abstraction, will be difficult, although it will not be as difficult as it would have been if those feeding off their corporate sponsors had ever engaged in serious theoretical inquiry and writing. Fortunately, the entire intellectual output of these mediocrities is mid-range at best. And remember: I have been generous with the analytics. I have included them equally within the limits to knowledge equation and granted them their appropriate dominance within the first and third stages of the dialectic (Chapter Three). I doubt if the Natural Right, and particularly the contributors to and water carriers for the above institutions, would ever be so generous with us. The Natural Left, in short, will have to fight for its place at the intellectual, and political, tables. But if it fights, it will be stronger than any objectively-based left group, if not stronger than all of the left groups combined.

We begin that fight, I suggest, by remembering the natural pyramid of intellectual endeavor. Modern knowledge still reflects the ladder of abstraction. The deepest moral and philosophical questions remain at the top of that ladder. It is not just that legally oriented groups such as The Federalist Society and the Liberty Fund, for example, disgorge incredible amounts of analytically biased jurisprudence. It is also true that such groups are as pretentious as they are biased, for they wrap the study of the law into a cocoon that seals off the more abstract and more fundamental philosophical questions, along with the real-world empirical realities, that lie conceptually above the jurisprudential subfield. In this sense, I am not an egalitarian. Jurisprudence, economics, political science, and all the other disciplines are but subfields and sorely need to be put in their place.

The worst pretenders, of course, are the economists, the cognitive biases of those such as the Chicago School being not only considerable in their volume but also much a part of an unwillingness, and inability, to abstract a set of economic dogmas into the larger questions that might transcend their work. In great part, it is the presumptuousness of the economic discipline, a field that would pretend to stand alone, that has maintained the primacy of the capitalism versus socialism argument as the core political debate. Stop arguing capitalism, or any brand of economics, with the analytics. Trump them, and do it by insisting on the intellectual primacy of those far-more-fundamental-than-economic questions that live at the top of the knowledge pyramid. Remind a conservative listener not only of the specific counterbalancing prescriptions of labor unions and antitrust protection in Adam Smith's economic work, but also of the Enlightenment influences of the earlier, moral writings of Smith, the latter setting the framework for the Scotsman's devotion to proportion in economics, and not the other way around. Few today read Smith's philosophical *Theory of Moral Sentiments,* beneath which all of Smith's economics, with its countermarket balances, lies.[10]

In view of the above, I submit that it is no longer debatable that there will only be equity and justice in the United States, and there will only be equity and justice in our rapidly integrating world, when subjective, subatomic political balances and harmonies are established within both our political philosophy and our political institutions. No objectively based political philosophy, and no objective group, ensures that, nor will it ever. For many of its residents, the politics of the United States, the wealthiest and the most well-educated nation in the history of the world, has fallen away from even the most minimal standards of justice and equity in the last years, in great part because it has not properly prescribed for it. That is why the American political system has fallen into oligarchy at the same time that it has created the most egregious distortions of American income and wealth since the 1880s. It has also created an egregious imbalance between economic and noneconomic values, the maintenance of that balance being the mark of a civilized society.

To say that the world is becoming an infinitely more complex place is a cliché. But it is hardly a cliché to argue that just as within every objectivity there is a subjectivity in any nation's politics, so too the subjective range will need consciously to be balanced in the twenty-first century within the entire global polity. Even within developed nations, the growing diversities of ethnicities, religions, and the like require that those who represent those objectivities are confronted with the full range of subjectively-based orientations. The rapid integration of our world means that nation-states and other global actors must contribute their own full range of subjective orientations to the global arena. If this does not happen, inequities even deeper than those we have already witnessed will cripple the world.

Regarding world peace, I do not know of any other way to ensure it, and at the same time equitably resolve the world's difficulties with respect to the environment, human rights, and the just treatment of the world's workers, other than to start at the core, and with a standard of subjective, subatomically derived political and economic equity. The subjective must philosophically precede the objective, at all levels. It must be a full participant in the finding and enacting of just standards in all areas. Put simply, there must be a subjective equilibrium within all objective atoms before there is justice among the atoms themselves that balances Kant's classically liberal view of peace among the nations. That is what subatomic theory requires, again at the global as well as the national levels.

Let it be clear that I respect the writings of those who have researched human psychology over many years in the Freudian, and even Marxian, developmental tradition. Surely, the environmentally based underpinnings of such writings contain great insight. I acknowledge that a return to philosophical essentialism, and the necessary and consequent return to the classical, or Idealist, dialectic, is more than a bit of a stretch for many who have spent their academic lives within the other tradition.

Having said that, I nonetheless believe that only a political philosophy that returns to an essentialist notion of an inherent psychological relativity, and that founds itself, in the first instance, on a plea for subjective equity across that relativity through a) an understanding of the Natural Left, b) an understanding of the Natural Left's role in support of the public sector, c) an understanding of the Natural Left's commitment to the fair representation of the synthetic cognition in all of its political structures and processes, will successfully navigate America's, and the world's, ever emerging dialectical contradictions. A fundamental understanding of the universal relativities, not some ersatz resolution of the vapid deconstructionist, existentialist, and "post-modernist" arguments that have pitted universality and relativity against each other as they occupied whole careers of both academic mesominds and the right wing moralistic community, is what will bring equity, and peace, to the world. The universal truth is relative and it is found within the subatomic subjectivities. It is time that this is understood, on the Boulevard St. Germain, and in the American academy.

Wilmette, Illinois

There are very few places left where you can still get a soft drink called a green river. When I was a kid, no drug store soda fountain would dare not have the carbonated lime phosphate drink among its offering of sodas, or what midwesterners still call "pop."

I remember the whole experience, and in remembrance, it is the sound of the phosphate mixer shooting out of the fountain into the inverted paper cone with a loud "psshhhh" that stays with me the most. The water hit the paper hard, and the syrup would splash around and sometimes spill. But when the green river was filled to the top, it was bubbling ferociously. Sometimes the soda jerk would put the straw in it for you. But mostly you preferred to do it yourself, after tearing off one end of the wrapper, putting the straw in your mouth, blowing the wrapper at your friend, and then swizzling the straw around in your soda for a while. The ice helped.

One of the few places that still serve a green river is on Broadway Street in Chicago, in a little delicatessen that still asks you whether you want a pickle, or chips, or a pop. But my favorite place is up on Green Bay Road in Wilmette. And yet, even there the green river is made with Seven-Up now. There is no "psshhhh" in what is now invariably a glass, and you sit in a booth because there is no counter. And it costs too much.

But at least you can sit there and look out the window at the bank of land that runs all the way from Chicago to Green Bay, Wisconsin, and know that this is where the native Americans walked, back and forth, for many centuries, until people came who, unlike the French, decided they didn't want to live with them and intermarry with them, and so pushed them farther West.

You can sit there and have a green river but think about another green river, when the nitrogen and the phosphorous run off into the water and the plant life goes nuts, and then there is too much oxygen trying to kill it all off, and that takes oxygen from everything else. The technical name is eutrofication, and you wouldn't want to drink from this green river because all the fish have died in it and it is past time now to do a great deal more about this than clean up certain sites that have the known runoff. We need to stop the nonsense all along the river, where the fertilizers drain a little bit at a time, all the time.

So you can sit with your green river pop in Wilmette, Illinois, and think about how beautiful the Baha'i Temple is, the Mother Temple of the West for the Baha'i faith, just down the street. Or you can think about the people who got you started thinking about politics. And so I muse a bit about Eugene V. Debs, who traveled tirelessly all across the Midwest organizing the American Railway Union, and then standing up to George Pullman in this nation's greatest labor strike.

Or I think about Governor John Peter Altgeld, who freed the last of the Haymarket prisoners and stood up to a president, Grover Cleveland, who had called in federal troops because he said Debs wasn't letting the mails through. The real reason was because Cleveland's attorney general, Richard Olney, was getting a check from the railroads at the same time he was getting a smaller check from the government. And then, at the end of his second term, Cleveland refused to support the next Democratic nominee, William Jennings Bryan, voting instead for a seventy-nine-year-old Civil War general, John M. Palmer, who ran as a "National Democrat" although his sole office had been governor of Illinois, as a Republican. After the election, Cleveland told his friends he was glad McKinley had won. Altgeld, who initiated many laws protecting women and children, humanizing prisons, and responding to the just claims of workers, couldn't run for president. He was born in Germany.

And then I recall the governor and U.S. senator Robert LaFollette, who was from Wisconsin and who fought the banks and the insurance companies, and the so-called Stalwarts in his Republican Party who loved the banks, the insurance companies, and everything else that had money. In 1924 LaFollette ran for president, won his own state, and beat the conservative Democrat, John W. Davis, in eleven other states, because he stood for something very different from Davis, and the Democratic Stalwarts.

Or I think about Jane Addams. who with her loyal friend, decided that women alone needed a place to stay, and a place to work, and an atmosphere that shel-

tered them from what a lot of men would have done to them, if they hadn't done it already. Disappointed as I am that The University of Illinois—Chicago tore down so much Chicago history in the Halsted Street, Roosevelt Road area, I am grateful that they at least saved two of Jane Addams's Hull House buildings, one her home and the other one of the old factory buildings. Bring your daughters there, just west of the loop, and show them what two very courageous women did a long time ago.

But I worry some, too. I worry mostly about the South, where I taught for thirty-four years. What is the model there? Will someone replace John C. Calhoun? I would like to think so, and I see one early evidence that someday all southerners will recognize what an extraordinary figure Martin Luther King Jr. was, and not just because of what he did for African Americans. Near the end of his life King spoke more broadly, to the status of women and to wages and working conditions. At the very end, he spoke about the Vietnam War, and it might have been what killed him.

Perhaps too many of us, myself included, have been solely focused on Dr. King's civil rights efforts to realize how comfortably he transcended his personal objectivity. On reflection, he may have been even more of the synthetic cognition, more of the Natural Left, than the Midwestern figures, Debs and Altgeld, LaFollette and Addams, whom I have always revered.

Of course, once in a very long time a figure comes along who transcends all groupings, and all periods, and even straddles the cognitions. He or she is capable of both cognitions, at a very high level of intellect and character. If you look closely, you will see that that person embraces the dialectic, with a deep sense of the forms of each of its stages.

IN ITSELF: Abraham Lincoln does not wish to patronize the southerner. He speaks, still, in a way that would not differentiate between the peoples of America's two great regions.

Speech on the Kansas-Nebraska Act, Peoria, Illinois. October 16, 1854

"Before proceeding, let me say I think I have no prejudice against the Southern people. They are just what we would be in their situation. If slavery did not now exist among them, they would not introduce it. If it did now exist among us, we should not instantly give it up. This I believe of the masses north and south."[11]

FOR ITSELF: The contradiction has come and Abraham Lincoln recognized it. Shortly after his famous "House Divided" Speech in what is now the Old Capitol in Springfield, Lincoln gave what is a far lesser, and lesser known, speech in Chicago. Lincoln reflected on the earlier speech, and the dialectic itself.

Speech at Chicago, Illinois. July 10, 1858

"I am not a master of language; I have not a fine education; I am not capable of entering into a disquisition on dialectics, as I believe you call it.... I am not, in the first place, unaware that this Government has endured eighty-two and a half years, half slave and half free.... I believe it has endured because, during all that time, until the introduction of the Nebraska Bill, the public mind did rest, all the time, in the belief that slavery was in the course of ultimate extinction."[12]

IN AND FOR ITSELF: The contradiction has been resolved. Reconciliation is possible. Only a rationalization of a new order remains, during which time the analytic cognition will return to the ascendancy, for a while.

"With malice towards none: with charity for all.... [l]et us strive ... to bind up the nation's wounds [and] to do all which may achieve and cherish a just and lasting peace, among ourselves, and with all nations."[13]

Notes

Introduction

1. Robert Lane, *Political Ideology* (New York: The Free Press, 1962).

Chapter One

1. Elizabeth Cady Stanton et al., eds., *History of Woman Suffrage* (New York: Gowter and Wells, 1881-1922); Frederick Douglass, *Narrative of the Life of Frederick Douglass, An American Slave Written by Himself*, ed. Benjamin Quarles (Cambridge: Harvard University Press, 1960).

2. See Tara E. Santmire, et al., "The Impact of Cognitive Diversity on Crisis Negotiations," *Political Psychology* 19, no. 4 (1998).

3. Steven Pinker, *The Blank Slate.* (New York: Viking, 2002).

4. My thanks to Prof. Clyde Wilcox of Georgetown University for his assistance with this point. He references Andrew Kohut, *The Diminishing Divide: Religion's Changing Role in American Politics* (Washington, DC: The Brookings Institution, 2000).

5. Ronald Inglehart, *The Silent Revolution: Changing Values and Political Styles among Western Publics* (Princeton: Princeton University Press, 1977).

6. *Economist,* May 5, 2001, 5.

7. See Friedrich Engels, "Ludwig Feuerbach and the End of Classical German Philosophy," in *Marx and Engels: Basic Writings on Politics and Philosophy,* ed. Lewis S. Fever (Garden City: Anchor Books, 1959).

8. Rudolf Bahro, *Socialism and Survival* (London: Heretic Books, 1982).

9. William Irwin Thompson, ed., *Emergence—The New Science of Becoming* (Hudson, NY: Lindisfarne Press, 1991).

10. Lovelock, "Gaia." In Ibid.

11. Kate Soper, "Greening Prometheus-Marxism and Ecology" In *The Greening of Marxism,* ed. Ted Benton (New York: The Guilford Press, 1996).

12. Mary Mellor, "Ecofeminism and Ecosocialism," in Benton.

13. The evolutionary psychologist Peter Singer, in his *Politics, Evolution and Cooperation,* (New Haven: Yale University Press, 2000), suggests that the political Left can be advanced by a relatively static notion of human nature. The point is available in William P. Kreml, *The Anti-Authoritarian Personality* (London: Pergamon Press, 1977). I recommend the work of the evolutionary psychologists John Tooby and Leda Cosmides: "The Psychological Foundations of Culture," in Jerome Barkow, Tooby, and Cosmides, *The Adapted Mind: Evolutionary Psychology and the Generation of Culture,* (New York: Oxford University Press. 1992). 19-136.

Chapter Two

1. Plato, *The Symposium of Plato,* trans. Robert Gregg Bury (Cambridge: Heffer, 1932). Plato, *The Phaedo of Plato,* ed. R. D. Archer-Hind (New York: Arno Press, 1973).

2. Immanuel Kant, "Critique of Pure Reason," in *The Philosophy of Kant,* ed. Carl Friedrich (New York: Modern Library, 1949).

3. G. W. F. Hegel, *The Science of Logic,* trans. W. H. Johnston and L. G. Struthers (London: George Allen and Unwin,1961), 790-91.

4. Roger Scruton, *Kant* (London: Oxford University Press, 1982), 2, 5.

5. Manfred Keuhn, *Kant: A Biography* (Cambridge: Cambridge University Press, 2001), 22.

6. Terry Pinkard, *Hegel: A Biography* (New York: Cambridge University Press, 1968), 26.

Chapter Three

1. John Locke, *An Essay Concerning Human Understanding,* ed. Alexander Campbell Fraser, (New York: Dover, 1959).

2. See "Perpetual Peace" in Immanuel Kant, *On History,* ed. Lewis White Beck, (Indianapolis: Bobbs-Merrill, 1963). For a more generous view of Kant's balance between what God has prescribed and man can advance, see Yirmiahu Yovel, *Kant and the Philosophy of History,* (Princeton: Princeton University Press. 1980).

3. G. W. F. Hegel, *The Phenomenology of Mind,* trans. J. B. Baillie, (London: George Allen and Unwin, 1949).

4. Judith Shklar, *Freedom and Independence: A Study of the Political Ideas of Hegel's* Phenomenology of Mind, (Cambridge: Cambridge University Press, 1976), 145.

5. See Hastings Lyons and Herman Block, *Edward Coke: Oracle of the Law* (Boston: Houghton-Mifflin, Riverside Press, 1929).

6. Ronald D. Rotunda, Dr. Bonham's Case, 8 Coke. Rep. C.P. 1610, *Modern Constitutional Law: Cases and Notes,* 6th ed. (St. Paul: West Publishing House, 1988).

7. Hastings and Block, Edward Coke, 357-63.

8. Bernard Schwartz, *The Bill of Rights: A Documentary History* (New York: McGraw-Hill, 1971), 18.

9. William Blackstone, *Commentaries,* (New York: Augustus M. Kelley, 1969), 10

10. John Ely, *Democracy and Distrust: A Theory of Judicial Review* (Cambridge: Harvard University Press, 1980). See Alexander Bickel, *The Least Dangerous Branch: The Supreme Court at the Bar of Politics* (Indianapolis: Bobbs-Merrill, 1962).

11. *Brown v. Board of Education of Topeka, Kansas,* 347 US. 483. (1954).

12. *Colegrove v. Green,* 328 US 549. (1946).

13. *Baker v. Carr,* 369 US 549 (1962); *Reynolds v. Sims,* 377 US 533 (1964).

14. *Griswold v. Connecticut,* 381 US 479 (1965).

15. *Roe v. Wade,* 410 US 113 (1973).

16. *Richmond v. Croson Co.,* 109 S. Ct. 706 (1989).

17. *Smith v. Allwright,* 321 US 649 (1944).

18. *Shelley v. Kraemer,* 334 US 1. (1948).

19. Robert Bork, "Neutral Principles and Some First Amendment Problems,"*Indiana Law Journal,* 47. no.1 (1971). 6.

20. William Rehnquist, in *Moose Lodge # 107 v. Irvis* 402 US 163 (1972).

Chapter Four

1. Robert Fendel Anderson, Robert Fendel. *Hume's First Principles* (Lincoln: University of Nebraska Press, 1966), 60-61.

2. G. W. F. Hegel, *The Science of Logic.* Vol. 2. trans.W. H. Johnston and L. G. Struthers. (London: George Allen and Unwin, 1961). 788.

3. Baron Charles Montesquieu, *The Spirit of the Laws.* (Cambridge: Cambridge University Press, 1989).

4. John Locke, "Essays on the Law of Nature," in Paul E. Sigmund, *Natural Law in Political Thought,* ed. (Cambridge: Winthrop, 1971), 91-95.

5. Paul Edwards, ed. *The Encyclopedia of Philosophy* (New York: Macmillan and The Free Press, 1967), 264.

6. William Blackstone, *Commentaries* (New York: Augustus M. Kelley, 1969), 4.

7. Daniel Boorstin, *The Mysterious Science of the Law* (Boston: Beacon Press, 1941).

8. Immanuel Kant, "To Eternal Peace," in Carl J. Friedrich, *The Philosophy of Kant,* ed. (New York: Modern Library, 1949).

9. Leonard Kreiger, *The Politics of Discretion: Pufendorf and the Acceptance of Natural Law* (Chicago: The University of Chicago Press, 1965), 88ff.

10. Jeremy Bentham, *The Theory of Legislation* (New York: Harcourt, Brace, 1931), 82.

11. John Austin, *Lectures on Jurisprudence* (London: Campbell, 1869), 2:1107.

12. Alexander Bickel, *The Least Dangerous Branch: The Supreme Court at the Bar of Politics* (Indianapolis: Bobbs-Merrill, 1962).

13. C. F. Puchta, *Outlines of Jurisprudence as the Science of Right: A Juristic Encyclopedia* (Edinburgh, 1887), 31.

14. Rudolf Stammler, "Fundamental Tendencies on Modern Jurisprudence," *Michigan Law Review* 21 (1923): 865.

15. Leon Duguit, "Objective Law," *Columbia Law Review* 20 (1920): 829.

16. Oliver Wendell Holmes, Jr., *The Common Law* (Birmingham: The Legal Classics Library, 1982).

17. Lon Fuller, *The Law In Quest of Itself* (Boston: Beacon Press, 1941), 118.

18. Hans Kelsen, "The Pure Theory of Law," trans. Charles H. Wilson, *Law Quarterly Review* 51 (1935): 517.

19. H. L. A. Hart, "Relativism and the Separation of Laws and Morals," *Harvard Law Review* 71 (February 1958): 594.

20. Adam Smith, *An Inquiry into the Nature and Causes of the Wealth of Nations* (Chicago: The University of Chicago Press, 1928).

21. David Ricardo, *The Works of David Ricardo* (London: J. Murray, 1846).

22. John Stuart Mill, *On the Principles of Political Economy and Taxation* (New York: E. P. Dutton, 1938).

23. John Maynard Keynes, "The General Theory of Employment," *Quarterly Journal of Economics* 51 (February 1937): 209-28.

24. G. F. McCleary, *The Malhtusian Population Theory* (London: Faber & Faber, Ltd., 1953).

25. See Joseph A. Schumpeter, *History of Economic Analysis* (New York: Oxford University Press, 1'954). 615-25.

26. See Alan Ebenstein, *Frederick Hayek: A Bibliography* (London: Palegrave, 2001), and Richard McKenzie, "The Neo-Classicists vs. The Aus-

trians: A Partial Reconciliation of Competing World Views,"*Southern Economic Journal* 47, no. 1 (July, 1980): 2.

27. John Kenneth Galbraith, *The Affluent Society* (Boston: Houghton Mifflin, 1958).

28. Daniel Fusfeld, "The Conceptual Framework of Modern Economics," *Journal of Economic Issues* 14, no.1 (March 1980): 1, 15.

Chapter Five

1. Aristotle, *The Complete Works of Aristotle,* v. 2, ed. Jonathan Barnes (Princeton: Princeton University Press, 1984), 2030-32.

2. See Leroy Rieselbach, *Congressional Reform in the Seventies* (Morristown, NJ: General Learning Press, 1977).

4. Anthony Downs, *Inside Bureaucracy* (Boston: Little Brown and Co. 1967).

5. Howard Aldrich, *Organizational Environments* (Englewood Cliffs, NJ: Prentice-Hall, 1979): 259-60.

6. Pitirim Sorokin, *Social and Cultural Dynamics* (London: Oxford University Press, 1957), 57, 28, 648.

7. Arnold Toynbee, *A Study of History,* (London: Oxford University Press, 1934), 321, 276.

8. Oswald Spengler, *Decline of the West* (New York: Alfred A. Knopf, 1922), 79.

9. Edward Gibbon, *Decline and Fall of the Roman Empire* (New York: P. F. Collier & Son, 1899).

10. Bernard Sanders, "Nation Can't Let Middle Class Fall," *Detroit Free Press.* Sept. 10, 2003, In *Sanders Scoop* (November 2003): 3.

11. Robert Kuttner, "Why the Economy Won't Boost Bush," *Business Week.* July 5, 2004. 32.

12. Bernard Sanders, *Sanders Scoop* (Summer 2000): 2.

13. "Prison population as recorded on December, 1999" *Bureau of Justice Statistics,* 2.

14. U.S. Census Bureau, *Income and Poverty,* 1999, Press briefing by Daniel H. Weinberg, Chief, Housing and Household Economic Statistics. Poor Population: 34.5 million, 1999, 32-3.

Chapter Six

1. James MacGregor Burns, *The Crosswinds of Freedom* (New York: Alfred A. Knopf, 1988), 90.

2. *Buckley v. Valeo,* 424 US 1. (1976).

3. *Dred Scott v. Sandford,* 60 US (39 Howard) 393 (1857).

4. *Marbury v. Madison,* 5 US (1 Cranch) 137. (1803).

5. *McCulloch v. Maryland,* 17 US (Wheat.) 316 (1819).

6. Hamilton, Alexander, James Madison, and John Jay, *The Federalist Papers,* no.10, ed. Garry Wills (New York: Bantam Books, 1982).

7. *Nebbia v. New York,* 291 US 502 (1934).

8. *National Labor Relations Board v. Jones and Laughlin Steel Co,* 301 US 1 (1937).

9. Croly, Herbert. *The Promise of American Life* (New York: MacMillan Co. 1909) 23.

10. *Standard Oil Co. v. United States* 221 US 203 (1911), *United States v. American Tobacco Co.*

11. *Muller v. Oregon,* 208 US 412 (1908).

12. N.L.R.B. v. Jones and Laughlin Steel Corp., 301 US 1 (1937).

13. *Schecter Poultry Corporation v. United States,* 295 US 495 (1936).

Chapter Seven

1. Anthony Downs, *Inside Bureaucracy* (Boston: Little Brown and Co. 1967), Howard Aldrich, *Organizational Environments* (Englewood Cliffs, NJ: Prentice-Hall, 1979), Pitirm Sorokin, *Social and Cultural Dynamics* (Boston: Porter and Savert, 1957), Oswald Spengler, *The Decline of the West* (New York: Alfred A. Knopf, 1922).

2. Bernard Schwartz, *The Bill of Rights: A Documetary History (*New York: McGraw-Hill, 1971) 1008-41.

3. Herbert Storing, *The Complete Anti-Federalist,* 11-14.

4. George Mason, in *The Essential Anti-Federlalist,* ed. W. B. Allen and Gordon Lloyd (Lanham MD: University Press of America, 1985), 11.

5. Akhil Reed Amar, *The Bill of Rights: Creation and Reconstruction* (New Haven: Yale University Press, 1998).

Chapter Eight

1. Consensus of presidential panel at the meeting of the American Historical Association, Chicago, January, 2001.

2. "Runaway CEO Pay," Global View from *Executive Paywatch* AFL-CIO Website.

3. "Permatemps Pose New Challenges for HR," from *HR Focus*, American Management Association, December 1999. 7.

4. The State of Working America, 2000-1,"*The State,* September 3, 2000, C 3.

5. David Coy Johnson, "Income Tax Enforcement Is Broadly Declining—New US Data Indicate," *The New York Times,* April 1, 2001, C2.

6. Thomas T. Lueck, "ATM Fees Unfair, Council Is Told." *The New York Times.* December 7, 2000, B11.

7. "Losing Interest: So Banks Boost Card Fees Risking Earnings Backlash," *Barron's.* 79 (December 13, 1999), 3.

8. "How Banks Make the Most of Bounced Checks," *The Wall Street Journal*, February 25, 1999, 3.

9. "Frankel Case Prompts Debate over Need for Federal Insurance Regulations," Associated Press, September 19, 2000.

10. Adam Smith, *Theory of Moral Sentiments* (New York: Garland. 1971).

11. Abraham Lincoln, "Speech on the Kansas-Nebraska Act," In *Abraham Lincoln: Speeches and Writings,* ed. Roy P. Basler (New York: The Library of America, 1989), 315.

12.———, "Speech at Chicago, Illinois," in Lincoln, *Speeches,* 447.

13.———, "Second Inaugural Address," in Lincoln, *Speeches,* 687.

Bibliography

Aldrich, Howard. *Organizational Environments.* Englewood Cliffs, NJ: Prentice-Hall, 1979.

Allen, W. B., and Gordon Lloyd, eds. *The Essential Anti-Federalist.* Lanham, MD: University Press of America,1985.

Amar, Akhil Reed. *The Bill of Rights: Creation and Reconstruction.* New Haven: Yale University Press, 1998.

Anderson, Robert Fendel. *Hume's First Principles.* Lincoln: University of Nebraska Press, 1966.

Aristotle. *The Complete Works of Aristotle.* Vol. 2. Princeton: Princeton University Press, 1984.

Austin, John. *Lectures on Jurisprudence.* Vol. 2. London: Campbell, 1869.

Bahra, Rudolph. *Socialism and Survival.* London: Heretic Books, 1982.

Barkow, Jerome, John Tooby, and Leda Cosmides. *The Adapted Mind: Evolutionary Psychology and the Generation of Culture.* New York: Oxford University Press, 1992.

Bentham, Jeremy. *The Theory of Legislation.* New York: Harcourt, Brace, 1931.

Bickel, Alexander. *The Least Dangerous Branch: The Supreme Court at the Bar of Politics.* Indianapolis: Bobbs-Merrill, 1962.

Blackstone, William. *Commentaries.* New York: Augustus M. Kelley, 1969.

Boorstin, Daniel. *The Mysterious Science of the Law.* Boston: Beacon Press, 1941.

Bork, Robert. "Neutral Principles and Some First Amendment Problems." *Indiana Law Journal* 47 no. 1 (1971).

Bureau of Justice Statistics, "Prison Population as Recorded on December, 1999".

Burns, James MacGregor. *The Crosswinds of Freedom.* New York: Alfred A. Knopf, 1988.

Croly, Herbert. *The Promise of American Life.* New York: Macmillan Co., 1909.

Doherty, Jacqueline. "Losing Interest: So Banks Boost Card Fees Risking Earnings Backlash." *Barron_s* 79, no. 50, (December 13, 1999).

Douglass, Frederick. *Narrative of the Life of Frederick Douglass, an American Slave, Written by Himself.* Edited by Benjamin Quarles. Cambridge: Harvard University Press, 1960.

Downs, Anthony. *Inside Bureaucracy.* Boston: Little, Brown and Co., 1967.

Duguit, Léon. "Objective Law." *Columbia Law Review* 20 (1920).

Ebenstein, Alan. "*Friedrich Hayek: A Bibliography.*" (London: Palegrave, London (2001).

Edwards, Paul. ed. *The Encyclopedia of Philosophy.* Vol. 8. New York: Macmillan and the Free Press, 1967.

Engels, Friedrich. "Ludwig Feuerbach and the End of Classical German Philosophy." In *Marx and Engels -Basic Writings on Politics and Philosophy, edited by* Lewis S. Fever. Garden City: Anchor Books, 1959.

Fuller, Lon. *The Law In Quest of Itself.* Boston: Beacon Press, 1941.

Fusfeld, Daniel. "The Conceptual Framework of Modern Economics," *Journal of Economic Issues* 14, no.1. (March, 1980).

Galbraith, John Kenneth. *The Affluent Society.* Boston: Houghton Mifflin, 1958.

Gibbon, Edward. *Decline and Fall of the Roman Empire.* New York: P. F. Collier & Son, 1899.

Hamilton, Alexander; James Madison; and John Jay. *The Federalist Papers.* No. 10. Edited by Garry Wills. New York: Bantam Books, 1982.

Hart, H. L. A. "Relativism and the Separation of Laws and Morals." *Harvard Law Review* 71 (February 1958).

Hastings, Lyon, and Herman Block. *Edward Coke: Oracle of the Law.* Boston: Houghton-Mifflin, Riverside Press, 1929.

Inglehart, Ronald. *The Silent Revolution: Changing Values and Political Styles among Western Publics.* Princeton: Princeton University Press, 1977.

Johnson, David Coy. "Income Tax Enforcement Is Broadly Declining, New U.S. Data Indicate." *The New York Times,* April 9, 2001, C2.

Kant, Immanuel. "To Eternal Peace." In *The Philosophy of Kant,* edited by Carl J. Friedrich. New York: Modern Library, 1949.

Kelsen, Hans. "The Pure Theory of Law." Translated by Charles H. Wilson. *Law Quarterly Review.* 51 (1935).

Keynes, John Maynard. "The General Theory of Employment," *Quarterly Journal of Economics* 51 (February 1937).

Kreml, William P. *The Anti-Authoritarian Personality.* London: Pergamon Press, 1977. *Psychology, Relativism and Politics.* New York: New York University Press, 1991. *Relativism and the Natural Left.* New York: New York University Press, 1984.

Krieger, Leonard. *The Politics of Discretion: Pufendorf and the Acceptance of Natural Law.* Chicago: The University of Chicago Press, 1965.

Kuehn, Manfred. *Kant: A Biography.* Cambridge: Cambridge University Press, 2001.

Kuttner, Robert. "Why the Economy Won't Boost Bush," *Business Week.* July 5, 2004.

Lane, Robert. *Political Ideology*. New York: The Free Press, 1962.

Lincoln, Abraham. "Second Inaugural Address," In *Abraham Lincoln: Speeches and Writings.* edited by *Roy P. Basler.* New York: The Library of America, 1989. "Speech at Chicago, Illinois," In *Abraham Lincoln: Speeches and Writings,* edited by Roy P. Basler. New York: The Library of America, 1989. "Speech on the Kansas-Nebraska Act." In *Abraham Lincoln: Speeches and Writings,* edited by Roy P. Basler. New York: The Library of America, 1989.

Locke, John. *An Essay Concerning Human Understanding.* Edited by Alexander Campbell Fraser. New York: Dover, 1959.

Lovelock, James. "Gaia." In *Emergence—The New Science of Becoming,* edited by William Irwin Thompson. Hudson. NY: Lindisfarne Press, 1991.

Lowi, Theodore J. *The End of Liberalism.* New York: W. W. Norton, 1969.

Lueck, Thomas T. "ATM Fees Unfair, Council Is Told." *The New York Times,* December 7, 2000.

Lyons, Hastings, and Herman Block. *Edward Coke: Oracle of the Law.* Boston: Houghton-Mifflin, Riverside Press, 1929.

Mason, George. In *The Essential Anti-Federalist.* Edited by W. B. Allen and Gordon Lloyd Lanham, MD: University Press of America, 1985

McConnell, Grant. *Private Power and American Democracy.* New York: Alfred A. Knopf, 1966.

McKenzie, Richard. "The Neo-Classicists vs. The Austrians: A Partial Reconciliation of Competing World Views." *Southern Economic Journal* 47, no 1, (July 1980).

Mellor, Mary. "Ecofeminism and Ecosocialism." In *The Greening of Marxism,*" ed. Ted Benton. New York: The Guilford Press. 1996.

Montesquieu, Baron Charles de. *The Spirit of the Laws.* Cambridge: Cambridge University Press,1989.

Pinkard, Terry. *Hegel - A Biography*. New York: Cambridge University Press, 1968.

Pound, Roscoe. "A Theory of Social Interests." *Papers and Proceedings of the American Sociological Society* 15 (1921).

Puchta, C. F. *Outlines of Jurisprudence as the Science of Right: A Juristic Encyclopedia.* Edinburgh, 1887.

Rieselbach, Leroy. *Congressional Reform in the Seventies.* Morristown, NJ: General Learning Press, 1977.

Rotunda, Ronald D. *Modern Constitutional Law: Cases and Notes.* 6th ed. St. Paul: West Group, 1988.

Sanders, Bernie. *Sanders Scoop* (Summer, 2000).

———. "Nation Can't Let Middle Class Fall," *Detroit Free Press,* Sep. 10, 2003. In *Sanders Scoop.* (November, 2003).

Santmire, Tara E. et al. "The Impact of Cognitive Diversity on Crisis Negotiations." *Political Psychology* 19, 4 (1998).

Schwartz, Bernard. *The Bill of Rights: A Documentary History.* New York: McGraw-Hill, 1971.

Scruton, Roger. *Kant.* London: Oxford University Press, 1982.

Shklar, Judith. *Freedom and Independence: A Study of the Political Ideas of Hegel's* Phenomenology of Mind. Cambridge: Cambridge University Press, 1976.

Singer, Peter. *A Darwinian Left: Politics, Evolution and Cooperation.* New Haven: Yale University Press, 2000.

Smith, Adam. *An Inquiry into the Nature and Causes of the Wealth of Nations.* Chicago: The University of Chicago Press, 1928.

———. *Theory of Moral Sentiments.* New York: Garland, 1971.

Soper, Kate. "Greening Prometheus-Marxism and Ecology." In *The Greening of Marxism,* edited by Ted Benton. New York: The Guilford Press, 1996.

Sorokin, Pitirim. *Social and Cultural Dynamics.* Boston: Porter and Savert, 1957.

Spengler, Oswald. *Decline of the West.* New York; Alfred A. Knopf, 1922.

Stammler, Rudolf. "Fundamental Tendencies in Modern Jurisprudence" *Michigan Law Review* 21 (1923).

Stanton, Elizabeth Cady, et al., eds. *History of Woman Suffrage.* New York: Gowter and Wells, 1881-1922.

Storing, Herbert J. *The Complete Anti-Federalist.* Chicago: University of Chicago Press, 1981.

Thompson, William Irwin, ed. *Emergence—The New Science of Becoming.* Hudson, NY: Lindisfarne Press, 1991.

Toynbee, Arnold. *A Study of History.* London: Oxford University Press, 1934.

Wasserstrom, Richard A. *Morality and the Law.* Belmont, CA: Wadsworth Publishing Co., 1971.

Index

ACT, 105
A.T. & T., 103
Acton, Lord, 92
Adams, Samuel, 4
Addams, Jane, 191
Agincourt, 32
Aiken County, SC, 117
Aldrich, Howard, 95, 147
Alfred, King, 48
Altgeld, John Peter, 191
Amar, Akhil Reed, 157
American Bar Association, 153
American Enterprise Institute, 187
American Historical Association, 167
American Legion, 98
American Railway Union, 191
American Tobacco Co. v. United States, 135
Americorps, 168
Anthony, Susan B., 3
Anti-Federalists, 147, 150–53
Anti-Federalist Papers, 151, 153
AOL, 172
Aquinas, Thomas, 69
Aristotle, 67, 69, 85, 86, 88, 113, 158
Articles of Confederation, 149
Asmolov, Alexander, 144
Attlee, Clement, 175
Augustine, 69
Austin, John, 73, 75
Automobile Manufacturers Association, 33
Baha'i Temple, 191
Bahro, Rudolf, 16
Baker v. Carr, 52
Bank of America, 171
Beaufort County, SC, 117
Beethoven, Ludwig von, 96
Bentham, Jeremy, 73, 75–6
Bickel, Alexander, 73
Bill of Rights, 98, 147, 150, 152, 156–8, 185
Bismarck, Otto von, 93
Blackstone, Sir William, 72
Bohr, Nils, 7, 181
Bonaparte, Napoleon, 37
Boone, Pat, 11
Boorstin, Daniel, 72
Bork, Robert, 56–7, 73
Bosnia, 168
Bradley, Senator William, 116
Brandt, Willie, 176
Brecht, Berthold, 168
Broadway Street, Chicago, 190
Brown v. The Board of Education, 51
Browne, Harry, 183
Brutus, 175
Bryan, William Jennings, 191
Buchanan v. Warley, 56
Buddha, 176
Burns, James MacGregor, 81, 125
Bush, George H. W., 167
Bush, George W., 9

Caeser, Julius, 175
Calhoun, John, 166
Cannon, Speaker Joe, 79
Carolignian Empire, 87
Carter Center, The, 182
Carter, Hodding III, 63
Carter, Jimmy, 182
Casper, Gerhard, 81
Cato Institute, 187
Center for the Study of Psychology in The Nuclear Age, 144
Cermak, Anton, 21
Ceska Beseda, 21
Charles I, 47, 53
Charleston, SC, 165
Charlotte, NC, 171
Chicago "Welfare Queen", 169
Chicago and Northwestern Railroad, xiv
Chicago Historical Society, xv
Chicago River, 102
Christendom, 180
Christian Science Monitor, 80, 116
Cicero, 72
Citigroup, 94
Columbia, SC, 164
Civil War, the, 88, 113, 166
Class of 1974, 79
Clemson University, 164
Cleveland, Grover, 173, 191
Clinton, Bill, 166–174
Clinton, Hillary, 169
Coke, Sir Edward, 44–47, 50
Colegrove v. Green, 52
Colson, Charles, 11
Committee on the Constitutional System, 81–84, 125
Committee for Science and Culture Of the Russian Parliament, 144
Compressed Distribution, 102–4
Condorcet, 14
Confederate Memorial Day, 165
Cooper Union, 135
Copernicus, 69
Corvair, 32
Coughlin, Father, 176
Croly, Herbert, 135
Cutler, Lloyd, 34, 81–84

Daley, Richard J., 21
Darrin, Bobby, 168
Davis, John W., 191
Dean, James, 179
De Leon, Daniel, xiv
Debs, Eugene, 191
Democratic Convention of 1968, 62
Democratic National Committee, 61
Democratic Party, 21–23
Democratic Socialists, 20
Descartes, René, 66, 96
Devlin, Lord, 76
Diderot, 14
Dillon, C. Douglas, 81
Domesday Book, 48
Douglass, Frederick, 3
Downs, Anthony, 95
Doyle, Arthur Conan, 170
Dr. Bonham's Case, 46
Dred Scott Case, 128, 134, 141–2, 158
Duguit, León, 74
DuPont, Pierre, 76
Duvaliers, The, 92

Eastland, The, 102–3
Edmund Fitzgerald, The, 103
Einstein, Albert, 16
Eisenhower, Dwight D., 33, 163
Electoral College, 186
Elizabeth I, Queen, 45
Ely, John Hart, 50, 54
Enlightenment, 69–70, 173
Enron, 172
Epicureans, 69

Essay Concerning Human Understanding, 38
European Union, 87
Evanston, IL, 21

Falwell, Rev. Jerry, 11
Federal Election Commission, 117
Federalist Papers, The, 109–110, 132, 150–1
Federalist #80, 109–110
Federalist Society, The, 188
Fermi, Enrico, 181
Feuerbach, Ludwig, 14, 180
Field, Stephen, 132–3
527 Organizations, 105
Foley, Thomas, 62
Ford Motor Company, 32
Ford, Henry II, 31
Fowler, Donald L., 60–1, 63
Fraser, Congressman Don, 61
Frederick the Great, 72
Friedrich, Karl, 39
French Revolution, 37, 70
Friedman, Milton, 77
Fulbright, Senator William, 81
Full Faith and Credit Clause, 149
Fuller, Lon, 75–6
Fusfeld, Donald, 78

Gaia, 16
Galbraith, John Kenneth, 78
Galileo, 69
Gandhi, the Mahatma, 176
General Electric, 19, 93
General Motors, 32
Germany, 104
Gibbon, Edward, 96
Giegerich, Wolfgang, 144
Glorious Revolution, 48, 106
Goethe, Johann, 96
Gorbachev, Mikhail, 96,186
Gore, Albert, 112
Graham-Rudman-Hollings Act, 167
Great Lakes, 102–3
Green Bay Road, 190
Green Party, 20, 183, 186
Griswold v. Connecticut, 159

Haiti, 168
Hamilton, Alexander, 109–110, 132
Hammurabi, 96
Hampton, Wade III, 164
Hardin, Charles, 80
Hart, H. L. A., 75–6
Harvey's Restaurant, 92
Havel, Vaclav, 176
Haverford College, 116
Hayek, Friedrich von, 77
Haymarket Affair, 191
Haynes, R. B., 165–6
Hegel, Georg Wilhelm Friedrich, 36–30, 35, 39–42, 62, 66, 69–71, 74, 179–80
Heisenberg, Werner, 16
Helms, Jesse, 169
Help America Vote Act, 141
Henry, Patrick, 151
Heritage Foundation, 187
Hiroshima, 181
Hitler, Adolf, 92
Hobbes, Thomas, 95
Hoffman, Paul, 31
Hollings, Senator Ernest, 80, 128
Holmes, Oliver Wendell Jr., 74
Holy Roman Empire, 93
Hooker, Richard, 72
Hoover Institution, 187
House of Lords, 175
House of Representatives, 150
Howard, A.E. Dick, 81
Hudson Institute, 187
Hughes, Charles Evans, 132–3, 135–7
Hume, David, 69

I.M.F., 187
I.R.S., 169
Illinois Green Party Conference, 2000, 20
International Association of Chiefs of Police, 32
Islamic Baghdad, 96
Israeli-Palestinian Conflict, 168

Jackson, Andrew, 4
James I, 45–6
Jay, John, 151
Jefferson, Thomas, Society at UVA, 116
Jevons, William, 77
Johnson, Lyndon, 32
Jung Institute, 144
Justinian, 72

Kansas City Convention, 62
Kant, Immanuel, 26–30, 35, 37, 38, 41, 66, 69–71, 73, 75, 180
Kassebaum, Nancy, 81
Kelsen, Hans, 75
Kemper Brothers, 31
Kennedy, John F., 174
Kennedy, Representative Patrick, 98
Kennedy, Senator Ted, 98
Kerouac, Jack, 179
Keynes, John Maynard, 77
Kierkegaard, Søren, 39
King, Martin Luther Jr., 3
Kremlin, The, 144
Kudlow, Larry, 9, 112
Kuehn, Manfred, 29
Kuttner, Robert, 113

LaFollette, Robert, 191
Lake Michigan, 103
Lake Ontario, 103
Lansing, John, 151
League of Women Voters, 98, 116
Leibniz, Gottfried, 38, 54
Lee, Richard Henry, 151
Lieberman, Joseph, 9, 10, 112
Legislationists, 72
Leibniz, Gottfried, 38, 59
Lenin's Tomb, 144
Liberty Fund, The, 188
Lincoln, Abraham, 172
Locke, John, 14, 17, 68, 69, 104, 118, 124–5
Long, Huey, 176
Lovelock, James, 16
Lowi, Theodore, 93
Lusitania, 102

Madison, James, 132, 152
Magna Carta, 48
Mao, Tze Tung, 92, 179
Malthus, Thomas, 77
Marbury v. Madison, 132
Marshall Plan, 31
Marshall, John, 132–3, 137
Marx, Karl, 179
Mary, Queen, 48
Maryland, 186
Mason, George, 151, 153
Massachusetts, 116
Mayflower Hotel, 92
McCain, John, 117
McCain-Feingold Act, 118, 127
McCarthy, Eugene, 176
McConnell, Grant, 93
McCulloch v. Maryland, 132
McGovern, George, 79
McGovern-Fraser Commission, 60–1
McKinley, William, 114
Medicare, 170
Mellor, Mary, 16
Menger, Carl, 77
Merrill Lynch, 94
Metropolitan Club, 92
Michels, Robert, 95

Machiavelli, 68
Mikulski, Senator Barbara, 62
Mill, James, 77
Mill, John Stuart, 77
Mises, Ludwig von, 77
Monroe, James, 152
Montesquieu, the Baron de, 70, 74
Moose Lodge # 17 v. Irvis, 58
Morris, Richard, 169
Morrison Hotel, 22
Morrison, Toni, 168
Moscow, 144
MoveOn.org, 105
Moynihan, Senator Daniel Patrick, 80
Muller v. Oregon, 135
Murdoch Rupert, 172
Myers-Briggs Tests, 29
Mysterious Science of the Law, The, 72

N.L.R.B. v. Jones and Laughlin Steel Co., 133, 136
N.A.A.C.P., 163
Nader, Ralph, 183
NAFTA, 187
Nagasaki, 181
National Defense Highway System, 33
National Safety Council, 32
Natural Law, 71–76
Naval War College, 144
Nebbia v. New York, 133
New England, 116
New Hampshire, 116
New Republic, The, 80
Newport Institute, 144
Newton, Isaac, 69, 96
Newtonian Physics, 42
Nicaean Christians, 69
Nixon, Richard, 174
Northwestern University Traffic Institute, 31

O'Hara, Congressman Jim, 61
Olney, Richard, 191
Orangeburg County, 117
Orwell, George, 181
Outfit, The, 170

Paderewski, Ignace, 176
Paine, Thomas, 4
Palme, Olaf, 176
Palmer, John M., 191
Parmenides, 96
PBS Nightly News, 182
Pericles, 185
Petition of Right, 47
Phaedo, The, 26
Phenomenology, The, 41
Pinkard, Terry, 29
Pinochet, Augusto, 92
Plato, 67, 97, 177
Politics, The, 86
Pol Pot, 179
Popper, Karl, 39
Popular Front, 179
Positive Law, 70–76
Post-materialism, 8
Pound, Roscoe, 74
Powell, Colin, 9, 10
Praxis of Good, 168
Protagoras, 68
Ptolemaic Alexandria, 96
Puchta. G. F., 74
Pufendorf, Samuel von, 73
Pullman, George, 191

Quesnay, François, 76

Reagan, Ronald, 169
Reconstruction, 163
Red Square, 144
Red-Green Coalition, 16
Rehnquist, William, 58, 131, 138–9, 160

Rehnquist, William, 58, 131, 138–9, 160
Religion in American Politics, 8
Rembrandt von Rijn, 96
Republic, The, 67
Republican Party, 20
Reuss, Henry, 81
Revolutionary War, 132
Reynolds v. Sims, 52
Ribicoff, Abraham, 62
Ricardo, David, 77
Richmond v. Croson, 54
Robertson, Rev. Pat, 11
Rockwell, Norman, xv
Roe v. Wade, 53
Roman Catholic Faith, 69, 114
Roman Empire, 96
Roosevelt, Franklin, 79
Roosevelt, Theodore, 175
Rousseau, Jean Jacques, 177
Russell, Bertrand, 71
Russian Orthodox Church, 144
Rutherford, Ernest, 7

Sanders, Representative Bernard, 11
Sanford, Terry, Governor, 61
Savigny, Frederick von, 74
Say, Jean Baptiste, 77
Schecter Poultry Corp. v. United States, 136
Scruton, Roger, 29
Seneca, 72
Seventh Amendment, 110-111, 155–156
Shays's Rebellion, 109–110
Shelley v. Kraemer, 55–58, 73, 139–40, 155–6, 161–2
Shelley's Case, *44, 45, 49, 51*
Sherman Anti-Trust Act, 135
Shklar, Judith, 180
Sierra Club, 116
Smith v. Allwright, 55
Smith, Adam, 76–7
Smith, Melancton, 151
Social Darwinism, 6
Social Security, 79
Socialist Labor Party, xiv
Soetendorp, Awraham, 144
Soper, Kate, 16
Sorokin, Pitirim, 95
South Carolina, 171
Spanish Civil War, 179
Spengler, Oswald, 96
Spirit of the Laws, The, 70
St. Basil's Cathedral, 144
Stagg Field, 181
Stalin, Joseph, 92
Stammler, Rudolph, 74
Standard Oil Co. v. United States, 135
Stanton, Elizabeth Cady, 3
State's Wrongs, 186
Stone, Clement, 142
Story, Joseph, 131
Strout, Richard, 80
Studebaker Motors Co., 31
Subatomic Moment, 112
Sutton, Willie, 171
Symposium, The, 26

Taft, William Howard, 137
Taney, Roger, 131
Teamsters Union, 18
Telecommunications Act of 1996, 172
Theory of Moral Sentiments, 189
Thompson, William Irwin, 16
Thrasymachus, 68–9, 71
Three Penny Opera, 168
Time-Warner, 172
Titanic, The, 102
Toynbee, Arnold, 96
Transportation Center, Northwestern University, 32–3
Travelers Insurance, 94
Treatise on Human Nature, 69

Truman, Harry, 79
Turgot, Robert, 76
Type 2 Undemocratic Elections, 100

Undemocratic Decentralization, 90–4
Uniform Commercial Code, 129
Union Pacific Railway, xiv
United Airlines, xiv
United Citizens Party, 20, 186
University of Chicago, 181
University of South Carolina, 164
Unsafe at Any Speed, 193

Vernadnsky, Vladimir, 16
Versailles, 169
Vietnam War, 59, 62, 179
Voltaire, Jean M. F., 72
Voting Rights Act of 1965, 141

Walrus, Leon, 77
Warp and Woof, 177, 185
Warren, Chief Justice Earl, 49–54
Washington Post, 117
Weimar Republic, 84
Welch, Jack, 93
Welland Locks, 102
Weschler, Herbert, 73
Western Electric, 103
Wexler, Ann, 63
Whole Group Equity, 115
William of Orange, 48
Wilmette, IL, 190
Wilson, Sloan, 179
Wilson, Woodrow, 175
Wittgenstein, Ludwig, 71
World Bank, 187
Worldcom, 172
WTO, 187

Yugoslavia, 168

Zeno, 148